The Nehru Years

The Nehru Years

An International History of Indian Non-Alignment

Swapna Kona Nayudu

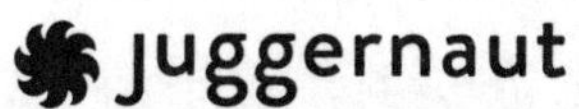

JUGGERNAUT BOOKS
C-I-128, First Floor, Sangam Vihar, Near Holi Chowk,
New Delhi 110080, India

First published by Juggernaut Books 2025

Copyright © Swapna Kona Nayudu 2025

10 9 8 7 6 5 4 3 2 1

P-ISBN: 9789353459604
E-ISBN: 9789353458232

The views and opinions expressed in this book are the author's own. The facts contained herein were reported to be true as on the date of publication by the author to the publishers of the book, and the publishers are not in any way liable for their accuracy or veracity.

All rights reserved. No part of this publication may be reproduced, transmitted, or stored in a retrieval system in any form or by any means without the written permission of the publisher.

For sale in the Indian Subcontinent excluding Pakistan

Typeset in Adobe Caslon Pro by R. Ajith Kumar, Noida

Printed at Thomson Press India Ltd

Contents

Contents

1

Introduction

When speaking of politics, do we think of non-alignment? If not, why is that the case? What have we forgotten about non-alignment and what do we remember incorrectly? What were the conceptual premises of non-alignment, what were its critical, liberatory, normative commitments? What was the relevance of non-alignment when it emerged and what does it tell us about the international relations of the twentieth century? This book offers qualitatively new ways to tackle these questions.

I situate non-alignment in a long tradition of thinking about politics and war as transformative of world order. Both politics and war are frames of analysis for non-alignment, which is fundamentally concerned with political thought, utopia, war, political ruin and the end of a possible future. The umbilical force that ties politics and war together has a grip on world order and hence, has always been of primary concern to non-alignment. Critique, as a method, is also foundational to non-aligned politics, so, in the first instance, the book is devoted to interrogating what critique does for non-aligned politics. This book will present non-alignment as critical of both politics and war and thus, also critical of world order. Rescuing politics from ideology, globalizing ways in which we think about war, embracing varied ideas of world order – these were urgent and compelling tasks for twentieth-century political thinkers from India. This book will also foreground this groundswell of modern international thought.

In this history, empire and the nation-state present as competing frames of analysis. This book presents non-alignment as a critical political vision, so there is a focus on the sources of this critique. This brings us to a discussion of the non-aligned engagement with the problem of empire. This book historicizes empire as a force with particular attributes in specific locations and time periods. Within that frame, I discuss non-alignment as a politics of anticolonial resistance. I argue that non-aligned critique has its origins in the critique of empire and cannot be fully understood outside of that intellectual practice. In order to develop a vision of postcolonial future, it was necessary for anticolonial individuals to explore the concept of the nation-state, also a key theme in the development of non-aligned thought. Even though it is true that non-aligned solidarities were often also built across national lines, it is also equally significant that the nation-state as a political formation was adopted and celebrated within non-aligned thought as a mode of political expression. In non-aligned thinking, relations between nation-states could concretize the links between multiple intellectual traditions that offered responses to the challenge of colonialism. Within this frame, I discuss non-alignment as a politics of aspiration. Consequently, the book is a history of non-alignment in the contexts of anticolonialism, decolonization and postcolonial diplomacy, which are treated as distinct and overlapping historical periods but also as modes of theorizing world politics through resistance and ambition.

What conceptual work does the idea of non-alignment do? Non-alignment was a political vision built through historical consciousness. So, its first task was to identify other political visions, their historical origins, their manifestos. Any political vision seeks to identify pathways to survival and success in shaping the world order. Of course, this leads to questions about why political projects fail, and what projects are not recognized as political to begin with – why some political visions become sanctioned, and many others don't. A failed political project is significant because it contains within it the seeds of an alternative political imaginary and possibilities of regeneration. In the twentieth century, a racial rule of difference attempted to foreclose political imagination to large swathes of peoples who were colonized. The anticolonial thought that arose as a consequence of and response to imperial power was then subjected to repeated erasure through historical narrative. This erasure of political thought has turned into an absence in International Relations theory that mustn't be viewed as real. Anticolonial thinkers are not historically absent but have been whited-out of International Relations theory in a process of selective redaction. This study of non-alignment is attuned to these histories, is built on them and privileges them. Non-aligned thought also allows us to escape empire, not just in its colonialist, European or Eurocentric forms, but by opening up a space to move beyond critiques of Eurocentrism[1]. The campaign to besmirch radical politics is much more cynical than can simply be grasped by only calling it "Eurocentric". Decolonizing International Relations theory should involve recovering older traditions of decolonial political thought. These traditions are exciting because they present a sustained engagement with questions of empire without being beholden to the idea of empire as the only terrain on which political thought could be given shape.

A history of non-alignment gives us a prescient view of politics and war as fundamentally constitutive of the world order, but also as provocations to think of world reordering. For non-alignment, politics and war as frames of analysis precede questions of empire and the nation-state, which are treated as objects of inquiry[2]. Thus, such a history shows us how political thought from the colonies can be profitably read as both – subverting empire in all its forms while also refusing the preponderance of empire as a structure for analytical thinking. Despite its preoccupation with the colonial question, non-alignment is able to step out of empire's long shadow by drawing attention to the international. Non-alignment is pertinent as modern international thought as well as an internationalist political project. I argue that the nation-state is a central actor in both imperial and internationalist ideas of world order, so it is consistently central to non-aligned thought. I discuss through ideas of Asia, Europe and Africa how ideas of the international were developed within non-aligned thinking. An internationalist vision drove the postcolonial diplomacy of newly decolonized nation-states that had become independent through anticolonial resistance. The path between a colonial past and an international future was charted through spirited diplomatic practice, which propelled nation-states into a dynamic present. Thus, the study of non-aligned diplomacy could ignite a rethinking of ways in which nation-states approach the international.

One of the anxieties driving this book was the ahistoricism of narratives about non-alignment and attendant inaccuracies. So, it was natural that the book began by suggesting alternative ways to study non-alignment. This book is an international history of Indian non-alignment because one of its core themes is the relation between India and the international. It is interesting to make India the site of political ideas for two reasons – engaging with Indian political thought from the twentieth century revises ways in which we understand the nation-state and the international as contiguous concepts but not necessarily in oppositional or harmonious terms. The story of twentieth-century Indian non-alignment is the story of unsettled theories of how India inhabited the world. In an opening chapter, the political thoughts of Rabindranath Tagore, Mohandas Karamchand Gandhi and Jawaharlal Nehru serve as an origin point for thinking about non-aligned politics. In the political thoughts of these three thinkers, the relation between India and the world is not entirely reconciled. These thinkers have disputed ways of relating the Indian political self with that of the larger international system. Tagore, Gandhi and Nehru are often reduced to some form of liberal thought. In this book, I will treat them as presenting radical ideas of India in the world. Their visions are germane to this discussion also because they are also incompatible with one another – their debates serve us well in shattering the myth of a monolithic Indian political tradition, and even less so, a liberal one. Shared commitments in this tradition existed in the realm of anticolonial thought which is vital to the theorization of the Indian nation-state in the international system, removed as it were from competing imperial-colonial ideas of the international. Moreover, for these Indian thinkers, the anticolonial had to be treated as a political actor, not only as a historical category and so, I suggest that Indian anticolonialism presented radical philosophic possibilities and widened the scope for twentieth-century politics beyond liberal internationalism.

I have discussed the nation-state emerging out of empire and expanding into the international as pivotal to India's non-aligned politics. But what about Indian non-alignment and war? For this, I turn to the person of Jawaharlal Nehru, India's first Prime Minister and Foreign Minister. India's colonial experience and the years right before independence in 1947, when India occupied a unique positionality between a colony and a nation, were a particularly generative experience for Nehru. In fact, even after India had become independent of British rule, anticolonialism remained central to Nehru's political thought. The agitation for independence was a formidable act of political agency. It became even more so after 1947, when India gained freedom, but most historical accounts only concede Nehru that radicalism as long as India was colonized. It was as though at independence, Nehru personified in him the State so starkly that he was not allowed to be a larger source for ideas. This has led to all sorts of distortions in interpreting his thought, so much so that writing on Nehru suffers equally at the hands of sympathizers and detractors. His foremost biographers, in an effort to rescue him from the charge of realpolitik, let it be believed that he was simply bewildered at the excesses of the post-war world. Proponents of this school of thought rely too heavily on Nehru's rhetorical practice to the extent that much meaning has been drained from his writings by selective reading intended to emphasize his liberalism. There is little understanding of his deployment of rhetoric as a certain kind of performance of anticolonialism. On the flip side, a focus on his rhetoric rather than on his ideas has allowed conservatives to endlessly pillory his liberal, and consequently for them, fantastical politics. Thus, even though criticism of Nehru's writings abounds on both sides, it offers not much more than a manipulation of his thought. I suggest that a most serious casualty of this approach has been a deep study of the Nehru period in India's international history[3].

Nehru is not a thinker for our century – as this book will demonstrate, his ideas belonged very much to the previous century, but the period he was alive in was itself illuminated by his thought, so he requires our attention even if we were to shed light on that past, with negligible lessons for the present. The persuasive hold of his politics in his own time cannot be denied. Indeed, his Olympian writing offers a way to understand Indian resistance to borrowed theories. Nehru located India in political traditions and offered up large themes, not least of which are his meditations on war. This line of thought runs through the pantheon of the influential political thinkers of that period, but I suggest that Nehru's use of particular historical ideas was intended to galvanize Indians towards the world and to arouse the world to India's power. India's rise to power in the mid-twentieth century is predicated in Nehru's political thought on India's theorization of war. This is not unworthy of deeper exploration, especially for widening the scope of International Relations as a discipline. Yet, attempting to locate Nehru's body of work in the larger canon of International Relations presents difficulties and raises questions about the constitution of that canon. The broader disciplines of history and political philosophy have made scant effort to situate Nehru in a political tradition – a lack felt equally by figures such as Rabindranath Tagore and Mohandas Karamchand Gandhi, who too are unable to escape the fiction of the seer and the saint. Such abridged readings of twentieth-century Indian thinkers have also served to domesticate them, their cosmopolitanism and worldliness notwithstanding. In the opening chapter of the book, I write about Tagore and Gandhi as forebearers of an intellectual lineage, put into practice by Nehru. This political expression united the role of the anticolonial, discomfort with ideological politics, a critique of the nation-state with the imagination of an Afro-Asian space and resistance to the Cold War – ideas that come together and not always cohesively or unproblematically in Nehru's non-aligned politics. Nehru's anxieties for what extraordinary circumstances war could bring, and the recognition that any circumstance surrounding a war *was* extraordinary – this resistance to the spectre of war is central to the non-aligned political project.

Perhaps that is why non-alignment is primarily thought of in Cold War terms. The first order of the book is to disrupt that assumption. For this, I turn to the fin de siècle origins of non-aligned thinking. I show that non-alignment is anti-imperial politics that predated and outlived the Cold War. Second, even though we cannot only think of non-alignment in the framework of the Cold War, non-alignment helps us to think about the Cold War in broader terms. A history of non-alignment is also a history of the Cold War. Naturally, as the concept of non-alignment was fundamental to India's international relations, it is prolifically used in the writing of India's political history, particularly in histories of the early years after independence. Even so, there has yet to emerge a serious discussion of what it has meant for India to be non-aligned. Why have Cold War histories been written for so long without a discussion of these themes? If now, more than ever before, public life depends on what we remember of the past, then why do we remember it so poorly? Primarily, this is a function of the origin myths surrounding non-alignment. There is extensive disagreement amongst scholars about its originary sources – I argue that it was the political landscape in India at the turn of the century that inaugurated non-alignment. This also means, rather more importantly, that I refuse the view that non-alignment is an artefact of the post-war period. Rather, I hold the view that the early life of the idea was an iterative process, with waves of unmaking and articulating political thought in the first stage, and that in later stages, the emphasis was firmly on the uptake of political action. These two phases roughly began in the late nineteenth century and came to a crescendo with the collapse of the Soviet Union.

The study of early Indian non-alignment in the period right after Indian independence has also become excessively braided with the Cold War. Mostly, this is a function of an uncomplicated view of non-alignment as Indian foreign policy, or rather, as not much else. This book treats non-alignment as a riposte to ideological politics. The Cold War was a period of time that coincided with the emergence of independent India in world politics. But it was also a system that was in direct contradiction to the kind of international politics that India sought to practice. It constituted the moment in which ideology politics became the dominant form that world politics took. Indian non-alignment was predicated on the belief that as both blocs led by the two superpowers were practising a form of ideological politics, they had more commonalities than differences, and were thus falsely opposed. A study of Indian diplomacy from this time offers an empirical corrective to the view that the Cold War was a competition between two antithetical political positions. At best, this history recognizes interventions by Indian political thought on world politics; at the very least, it allows for an escape from thinking of International History as national narratives locked into place by the Cold War allegiances of their respective states. Indeed, global histories of this period are increasingly concerned with India as an international actor; histories of modern India should also feature India as an international actor. This widens the scope of modern Indian history, but also of the study of the postcolonial condition of India. The Indian experience shows that the global struggle against the Cold War as well as national and transnational struggles for decolonization were intrinsically linked. Much of the history of the Cold War is thus, first, the history of decolonization. Such an examination of non-aligned politics also yields dividends for the writing of Cold War history itself, particularly in interrogating the narrative modes in which these histories are written. The idea of the Long Peace, for instance, is enraging and exhausting because of its blindness to the Indian experience of the Cold War. The Cold War sometimes stayed cold because of the enormous and world-altering contribution of Afro-Asian nation-states in regulating great power politics. Non-alignment provided a recess when capitalism and socialism were attempting to outweigh each other, even though capitalism already had, in the 1940s, pretensions to outlasting socialism.

Political scientists and historians in the 1960s looked to the political successes that non-alignment has enjoyed as an idea, often writing analytically sophisticated studies, locating non-alignment in international history, politics and law. Sadly, this approach was buried in the following decades by the relentless cataloguing of its failures. Yet, one has to only look to the history of India at the United Nations (UN) to observe the innovativeness with which non-alignment was reproduced in that site. The founding of the UN brought new possibilities for transformative politics, and India occupied a leading role in that process through diplomacy and peacekeeping – both projects that deserve histories of their own but are also indispensable to this larger narrative. Descriptions of non-alignment are often inattentive to this aspect, or significantly underplay its originality. *The Nehru Years* is an international history of Indian non-alignment from the founding period following India's independence in 1947 and is wrapped up in 1964, with Nehru's death, signalling the end of the first long period of independent India's international relations. In the book, I use non-alignment/non-aligned politics/non-aligned political action to denote a particular understanding of world politics, a willingness to engage with this politics and the actual action itself.

The ways in which we think of both the political philosophy driving non-alignment and the historical manifestations of that politics are so closely intertwined that the chapters in the book are organized to make those connections more explicit. The chapter titles in the book are borrowed from Nehru's descriptions of the events under study. They are doubly interesting because they are signal terms marking the political environment in which Nehru thought non-alignment was operating. When he said, "India ploughs a lonely furrow", he was identifying non-alignment as isolating India, an effect Nehru sought to overcome through diplomatic practice. The Korean War took many surprising turns, but the armistice negotiations quickly fell into a lull; so unexpected was an agreement between the two superpowers that Nehru called it an "outbreak of peace". In 1956, as events proceeded quicker than non-alignment could reconcile with, Nehru spoke of the inability of foreign policy to distinguish between right and wrong under "the fog of war". Finally, as Indian troops sustained casualties in the Congo, and African states were estranged from Indian involvement in that crisis, we recall Nehru's pronouncement decades ago that a "patched-up unity" only produced "bad ethics and worse policy".

The opening chapter, Chapter 2, is a conceptual history of Tagore, Gandhi and Nehru's international and political thought. The historical chapters that follow are built around Nehru's ideas of Asia, Europe and Africa, which offer specific ideas of the international. Chapter 3 is a study of India's involvement in the Korean War, particularly in the later stages of that war and in bringing it to a close through the successful negotiation of an armistice agreement between 1950 and 1953. A history of India's role in the negotiations following the Korean War is insightful because it outlines India's mediatory diplomacy. Next, in Chapter 4, I discuss the year 1956 as bringing together two crises that coincided in time almost to the hour but were starkly different in their causes and consequences. In the Suez Canal Crisis, India again assumed a mediatory role. The anticolonial fervour of the crisis and Indian empathy with the Egyptian cause did not stop India from mediating with both sides, contributing to the closing of the crisis. On the other hand, in the case of Hungary, Nehru exposed himself to severe criticism, both international and domestic, for India's delayed and ambiguous response to Soviet actions in suppressing the revolution. Both these events are discussed in conjunction as an attempt to read them as a discursive moment, one in which Indian non-alignment as an approach to world politics encountered its first challenge. The next crisis we discuss goes even further away from the critical stance adopted by non-alignment in the early 1950s. In Chapter 5, I discuss the Congo Crisis, one where India was involved between 1960 and 1964. It is my contention that the advent of peacekeeping and the UN's reliance on India's troop contribution for its continued survival and success in the Congo exposed India to rapid alienation from

African member-states and led to the loss of Indian lives. Reversals to India's foreign policy were soon overshadowed by problems on India's borders with China and eventually, the Sino-Indian War. The epilogue offers some final remarks on how we may approach non-alignment critically, and on lessons learnt from a diminished political vision.

2

A Lonely Furrow

Tagore, Gandhi and Nehruvian Non-Alignment

A genealogy of non-alignment depends to a large extent on what we think non-alignment is. If it is treated as only a foreign policy, then its value lies in its versatility and in its continued relevance to furthering a nation's interests. As this is a history of non-alignment as a political vision, I shall trace its origins to the thought of Rabindranath Tagore – modernist, philosopher, poet, and Mohandas Karamchand Gandhi – anticolonialist, ethicist, political thinker. Together with Nehru's own historically oriented political philosophy, for non-alignment, Tagore's and Gandhi's ideas were formative and influential. Both thinkers had long engagements with the core concepts that non-alignment is concerned with the interplay between empire and nationalism, the imagination of the international as a space of movements and flux, and the nation-state as essentially problematic. Nehru's own historical consciousness developed through his exposure to the intellectual currents of the early twentieth century and especially to socialist anticolonialism, Tagore's commentaries on the dangers of nationalism and the promise of cosmopolitanism, Gandhi's commentaries on the evils of empire and the state as well as his methods for political redemption through ethical practice. Nehru then made attempts to integrate these multiple commentaries into what was, essentially, a theoretical approach to international relations. Influences on Nehru's international political thought can be used as a basis for interpreting India's non-aligned diplomacy in the early Cold War period. I discuss these influences, Nehru's theory of the state and introduce India's non-aligned approach in Asia, Europe and Africa.

Is Politics Ultimately Doomed?

Nehru's predilection for history predated the attainment of Indian independence (1947) or the beginning of the Cold War (1945). Indeed, Nehru's major pre-independence works were all histories – in *Glimpses of World History* (1934), Nehru offered a view of the world, and its contending ideologies; in *An Autobiography – Towards Freedom* (1936), he traced his own life alongside the development of the Indian anticolonial movement and then located both in the timeline of world history, and finally, in *The Discovery of India* (1946), he recounted India's history from ancient times to the twentieth century to highlight India's identity as a nation. Throughout this work, he located the self, the global and the nation as being analogous[1]. Subsequently, however, in his writing post-independence, there was a discernible shift towards separating these concepts from one another, seeing the nation-state as more than a collection of individuals, and the international as more than a collection of nation-states[2]. Nehru's early theorization of the nation-state had developed in the period before India became independent of British rule, so it was natural that in his view the nation-state was an entity taking form in a later time, in the image of a post-imperial future. For theorists of International Relations, this postcoloniality of the Indian nation-state is assumed as the plane on which India experiences international relations. The nation is reified in the form of the state, and the state in India, on coming into existence in 1947, immediately acquires a postcolonial character. Beyond that, there is a lack of theoretical reflection on the relation between the Indian nation and the Indian state, how this may have translated into an Indian encounter with the international as a space or whether these encounters bear any significance for International Relations. To fully grasp the origins of twentieth-century Indian internationalism, it is useful to assume that "states have given birth to nations at least so often as nations have given birth to states"[3]. It has been argued that in his image of the future, Nehru distinguished the concepts of nation and state, and employed the past of the Indian nation to advance an idea of the state India could become. The Nehruvian idea of the state

Prime Minister Nehru Meets Indian Delegation
Pandit Jawaharlal Nehru greets members of the Secretariat of the Indian delegation to the UN during his visit to the UN headquarters at Lake Success, NY, 19 October 1949. (Bettmann via Getty Images)

Hammarskjöld Meets Nehru
UN Secretary General stops in New Delhi for talks with Prime Minister Nehru on his way to China for talks with Premier Zhou Enlai. New Delhi, 13 January 1955. (United Press Photo/AFP via Getty Images)

– its character, its function, its power – also inspired a retelling of the Indian national story, with an emphasis on certain aspects more than on others. Indeed, the "status of the past" was a crucial element in shaping a future for India[4]. Nehru, not unlike other postcolonial elites, had chosen the nation-state to form the core of his political project, which is not surprising, yet the process by which he came to do so is significant in itself[5].

Indeed, the nation and the state, in their conjoined form, were at the centre of the Nehruvian political project. The nation-state was not unthinkingly adopted by Nehru, and it is crucial to fully grasp this idea of India to come to terms with Nehru's placement of India in the world. The international was for Nehru a lived reality, one that he occupied as a public figure in India's independence movement, taking on both national and international roles, much like the colonialists he had been fighting[6]. By the 1910s, Nehru was involved in the nationalist discourse gaining currency in India and the anticolonial internationalism of the wider world. This made available to him different narratives of history from which he could cast a mold for his own thought[7]. On the basis of early exposure to diverse historical narratives, Nehru repeatedly attempted "a second first reading" of the history of India[8]. The first such attempt was rooted in a primarily economic theory of socialist thought – it was the Marxist critique of the exploitative nature of a capitalist society[9]. Nehru was an enthusiastic votary of socialist thought and of the anticolonial discourse of Marxism, announcing on the eve of Indian independence, "I hope, India will stand for Socialism and that India will go towards the constitution of a Socialist state and I do believe that the whole world will have to go that way"[10]. The subsequent influence of socialist thought on India's political economy is very well-documented[11]. However, at the beginning of the twentieth century, when India was still under colonial domination, the Marxist trope of "exploitation" carried even more significance. In an imperialist international society, the concept of the exploitation of the weaker people within one nation was being amplified and replayed as the exploitation of the weaker nations of the world. Globally, Marxists attempted to influence anti-imperial struggles quite directly, as is evident in the League Against Imperialism, an anti-imperialist meeting organized by the Comintern in 1927, held in Brussels, Belgium[12]. Thirty-seven colonies were represented amongst the League's members; Nehru attended this meeting and encountered for the first time Marxist thought with an anticolonial impulse[13]. Subsequently, this confluence of narratives came forth more sharply in his own political thought[14]. Although the League eventually failed over disagreements amongst members, it provided a model for future organizations. Indeed, the similarities in basic structure with the Non-Aligned Movement (NAM) are quite evident[15].

The second of Nehru's attempts at reading anew the history of India came from his involvement in Indian anticolonialism. In Nehru's view, even if the independence movement were successful, India would merely transition from being a colony to having had a colonial past, as the main objective of the movement was only to secure the independence of India from colonial rule[16]. Having secured that objective, anticolonialist thought was unlikely to have an enduring influence on independent India, or on India's status in the larger world. India was tied to the colonial framework through which it had entered a period of modernity – India's political identity had been constructed in relation to the empire. It was unlikely the freedom movement would remake the image of India in the world, so a new identity would have to be forged for India, but this could be on the basis neither of political nor of economic history, because these were both histories of subjugation. An emphasis on the political or economic aspects of India's history would have resulted in a view that one's cultural past was too dislocated to inform a sense of politics; it would be seen as a "history of lack, a history that always falls short of true history"[17]. On the other hand, an accentuation of India's cultural past could lead to the sort of militant nationalism that fascist movements relied on[18]. An alternate approach to reorienting India's history was presented by Mohandas Karamchand Gandhi. With the advent of Gandhi, whose politics was fashioned fundamentally differently, the economic and cultural aspects of the anticolonial critique were minimized in favor of a moral attack on the evils of colonialism and an exhortation to the British to redeem themselves through the practice of ethical politics. Gandhi had been in South Africa until 1915, so when he arrived back in India, at about the time he first met Nehru, he was preoccupied with the issues Indians were facing in South Africa. But over the next two years, Gandhi went on to engineer a farmers' agitation against forced indigo cultivation, his first act of civil disobedience and a pivotal event in the course of the Indian freedom struggle that also signaled his unequivocal arrival on the Indian political scene. Through acts of political protest, over the next three decades, Gandhi impugned the founding logic of the British Empire. Gandhi also shaped modern Indian political thought, drawing attention to questions of violence as manifest in human relations and in relation to man's morality, but also in its larger form as the problem of empire[19]. Gandhi's treatment of violence and non-violence made him suspect of empire and of nationalism – after all, what was empire but colonial nationalism, the power-riddled urge to conquer territories and peoples in the name of the sovereign, "a danger whose reality was always to be found elsewhere"[20].

The early twentieth century was a time of great political ferment in India, a time for the articulation and remaking of the language of modern Indian political thought. The sources of this language were myriad, and not necessarily all of political origin. The work of Rabindranath Tagore, for instance, drew on social and cultural idioms. Indeed, moving even further away from Gandhi's already quite radical positions, Tagore's thinking was critical not just of empire and nationalism but also of politics itself. Tagore was a social reformer, an educationist, a poet who was widely travelled – perhaps more than any other Indian public figure of that time. Tagore travelled to and lectured on poetry, philosophy and spirituality in China, Japan, Iran, Yugoslavia, Mexico amongst other places, becoming the first non-European to win the Nobel Prize in 1913. Although most of his lectures were highly acclaimed and well-received, there was also some resistance to his lectures on nationalism, delivered mostly in Japan. Published as the treatise *Nationalism*, Tagore in his talks, put forth the view that politics as a method of achieving social cohesion, was deeply problematic. Tagore said he was wary of the "profound inauthenticity"[21] of politics and in his arguments against nationalisms, both European and Japanese[22], he expressed an anxiety that a political form of life would unavoidably lapse into an "aggressive, competitive and acquisitive practice of imperialism"[23]. Tagore's critique of nationalism also critiqued politics because Tagore saw nationalism as nothing more than the manifestation of politics. This also coloured Tagore's view of how the international as a place of encounters and movement should be organized – if people had to organize themselves politically, that would dilute the social texture of their being; if they found themselves organized as nations, that would homogenize them. Rather than inspiring innovative ways to make connections and sustain movement and growth between communities, this would lead to a tedious sameness between worlds. Politics was wont to rely on nationalism, and Tagore was certain that nationalism would phase "India's entry into the universal"[24]. Thus, suspicious of nationalism and colonialism, Tagore also approached politics with cynicism.

Gandhi and Tagore are pivotal in modern political thought because they are dissatisfied not only with the core elements of politics but also with politics itself as somewhat irredeemable and fulfilling a limited function. Faced with the question of whether politics was ultimately doomed, Gandhi and Tagore's views on how to address this fundamental problem were starkly at odds. Both viewed the nation-state as undesirable and sought to put forth a community-based conceptualization of social life. Both relied on the idea of community-led reinvigoration of a social space, but they employed the concept differently. Gandhi saw the village as the ideal representation of social life, whilst Tagore was more focused on the flows between global communities. They both placed an emphasis on the social over the political, the cultural over the national. For Gandhi, this was to be achieved by replacing the state with smaller units, a kind of conglomeration of village republics. Tagore sought to reconcile the political with a redemptive cosmopolitanism[25]. The nation-state, in India and elsewhere, would become a repository of the aspirations of its people, and because those aspirations were universal and were also always simultaneously being expressed elsewhere, India's role in world politics could serve to legitimize the shared character of these aspirations. Through this transnational interconnectedness, India could enter the international space while remaking it in sharp contrast with earlier imperial ideas. Tagore's cosmopolitan political thought is significant because it disrupts a hegemonic core-periphery structure in two ways – first, in Tagore's thought, Indian anticolonialism was not only in conversation with its European colonizers but also with other anticolonialisms, thus engaging with conversations between peripheries, between the core and the periphery and across various core-periphery relations[26]. Second, by reorienting the role of the Indian nation-state away from power politics and towards transnational solidarities, the essentially cosmopolitan character of India, a vast geographical entity with a multitude of diverse cultures, could be safeguarded. Indeed, if it espoused this political approach, India would remain a "land without a centre"[27]. It is this "idea of India: and Jawaharlal Nehru" that is carried forward in Nehru's own international political thought, albeit with different inflections of emphasis[28].

Both Tagore and Gandhi developed critiques of the form of the nation-state. For Tagore, politics was deeply problematic because it encouraged the organization of peoples as nations, it diminished the scope for social organization and therefore, led inevitably to imperialist modes of thought[29]. Tagore's antidote to this condition was to inspire the free movement of people outside the borders of the state. In emphasizing the interconnectedness of people, he sought to make the political character of the Indian nation-state somewhat circumscribed. A nation-state whose sovereignty was secured within its borders, would be elevated in international affairs if it could blur its intellectual boundaries for the free movement of ideas. The East and the West had to be treated as conceptual categories. Neither would India be "blind, foolish, insensate begging at the door of Europe, with our critical sense entirely benumbed"[30] nor would there be "a wholesale suspicion of the West"[31]. For Tagore, the idea of the international was "including but not restricted to the West"[32]. Tagore's international thought warns against India being ghettoized because of its location outside of the West and also against its non-western cosmopolitanism being understood as a colloquial political language. This, of course, is the most recognizable characteristic of Nehruvian non-alignment – the Indian non-aligned position in world politics arises out of a breach in the split between the West and the non-West. In line with Tagore's views, Nehru too thought that the essence of the problem of peace was the problem of empire and thus, his internationalism was explicitly positioned as being more than just thinking within parochial confines[33]. Although non-alignment often takes on the semblance of advocating internationalism, in reality, non-alignment was also to a large extent, contingent *on* internationalism[34]. Instead of "confining India within local horizons", Tagore had overthrown an understanding of the East and West as opposite, highlighting their coeval origins[35]. In so doing, he prefaced Nehru's non-alignment, whose motif was to politicize geography differently.

For Gandhi, the danger of the state was not so much in its capacity to make a certain sort of politics possible. Certainly, he was deeply aware of the state as a repository of violence, writing in 1935, "The state represents violence in a concentrated and organized form. The individual has a soul, but as the state is a soulless machine, it can never be weaned from violence to which it owes its very existence"[36]. Yet, for him the critique of the state was founded not in the processes it set in motion, but in the processes that were required to birth the state. Thus, he positioned the non-violence of the anti-imperial struggle for freedom against the violence of the imperial state. Violence, he saw as deeply entrenched in both state and society, but while the state's existence was tied to the "violent politics of life"[37], society was more capable of redeeming itself through "the formal recognition of a force that already sustained society" – that of non-violence[38]. Gandhi's critique was not solely confined to a study of non-violence as his method. With each wave of anticolonial protest in India, he was able to further refine his own critique. At an earlier stage, he was chiefly concerned with the recovery of "a line of moral inquiry"[39]; later, he goes so far as to suggest there were possibilities for ethical action present in politics[40]. Over the years, Gandhi adopted a position that was increasingly wary of politics and remained committed to ethics as a formative discourse. Earlier anxieties with regard to the state inform the profound anti-statism of his later years[41]. In 1939, he wrote, "In an Ideal state there will be no political institution and therefore no political power"[42]. By divorcing politics from it, he was able to undermine the centrality of the state in two ways – first, by offering a model of government even more diffused than the federalist structure, through his vision of village republics; second, by highlighting the possibilities for moral action not in a collective form of politics, but in an individual form of life. For Gandhi, the state was essentially a symptom of crisis. The crisis in question was the loss of sovereignty over self because the existence of the state meant that sovereignty had to be understood solely in those terms. By prioritizing the state over other forms of social interaction, the possibilities for moral action by individuals would be diminished[43]. Such a compromised morality would only exist in the "shadow of politics"[44]. Therefore, in order to secure the conditions for moral action, Gandhi "fragmented sovereignty"[45]; he sought to agitate the alliance between state and sovereignty by privileging the self. In many ways, Gandhi disrupted the idea that sovereignty belonged only to the state, and that the sovereignty of the state was the basis on which to analyze power, anticipating Foucault's oft-quoted call for the king's head in political theory[46].

Having thus formulated a radical critique of politics, Gandhi also developed a theoretical perspective on war. Gandhi's philosophy drew a distinction between politics and war. He was interested in two aspects of the relationship – the politics that makes war seem necessary and therefore possible, and ethical action in the midst of a state of war. The study of the first aspect led him to believe that with regard to war, "the logic of its necessity seems always to trump the tragedy of its effects"[47]. He saw politics as having a vacuous presence, preoccupied by its instrumentality[48]. He saw the state as being hopelessly infatuated by such a politics, incessantly calculating its "larger purposes"[49]. Having already established the moral vacancy of politics, his attention was to identify the potential for moral action *within* the conditions in which war was being waged, by sequestering it from politics. Although war was justified by the invocation of another better future, in itself it was devoid of the "permanent idealism of politics and peace"[50]. Therefore, Gandhi was interested not in a morality that sanctions war as a means of politics, but morality as a possibility in times of war. This morality could be found in that twilight zone where politics was not in a "pacific instantiation", but where a total loss of human life had not yet occurred[51]. Here, he thought the conditions of moral action could assert themselves with complete autonomy: they were not constrained by the normality of politics. When states went to war, their moral choices stood completely exposed. Therefore, when he said that "India shall survive this death dance and occupy the moral height"[52], he was referring not only to the possibility that India would not go to war, but that in the event *other* states went to war, India would find ways in which to fully exercise its moral agency. In Gandhi's view, if morality was not in any way contingent on politics, if indeed, politics was perilous to the scope of morality, then a state of war where politics had broken down could create more generative conditions for the exercise of morality.

Two aspects of Gandhi's political thought have been discussed here – the first is the assumption that politics makes the state and second, that war, as distinct from politics, permits morality. The state was essentially prone to violence, in Gandhi's critique, and to imperialism, in Tagore's analysis. These critiques were fundamentally opposed to the creed of politics that made the state possible, but in so doing, they tied the two concepts together; both agreed that the state was the site where politics took place, while Gandhi also theorized it as the site of war. Gandhi chose first to bring forth the ethical content of politics, and then to focus his attention on ethics alone. In part, this was because the frame of reference within which Gandhi was working was that of the problem of modernity. For him, the framework of empire meant "the forcible imposition of European modernity on India"[53]. In order to move out of that framework, it was necessary to bring about a sense of India's own modernity. For Gandhi, this could only be done outside the orbit of the state[54]. But, by suggesting these ideas in conjunction, Gandhi generated possibilities for a new vision of the state, a prospect taken up vigorously by Nehru. Nehru's engagement with the state was primarily in conversation with Gandhi's critique of it. Nehru's vision reflected the overall anxieties present in Gandhi's political thought but rejected its underlying assumptions.

The most significant assumption in Nehru's thought was to treat the state as a desirable entity. When located within the narrative of the state in Tagore and Gandhi's thought, this assumption strikes a discordant note. For instance, it has been suggested that Nehru's "étatisme" was "an entirely novel ideological reconstruction of the elements of nationalist thought that was then being undertaken in the final, fully mature, stage of the development of nationalism in India - its moment of arrival" and "a reconstruction whose specific form was to situate nationalism within the domain of a state ideology"[55]. Placed in the context of the independence movement, Nehru's statism is analyzed as a logical, even inevitable outcome. In fact, this perception is quite popular with writers taking the view that "…for an Asian country newly liberated from more than a century of rule by a European power it would have been unthinkable not to espouse those causes"[56]. Other readings have suggested the contrary – that Nehru's attempts at conceptualizing the state differently are unique, that "the political history of Asia and Africa are full of examples of states which simply inherited colonial bureaucracies, with a tired political imagination" but that this was not true of Nehru who sought to invigorate the concept of the nation-state[57].

In either reading, the estimation is that Nehru was "at times Gandhian, at others Nehruvian", that is to say that while Nehru adapted some of Gandhi's political thought, he also made sharp departures from it[58]. These departures are about the content of the state. My emphasis in the following section is on what I consider his most significant departure – one in which he places his conviction in the form of the state, in arguing for the state, in making the argument that the state was essential and inevitable. Nehru does this not only by repudiating the European model of statehood but by imagining a form that would be particularly suited to accommodating the paradoxes of the Indian nation, while functioning in a western-dominated international system. By overlooking this element of translation and redefinition in Nehru's theorization of the state, we have an incomplete picture of his political vision. We are also inclined to ignore his critique not only of nation-states, but also of the world order they occupy. The Gandhian and Tagorean critique and rejection of the nation-state was acknowledged by Nehru but the inherent contradictions present in those commentaries made it impossible for Nehru to endorse those views – as Kaviraj puts it, "After all, the independence movement was about the capture of the state, and it was anomalous to suggest that the state that was captured with such effort should then be reduced to insignificance"[59]. Placing too much emphasis on the discontinuities between Tagore, Gandhi and Nehru suggests that while Nehru manipulated the form of the state, he was really only disagreeing with those who came before him. I suggest a different reading of Nehru's attempts to build a theory of the state, one based on his repudiation of the idea that politics was ultimately doomed.

India in the Cold War

By developing the radical ethical positions taken up by Gandhi and by locating them in Tagore's idea of the international, Nehru re-imagined the state itself as capable of exerting moral force and to imagine it as the location of politics, which was increasingly becoming "the dominant medium of public life"[60]. India's experience of the "operative calculus of imperial power"[61] had forged a deep suspicion of narratives rooted in emancipation and Gandhi's broadly ethical framework had discarded the politics of the state. For Nehru, it was necessary to situate this moral force in a way that did not mean either the state taking on an emancipatory role or emphasizing only the ethical dimensions of public life, thereby displacing its own political function. To lay the foundations of this new theory, Nehru challenged Gandhi's view that for man to be able to act morally both in politics and in war, these actions would have to take place outside of the remit of the state. For Gandhi, the state embodied moral ambiguity, the loss of ethical ambition. For Nehru, the state could be salvaged as a political actor, indeed, the state could buttress political action provided there were ways in which the state was not estranged from politics.

The relation between politics as action and the state as an actor could be restored. The breakdown of this relation was a characteristic of modernity and had also affected it, so a revised postmodern approach could also resolve the self-estrangement of politics. If in India, there was "more to politics than the forceful machinery of the state", then such a politics could also take a critical view of war as excessive and amoral while also acting politically through the medium of the state[62]. This postmodern, statist and critical political vision informed India's international relations and the conduct of Indian external affairs and came to be known as non-alignment[63].

Nehru was so unabashedly critical of the Cold War's ideological camps that his policy was, in fact, *anti*-alignment. In the Gandhian intellectual tradition, negotiation was crucial as a political method and had served Gandhi well in his dealings with imperial authority. Nehru included this approach in his international thought, not just in terms of how India would participate in world politics but also in describing Indian unacceptance of an alliance-based world order. For this, he relied on the history of India's anticolonial movement, saying, "[Gandhi] created connecting links between conflicting elements. I would not say that all conflicts are thus avoided. But the door is always open. And remember also that Gandhi was absolutely unbending when it came to giving up a principle; when it came to surrendering a vital position. But he never closed the door to the other party wishing to enter, to talk to him and to discuss matters. He fought the British, but he was always friendly to them. That dual conception is not quite understood. That is why we cannot understand or appreciate the Cold War mentality"[64]. In invoking Gandhi's position as being anticolonial but not anti-British, Nehru's larger implication was that the danger of an ideological conflict was seldom only the wars, hot or cold, that it caused but was also that conflict per se would perpetually frame the political relationship between the parties to the conflict. Nehru also found the concept of a Cold War absurd and regressive: "The Cold War approach seems utterly illogical because a cold war has some meaning only as a prelude to a hot war. If the hot war is not to take place, then some other method has to be evolved. But the cold war prevents other methods being evolved"[65]. To introduce alternative methods of conducting world politics, Nehru questioned the two dominant ideologies of the Cold War and in order to create space for non-alignment as one such alternative approach, he insisted that there was "no justification for saying there can be only two ideologies in the world" and that such a view presented "too great a limitation of the power of thinking, or of action"[66].

Given the realities of the Cold War, Nehru leaned on his earlier engagement with Tagore's and Gandhi's ideas to theorize non-alignment. Nehruvian non-alignment relies very heavily on the imminent prominence of Asia, and even more so, on that of India. It put forth a critique of Europe as a historical category, but portrayed Asia as a sociological one. While Europe's history was in Nehru's critique the history of war, colonialism and empire, the relations between peoples and their futurist visions would define Asia. Asia was on the verge of forming multiple modernities and if it counted somewhat in world affairs then, it would count much more in the future[67]. Nehru also framed Asia's past and India's future as diametrically opposed[68]. Using anachronism as a method, he projected India's future influence as if it were already a true fact. Although it has been suggested that essentially Nehru was punching above his weight, or that it was the appeal of his own personality that resulted in this outcome, I suggest that in fact, this was a position he was consistently vested in[69]. By stating that India was seeking "synthesis" and disliked an "upheaval of so much that is old", he was alluding to a narrative of continuity, to be achieved in the present and in the future[70]. This language of continuity was integral to the Gandhian method too[71]. In imagining India, the past did not have to be forsaken; it had to be reshaped in order to make the future possible. This was one way to counter the problem of maintaining continuity with the past while moving away from the burden of history. This was also a way to stress the importance of Asia that would have "a greater influence on the future shaping of world events" adding that Asian powers were now "awake; their people are moving, and they have no intention whatever of being ignored or of being passed by"[72]. Nehru began to present India as the locus of this temporal-geographical critique of world politics, identifying India as the source of non-alignment, which was now "an integral part of the international pattern", and "widely conceded to be a comprehensible and legitimate policy, particularly for the emergent Afro-Asian states" [73]. In this way, Nehru established India's new identity around India's relations with the rest of the world[74]. It could be said that India came to occupy a "special place which could not be identified as being either with the "haves or the have nots"[75]. Indian diplomats were referring to non-alignment as "an ugly word", a "negative" concept but one that became "positive when you use it the way we do"[76].

Gandhi's vision "represented something more than the immediate past"[77]. It was not only the ethical commitment in Gandhi's politics, but also the central concepts in Gandhi's thought – war, peace, politics, violence, morality and truth. Gandhi theorized ideas as relational towards each other in an entirely novel, and perhaps too radical manner. Gandhi was also able to make these ideas widely accessible[78]. Through the experience of anticolonial action in India, the universality of Gandhi's methods became increasingly evident. Gandhi's political epistemology suggests that by insisting on the fundamentality of certain concepts (such as violence), Gandhi rejected those concepts that he saw as problematic (such as the state), and neglected others that he saw as directly related to the concepts that he had rejected (such as the international). The international was one of the least problematized concepts in Gandhi's politics, not because it was essentially unproblematic but because it was in his view, theoretically braided with the state. Arguably, Gandhi had offered even in the very early years after his return to India, an unparalleled critique of Britain's colonial nationalism. Yet, he had even then misread concurrent attempts at colonial internationalism, mistaking colonial internationalists for reformers of international society, unable to fully grasp the manner in which certain institutions would eventually set a template for post-war internationalism[79]. Nehru, whose political thought was deeply influenced by the history of the twentieth century, saw the international become the dominant mode of imagining the state, especially following processes of state formation in Europe. The Cold War represented an interregnum in that process. The breakdown of empires and the "balance of terror" was followed by rapid decolonization[80]. As new states emerged in Asia and Africa, they formed the Third World, a concept that became even more prominent in the 1950s[81]. These states were occupied by the question of sovereignty – acquiring, consolidating and defending it. For Nehru, this meant that the sovereignty of one state was not only conceptualized in relation to the sovereignty of another but also in relation to the international. The idea simply was that if more states ascribed to this view, then the international could be a site of peaceful co-existence while allowing states to "meet any possible contingency that may arise" without having to enter either Soviet or American spheres of influence[82]. Nehru's non-alignment, a "straightforward, honest and independent policy", was thus an act of civil disobedience[83].

A discourse so deeply critical of the structure of international relations carried in it the possibility of isolating India. The international commitment that was an integral part of non-alignment itself came into question; the question being asked of all non-aligned nations was if they believed they were "playing their full part as citizens of the world by sitting on the fence between two power blocs and enjoying the best of both worlds", and India was no exception to this skepticism[84]. In 1947, Nehru had warned the Constituent Assembly that by taking this course, India would have to "plough a lonely furrow"[85]; by 1949, he was anxious that Indians were possibly "too sure of our stability, internal and external"[86] as neither of the big blocs looked upon India with favor[87]. Only a few years later, the formation of the NAM reinvigorated the idea of the Third World by giving voice to "a common consciousness among the newly independent countries of the Third World"[88]. Although both the Third World and the NAM shared basic premises, they were distinct in one extremely important way – the members of the NAM abjured military pacts with either bloc, but also with each other. As Indian diplomat V. K. Krishna Menon once put it, "a non-aligned nation must be non-aligned with the non-aligned to be truly non-aligned"[89]. Nehru, reluctant from the start to overly associate Indian non-alignment with the larger NAM, distanced India from what he possibly saw as a limiting discourse, an institution that was more a reflection of the historical momentum of the time than an abiding normative commitment to reordering world politics. As the NAM grew by the mid-1950s, every effort at expanding brought to the fore divisions amongst members, not in the least between India and Indonesia. This unravelling of NAM was also hastened by relaxations towards non-alignment in Nehru's own position. In part, this came from the consolidation of Indian territories (such as in Kashmir, Hyderabad or Goa) and India's policies regionally (such as in Nepal or Bhutan)[90].

In 1927, Nehru had outlined India's future foreign policy as being opposed to the use of force on foreign territories, claiming that India had "no interests…anywhere which require the protection of armed force" and that even if India had such interests, it was better for them to "suffer than to be protected at the point of the bayonet", adding that the "only interests we wish to develop in any country are such as are acceptable to the people of that country"[91]. Two decades later, when Nehru took office as India's first Prime Minister, India was a founding member of the UN. The UN presented a challenge to Nehru's conceptualization of the international, as he began to fear that transnationalism would strengthen nationalisms, not diffuse them[92]. Over the next ten years, India's response to mitigating superpower rivalry and a surge in ideological politics at the UN was to participate in mediation. Writing to India's ambassador in the US, Nehru said, "What do we try to do? To soften and soothe each side and make it slightly more receptive to the other"[93]. In part, Nehru could have seen this as a sort of affirmation of India's still new identity. But it also seems likely that this was an attempt at securing India's friendly relations with the west to bring about "the peaceful transformation of an untenable relationship"[94]. Looking back at the end of the Nehru era, Krishna Menon summarized the significance of non-alignment as having established India, "not as a major power, but as an important quantity in world affairs", having prevented India "from becoming a satellite state" and, as having "put a brake on war"[95]. India also committed in a very substantial way to UN peacekeeping. India was one of the first contributors to the UN Peacekeeping Force and also one of the beneficiaries of it, when the United Nations Military Observation Group was deployed to maintain peace in India and Pakistan in 1948. The same year, Nehru had announced that "the less we interfere in international conflicts, the better, unless our own interest is involved, for this reason that it is not in consonance with our dignity just to interfere without any effect being produced. Either we should be strong enough to produce some effect or we should not interfere at all"[96].

Conflicts where, through mediation and peacekeeping, India did produce an effect were the Korean War (1951), the Suez Canal Crisis

Nehru Visits the UN
From left to right – Andrew Cordier, Under Secretary in Charge of the UN General Assembly, Carlos Peña Rómulo, President of the UN General Assembly and Jawaharlal Nehru, Prime Minister of India, in front of the UN building in New York, US, 19 October 1949. (Keystone-France/Gamma-Rapho via Getty Images)

(1956), the Hungarian Revolution (1956) and the Congo Crisis (1960). The following three chapters look at one event each, with 1956 being treated as one historic moment that found expression in two crises. How was Indian non-alignment received globally? How did Nehru's ideas of Asia, Europe and Africa affect the practice of non-aligned foreign policy? What do each of the events tell us about the non-aligned response to internationalism, nationalism and race? The following chapters will foreground these questions. The analysis of archival material might reveal certain continuities between events, even if there are discontinuities in their specific historical contexts. Histories of India's international relations are usually so concerned with establishing the retrospective significance of particular events that they neglect a study of the central idea that informed India's response to them. This book addresses this problem by offering a history of India as an international actor. I present India's non-aligned political practice as a phenomenon from which to derive conclusions about the relationship between politics and war more broadly.

3

The Outbreak of Peace

India and the Korean War, 1950–1953

This chapter discusses India's engagement with the Korean War, particularly between the crossing of the 38th Parallel by the North Koreans in 1950 and the signing of the armistice agreement at Panmunjom in 1953. I begin by discussing the contextual specificities of Asia and the interface between India and Asia. I have previously discussed at length Nehru's articulation of the international; I now look specifically to his understanding of Asia. This is followed by a narrative of the Korean War, with particular attention to the substantial role of non-aligned India in bringing the war to a close. I study the way India navigated the international as a space and how the Nehruvian conceptualization of international relations made these moves possible. I will finally end with a discussion of how India's approach to the Korean War presented a challenge to the Eurocentric imagination of international relations and was an attempt to shape the UN as a global platform where issues could be dealt with politically, not militarily. This made it possible to move away from securitized discourses, both of nationalism and internationalism. Thus, the Korean War represents a moment of great historical significance not just for the states directly involved in the conflict, but also for states such as India[1]. As such, this account provides a corrective to histories of the Korean War that were already considered revisionist but neglected India's involvement in the peace process[2].

India, Korea and Asia

The intellectual networks between India and the rest of Asia in the early- and mid-twentieth century developed in the context of and in response to the Empire. A strand of intellectuals in colonial India routinely expressed their anti-imperial positions in an Asian idiom[3]. This form of historicized expression was developed by three simultaneous methods – the nationalist, the Asianist and the cosmopolitan. While nationalists operated within their respective countries, early Indian pan-Asianists such as Rasbehari Bose and Taraknath Das based themselves in other Asian countries such as Japan and China[4]. Intellectuals such as Tagore, who emphasized universalism and were less interested in Asian essentialism, promulgated the cosmopolitan position. When Tagore's seminal work *Nationalism* was published, it used both Asian and European examples to illustrate the ills of nationalist thinking. Indeed, Tagore's anti-imperial stance was inherently a political position, and he is a significant early figure in the India–Korea political relationship. In 1924, Tagore travelled to Japan and expressed his support for the anticolonial movement in Korea. The political dimension of his activism became more apparent when five years later, in 1929, he further extended that call, writing a poem asking Koreans to overthrow Japanese colonial rule, reclaim their national history and strengthen the idea of Asia. Again, in 1938, Tagore exchanged public letters with the Japanese poet Yone Noguchi, publicly denouncing the militaristic nature of Japan's relations with Korea[5].

Tagore used the example of Korea under Japanese rule as a warning against nationalistic projects, which according to him would inevitably lead to imperialism, but also to say that this was possible even outside of Europe – after all, this was one Asian state subjugating another. His position met with resistance and criticism amongst Japanese nationalists, but also, interestingly, in China, where his repudiation of nationalism and politics provoked nationalist fervour – "We cannot but oppose Dr. Tagore, who upholds these things that would *shorten the life of our nation*" said one widely circulated pamphlet[6]. The nationalist discourse within Asian nation-states, such as Japan and colonies, such as India, would often overlap with the discourse of Asian nationalism, and the lines between the two were blurred for some years, especially as they were both agitated by a "war against colonialism in politics and against 'orientalisme' in science"[7]. A leitmotif of Asian nationalism as conceived in India was the discourse of unity between India and China, on account of civilizational and socio-religious commonalities. At the Brussels Congress in 1927, Nehru invoked that discourse and cast it in a political mould by saying, "India and China must now resume the ancient personal, cultural, and political relations between the two peoples. British imperialism, which in the past has kept us apart and done us so much injury, is now the very force that is uniting us in a common endeavour to overthrow it"[8]. In Gandhi's reading, it was vital for India to observe and learn from the anticolonial movements in Russia and China: "not simply the greatness of the past history of these nations that attracts us…it is because we believe that there are movements going on in those countries"[9]. Over time, the nationalist discourses within both India and China became more prominent as independence movements gained momentum.

In parallel, Asianism suffered, as tensions between China and Japan became more obvious, especially when Japan invaded Manchuria in 1931. This event was significant for two reasons – first, India in the throes of a non-violent anticolonial independence movement was dismayed by Japanese actions, and Indians felt there was "little to choose between imperialism, Western or Eastern"[10]. Second, China's response to Japanese action demonstrated the differences between Indian and Chinese anticolonial methods. Gandhi, who was usually inattentive to the idea of Asia, was moved to make a statement, "China's is not active non-violence… I must say it is unbecoming for a nation of 400 millions, a nation as cultured as Japan, to repel Japanese aggression by resorting to Japan's own methods"[11]. India now had a renewed reading of Chinese politics, one that was divorced from a larger reading of Asia[12]. With India, China and Japan all breaking away from each other in significant ways, it was only a matter of time before the Asianist discourse was to dissolve completely. Over time, the weaknesses of Pan-Asianism became even more apparent. The organization of the Pan-Asiatic Conference of 1926 and the Asian Relations Conference of 1947 brought to the fore tensions between the different ways in which Asian states were responding to modernity, independence from colonial rule and nationalism, as also the competitive attitude they held towards each other[13]. Nevertheless, the encounter of the different "Asias" inhabited by Japan, China and India aided Nehru's internationalism by providing a conceptualization of "Asia" as a distinctive space. This was premised to a large extent on the histories of China and Japan, and on the history of Japanese imperialism towards China and Korea[14].

Most Asian states experienced the radicality of the twentieth century while still not being full-fledged states[15]. The framework of Empire had dominated the nineteenth and early twentieth centuries, and inter-Asian relations often took place within that framework.

As Asian nation-states were in fact, becoming nation-states, forging national identities, and responding to the realities of decolonization, they were emerging into a world dominated, but also shaped by, other modernities. Not only did Empire become a less predominant framework within which these relationships were taking place, it was also categorically invalidated in two attempts, one not quite so successful and the other more enduring. The League of Nations (founded in 1919) and the UN (founded in 1945) represent two waves in which Empire lost its stronghold over the imagination of politics and opened ways in which that politics could be re-imagined. This points out what we already know – that the end of World War II brought with it a wave of decolonization, and the formation of an international organization with which to replace it, even though some studies have suggested that one of the founding ideas of the UN only meant for it to ensure the continuation of the fundamental ideas of the colonial project[16].

This reading dismisses off-hand the substantial role Asian diplomacy had to play in the remaking of the international. The specific relationship between Asia and Europe came to shape the international – first, as an interface between Europe and Asia, and second, as a conjunctural moment between the two modernities that they represented. The international became an arena where ideas came into circulation but were also now open to contestation. Not only did this represent a significant departure from the idea of the Empire, but it also invested the international with a character that was essentially political. Within this newly evolving space, Asian thinkers were making new historical and philosophical claims – it is interesting to note that these thinkers were not interested in Asian essentialism at all but were interested in what would become global Asia – a source of new imaginations. Tagore attempted a re-imagination of Asia as a vibrant participant in the international where cultural and people-to-people flows would act against nationalist impulses. Yet, he was unable to understand the deeply political nature of subjugated peoples and their aspirations to political expression and national identity. Gandhi took that idea forward, and successfully and repeatedly choreographed it to achieve political mileage, and eventually, secure anticolonial objectives. Yet, as also previously discussed, he was in opposition to the state and to Western modernity, and indifferent to the international as a sphere. Thus, in very different ways, both Gandhi and Tagore defined anticolonialism and Asian nationalism for an Indian audience. In so doing, they presented the conditions in which it became possible for Nehru to first, imagine the international, but also then, to define Asia's position within it, and indeed, to conclude that the international was incomplete without the integration of Asia.

The processes of decolonization, for Gandhi and Tagore, were to bring about not only freedom from colonial control but from a fundamentally asymmetrical relationship where not only was the balance of power perpetually tilted in one direction, but it had also become the only metric by which this relationship had been measured. To move away from that logic, Nehru projected, first in the case of India, and later for Asia, a discourse of futurity. Nehru used the "Greatness of Asia" only partly as invocation to civilizational heritage. More importantly, he emphasized what was yet to come, as is evident in his reiteration of the idea of the "Asian century". Having thus articulated the international quite early on, Nehru also became an enthusiastic votary of it. India, in the Nehru years, was actively involved not only in its own external affairs, but also in international affairs in general. Early Indian participation at the UN was mind-bogglingly substantial for a state with very limited means. India was also at the forefront of much of the agenda setting at the UN[17]. Not only was Korea "the first international test"[18] India had to face, but it was also in many ways the first test of the concept of the international, which Nehru played such a large role in articulating. Thus, it was almost logical for India to be involved in the resolution of the Korean War, and in achieving it through the instruments of the UN. Even more so, the Korean War represented an avenue for India to integrate both Russia and China into the international. Although Russia was represented at the UN and China wasn't, the issue of UN representation bore significance not only because of its inherent complexity but because the UN was meant to be the arena where competing or contradicting modernities would open themselves up to each other through political contestation over issues. In a sense, therefore, the strengthening of the UN would entail the accommodation not only of numerous states, but also of the discourses of modernity they personified; those discourses would be juxtaposed against one another and in so doing, the UN would constitute an embodiment of the international as a space where all modernities, Asian and European included, could make a move towards an advanced version of their own modernities.

When seen as part of the "struggle to make Asia"[19], it comes as no surprise, therefore, that Nehru placed such stock in bringing China into that framework. Often seen as logically anomalous, his support for Chinese membership of the UN and his conception of India's role as being quite central to the organization make perfect sense from the point of view of the forceful and equal representation of Asia at the UN or indeed, within the international. It was necessary for Asia to resemble some sort of loosely cohesive unit, but this could not be achieved with China on the outside. The anticolonial discourse of politics in India was inherently so opposed to dichotomous categories, that Nehru saw as completely illogical the First World/Second World binary. The only way in which it would have been possible to regard Russia and China as presenting a discursive challenge to Eurocentric imaginations of politics would be if they participated in a conversation that was political. The Cold War had replaced that with an emphasis on the aspects of the international that were solely concerned with defence and security. Nehru saw the Korean War as an outcome of this animosity and sought to manipulate it in such a way that would end the war on the Korean peninsula, diminish the effects of the Cold War in Asia, and strengthen the international through the participation of India, Russia, and China at the UN. Non-aligned India was best placed to act in a catalytic role, because India was at once Asian, international, yet neutral with respect to the Cold War. Nehru's was not the only assessment to reach this conclusion.

When in 1953, K.P.S. Menon went to Korea as Chairman of the United Nations Commission On Korea (UNCOK), Tagore's poem for the Korean people was often recited back to him, which he took as testimony to the societal ties between India and Korea[20]. The unfortunate fact, of course, was that Tagore's message was still relevant in 1950s Korea and that colonialism had merely been replaced by another form of dominance. Although Tagore's poem reflected the pathos that characterized his deeply spiritual writing style, it also called for Korea to imagine itself sociologically, as a constituent of Asia and as a society of the future. Although Tagore's own larger discourse was anti-nationalistic, by defining the purpose of a Korean collective, Tagore's message resembled a political call to arms. Essentially, Tagore was attempting a move away from the highly securitized identity thrust upon colonies and was appealing to a socio-cultural identity amongst them. Yet, he had envisaged this socio-cultural identity along international lines, not national ones. For Nehru in the 1950s, "nationalism" and "internationalism" both represented parallel expressions of the political[21]. From the 1940s to the 1960s, Nehru's nationalism and his internationalism grew simultaneously. As an early biographer puts it, "It is rather interesting to note that as his role as a nationalist became more and more intensified, his faith in internationalism grew deeper and deeper. He could combine the philosophy of nationalism with that of cosmopolitanism or universalism. In India, as well as in the world at large, he held the above synthesis almost as a political doctrine of his own"[22]. Nehru developed a critique of the nation-state, but also sought to accommodate it within the larger system of states. As discussed previously, his critique was statist and modern, and he saw the international as an arena where states would be able to mitigate their nationalistic impulses. Therefore, in the early years, India's involvement in and commitment to the UN represents a continuation of the anticolonial discourse in India.

The Problem of the Independence of Korea

One of the features of Nehru's approach to international affairs was his awareness of a nation's portrayal in history. From this vantage point, Korea represented an example of a nation unable to escape its history of subjugation. In the aftermath of Japanese defeat in World War II, the US and the USSR took control of the Korean peninsula, divided along the 38th parallel. The US-USSR Joint Commission was set up in 1945 to deliberate on the future of the Korean peninsula. However, the commission reached an impasse as both nations were unable to reach an agreement on the formation of a Korean government. As a result, the US sponsored a resolution on 17 September 1947 to bring the "Problem of the Independence of Korea" to the UN. The United Nations Temporary Commission on Korea (UNTCOK) was set up on 14 November 1947 through a US-proposed UN General Assembly (UNGA) resolution. Although India had no direct interest in the Korean issue, India was in the process of establishing itself as an active member of the UN. Nehru saw Korea as an extension of the Cold War rivalry between the two superpowers, and therefore, non-aligned India became very vocally involved in the resolution of this deadlock, and a member of the commission. Being told that India had to "shoulder more responsibility", K.P.S. Menon, of the Indian Foreign Service was sent as Indian representative; eventually, he was elected Chairman and served in that post from January to March 1948[23].

The issue before the UN at this point was to achieve "the obliteration of the 38th Parallel" and the UNTCOK emphasized that it had "no political prejudices", "no ideological predilections" and did "not constitute a bloc"[24]. Evident from this message was the influence of the Indian non-aligned position on the Commission itself. The Commission ran into difficulties from both sides, when Syngman Rhee, the first President of South Korea, refused to take the initiative to bring the war to a close, and the Soviets decried the work of the Commission. As a result, the UNTCOK oversaw elections in South Korea in May 1948, but was not allowed to do so in North Korea. In the final report of the UNTCOK, Menon highlighted the problems of Korea, "a hermit nation which has been thrust into the play of international forces through no fault of its own" and called upon the Great Powers "on whom a solution would finally rest" to "emerge out of this episode with enhanced prestige in the eyes of the world and in particular in the eyes of those great Asian States"[25]. The language of the report stresses the Asian context of the problem repeatedly and as such, represents a significant departure from previous UN documents relating to Korea. In December 1948, the General Assembly accepted this report, dissolved the UNTCOK and replaced it with the UNCOK, tasked with the removal of all barriers to the unification of Korea, observation of the actual withdrawal of the occupation forces, and active from 12 December 1948 to 7 July 1950.

Although all attention was focused on US-USSR differences at this time, Nehru also understood the inconsistencies *within* those positions, pointing to the fact that both states were "in a cleft stick"[26]. It became evident to him that China's involvement in the question of Korea was unavoidable, and that China's membership of the UN was crucial to that process. Therefore, when both the Republic of Korea (South Korea) and the Democratic People's Republic of Korea (North Korea) applied for UN membership in 1949, India refused to recognize either of these governments, as this would take away from the larger objective of achieving unification on the peninsula[27]. Instead, Nehru pressed for the admission of China into the UN as "essential to the very existence of the UN as a true world organization"[28]. Nehru also had a clear appreciation of the differences between the Russian and Chinese positions regarding what China saw fundamentally as an issue that threatened Chinese national security, but Russia saw as an episode of Cold War rivalry[29]. On India's role in the matter, Nehru held a rather sober view: "...our opportunities and our power to influence events are very much limited"[30]. But he did emphasize partnership with the Commonwealth in the matter and the idea that India could serve to placate the Chinese and open an avenue for resolution of the Korean situation, a possibility he thought would be much bettered by the arrival of KM Panikkar in Peking in May 1950[31]. Clearly, Nehru realized that the international community would not be able to restrain China if there were to be a military conflict on the Korean peninsula. The only way in which that scenario could have been avoided would have been to bring China under the aegis of the UN. Even before he could press on in this direction, on 25 June 1950, North Korean forces crossed the 38th Parallel into South Korea, marking the beginning of the Korean War.

Thereafter, the events of the summer of 1950 proceeded in very quick progression. The Truman administration proposed a resolution to the The United Nations Security Council (UNSC), branding the North Korean attack an "act of aggression". The UNSC met under the presidency of Sir B.N. Rau, an eminent Indian jurist and India's Permanent Representative to the UN, who along with the British delegation was able to change the phrasing to "breach of peace"[32]. India agreed to support the proposal and the resolution was subsequently adopted[33]. Two days later, the US proposed a second resolution, asking for "assistance to the Republic of Korea as may be necessary to repel the armed attack and to restore international peace and security to the area". Rau was unable to receive instructions and therefore, India abstained when the resolution went to vote. In North Korea at the time, Kim Il-Sung made public statements assuring his people that Nehru was backing him[34]. This led to speculation amongst the western bloc about India's neutral stance. Therefore, even after the resolution had been adopted, US Ambassador Loy Henderson decided to approach Nehru for his support[35], while Vijaya Lakshmi Pandit was approached in Washington, DC[36]. The Americans justified their resolution by insisting that not stopping the aggression would damage the legitimacy of the UN; they were able to convince Nehru, who subsequently conceded to supporting the UNSC resolution[37]. North Korea came down heavily on India, with national broadcasts calling India "a beggar in a bumper year, which has decided to live of its two masters, the United States of America and Britain"[38] even though India had been distancing itself from South Korea all throughout. Nehru protested these allegations and explained Indian support for a state set up under the aegis of the UN but faced criticism even on the home front for what was widely regarded as a volte-face on non-alignment. Questions were raised asking whether the support of UN Resolution on South Korea was "a direct contravention of the spirit of this non-alignment policy"[39]. The Government of India responded by saying they were "opposed to any attempt to settle international disputes by resort to aggression" but this decision did not "involve any modification of their foreign policy"[40].

Immediately after the North Korean forces had crossed the 38th Parallel, President Truman had moved the Seventh Fleet into the Taiwan Strait. In January 1950, the US Government had announced that it would not intervene in the event of an attack on the Taiwan Straits. Going back on that statement, President Truman issued a fresh statement linking the Formosa issue to that of the Korean War[41]. The American strategy was to signal to the Soviets by a way of a limited and overt military move that they intended to use force if necessary but that they were willing to leave room for negotiation. The inadvertent consequence of this move, though, was to draw China into what was now very clearly a confrontational situation. All along, India, and with great emphasis, Nehru had been calling upon the western powers to recognize the role that China had to play in this conflict, and in that direction, to consider decisively Chinese membership of the UN. Instead, the Americans had linked Korea with an issue as sensitive as Formosa. Expectedly, the government in Peking denounced this action as an act of aggression being committed against China, especially when the UN decided not to support the American action. Yet, the Chinese had made no military movement, and this led to renewed sympathy for China's cause amongst Asian states, who increasingly saw Truman's manoeuvre as an act of aggression against China. Nehru was deeply annoyed at the American approach and said it was "exceedingly maladroit of the USA Government to mix up the Korean issue with Formosa, Indo-China" but that India would "like to treat them separately"[42].

The US then put in a third and additional proposal at the UNSC, eventually adopted on 7 July 1950, calling for the formation of a Unified Command, with the American Commander of Forces, General Douglas MacArthur in charge. In effect, the Unified Command replaced the UNCOK. India was quick to announce no military help but sent a field ambulance unit[43], the Indian Army's Medical 60 Parachute Field Ambulance (60 PFA). Nehru placed great emphasis on this aspect of Indian policy: "There can be no question of our sending any troops to Korea even for patrol duty. If there is an intensification of the conflict in Korea, this will be a tragedy. But there will be no reason why we will change our policy."[44] In later years, when the ambulance unit was up for revision, Nehru reemphasized the humanitarian nature of India's contribution, declining even in passing to make a commitment from India that foresaw continuing war in any way: "Are we going to send them for two years in the expectation of two years of war?" The entire time, Nehru was writing to Indian diplomats in China, the Soviet Union, the US and at the UN, reminding them of "the main objective of bringing peace and security to the Korean people", which he was afraid war-mindedness had made others forget[45]. India's approach to desecuritize the issue by sending a medical ambulance received criticism on the grounds that "India had sent no troops because a large part of the Indian troops were tied up in Kashmir in the dispute with Pakistan…"[46] Yet, it was in fact India's policy at the time that "India's defence forces [had been] organized essentially for home defence and not for service in distant theatres of war"[47].

As the great powers seemed no closer to a solution, India became more active in the pursuit of a solution. Vijaya Lakshmi Pandit, India's Permanent Representative to the UN, spoke of this in no ambiguous terms: "…the Great Powers instead of coming closer, are drifting apart. We, in India, for our part are aware of no compulsion to identify ourselves systematically, with either or any of the different groups. On the contrary, we consider it of paramount importance that the distance between them should be narrowed down. We believe that our conduct should conduce to that end…"[48]. Nehru appealed to Stalin to end the war, and received a response, leading to speculation in the western press that Nehru was suited for the task of global mediator[49]: "What is needed in Korea is a new mediator of world stature and repute. The one who measures up to that standard is Pandit Nehru"[50]. The MEA had "no special suggestions at present for unifying Korea" and considered it "a forlorn business"[51], but saw this more as an excellent opportunity for the UN to assert itself. Accordingly, India sent through Rau a proposal for a committee of non-permanent members that would take into consideration all resolutions on Korea so far made[52]. However, both sides denounced the plan, saying it would lead to a delay in the resolution of the Korean problem, and that only most interested parties should be involved in the situation as it stood[53]. Although unsuccessful, the Indian proposal brought to the fore the militaristic positions taken by both camps. As a newspaper article put it, "It is impossible at any time and in any circumstances to have peace in and around Korea without the cooperation of her two powerful neighbours, China and the Soviet Union. On this premise, Pandit Nehru based his mediation proposal for the admission of China to the UNSC. Although Nehru's overtures were rejected, they did at least clarify the strength and weakness of the Russian and American positions"[54]. India had grasped the entry of the Cold War into the Korean problem, and as Nehru said in August 1950, "the fate of the world seems to hang in regard to war and peace by a thin thread which might be cut down by a sword or blown off by a gun"[55]. On 15 September, General MacArthur staged the first of the Inchon landings. The UN troops drove the North Koreans back into North Korea but didn't appear to be stopping at the 38th Parallel. China considered any crossing of the line an aggression on Chinese authority and issued warnings to that effect. Two more events seem to have convinced China of the need for intervention: the first was General MacArthur's visit to Formosa, and his announcement with Chiang Kai Shek regarding joint defence of the island; the second was the Veterans of Foreign Wars (VFW) episode, when General MacArthur had said in a letter that the US "must retain control of Formosa at any cost" and had warned against "defeatism in the Pacific"[56]. The US distanced itself from this statement immediately, and President Truman issued strong warnings to General MacArthur about retracting it. However, the episode had already created misgivings about American ambitions in the Pacific, and the Chinese drew their own conclusions from it. Having announced in July 1950 their intention of retaking Formosa, they now found themselves in direct conflict with the Americans.

Nehru was at this time alarmed at the prospect of China entering the war and sought to warn the world at large, and the Americans in particular that this was set to happen[57]. His thinking was reinforced by Panikkar's regular telegrams from Peking that were stressing that China would intervene[58]. On 26 September 1950, Panikkar sent an urgent telegram to Nehru alerting him to the possibilities of Chinese intervention[59]. Nehru then addressed a letter to Zhou Enlai pleading for restraint. Finally, on 3 October 1950, Zhou Enlai called for Panikkar and told him in no uncertain terms that "US troops are going to cross the 38th Parallel in an attempt to extend the war" and that in that eventuality, China would intervene[60]. Zhou Enlai and Panikkar then discussed the crossing over of some troops into North Korean territory, and Zhou indicated his view that the US Government was unreliable, referring to the need to "localize" the conflict. Panikkar reassured Zhou that the Government of India was doing whatever it could, and that Rau had read out in the General Assembly Zhou's Report of 1 October 1950. Panikkar concluded by saying, "Our government is doing its best to exert pressure" but went on to ask if by "localization", the Chinese meant confining the armed conflict south of the 38th Parallel or if they meant a complete halt to the Korean armed conflict. Zhou Enlai clarified this point: "The Korean armed conflict ought to stop immediately, and foreign troops ought to be withdrawn [from Korea]. This will be advantageous to peace in the East. Our idea for localizing the Korean incident is just to make efforts to keep the aggression of US troops from expanding into an incident of worldwide dimensions." Panikkar took this as a formal policy declaration and relayed the message to Nehru, through whom he hoped it would reach the British, and the Americans. In hindsight, he realized that "Eden endorsed those views but the Americans had nothing but contempt for Zhou's warning and my assessment "[61]. This might not have been completely true, as the record now shows that indeed, Loy Henderson, then US Ambassador in Delhi approached G.S. Bajpai regarding the possibility of exploring all avenues for cessation of hostilities including him personally meeting with and talking to the Chinese Communist Ambassador, a proposal that shocked Bajpai[62], who relayed it to Nehru, who in turn suggested the Government of India could act as a conduit[63].

On 8 October 1950, a UN offensive was launched north of the 38th Parallel. Two days later, the Chinese Communist Ambassador relayed to Henderson, through the Government of India that it was not a good idea for the US and China to have informal talks pending formal relations between the two countries; as a result, the Government of India immediately distanced itself from this process[64]. By 22 October 1950, the Chinese were attacking South Korean and UN forces. A US-sponsored resolution in the UNSC asked China to withdraw its forces, but India proposed a counterproposal with British support asking a Chinese representative to present their position to the Security Council. The proposal passed but was disregarded by the Chinese who continued to invest heavily in the war[65]. As a result, the US then sponsored a resolution asking for the UNSC to brand China an aggressor; the proposal was vetoed by the USSR, while India abstained at voting[66], saying it "was unrealistic to so accuse a state not bound by the United Nations charter"[67]. Once the General Assembly reopened, without the fear of a Soviet veto and with the confidence of military advancements on ground, the question being asked was whether the UN force should press ahead and achieve the unification of Korea by the use of force. At this time, the British delegation put forth a proposal suggesting the occupation of the entire peninsula by UN forces, and the establishment of the UNCURK to facilitate that objective[68]. Nehru was in complete opposition to this idea, and instead of adopting a "flamboyant attitude", stressed "the temper of the approach"[69]. He proposed a sub-committee to move towards a ceasefire and withdrawal of all foreign forces[70]. Although the Indian proposal evoked widespread Third World support, the western bloc voted against it[71]. This, however, did not stop Nehru who wrote to V.K. Krishna Menon saying, "No question of prestige would deter me from taking a step which might help in [the] preservation of peace"[72]. Accordingly, India took two initiatives – the first was to put up a draft proposal demanding the peaceful settlement of all East Asian issues. The Americans, who refused to discuss anything until the fighting in Korea had stopped, immediately shot this down[73]. The second initiative from the Indian side was to propose a ceasefire, to be monitored by a Ceasefire Committee, which eventually came to consist of Rau as its Chairman and Nasrollah Entezam (Iran) and Lester Pearson (Canada) as the other members and made provisions for negotiations on Korea and Taiwan right after the cessation of hostilities. Rau said at the Ceasefire Committee that negotiations on Taiwan and Chinese representation at the UN would take place once the ceasefire had been achieved, which the US supported, followed by the Commonwealth members, followed by the adoption of the resolution[74]. Sadly, the Indian proposal was rejected by Peking, leading to a worsening of the military situation and in the face of escalation, the US successfully asked for China to be branded aggressor and for the imposition of sanctions against China[75].

Particularly significant here was not whether Indian proposals had been successful at all, but that they had bought precious time in which American cries for war had somewhat subsided[76]. Nehru disagreed with the American attitude and tried to mediate through Attlee, writing to him to say that any sort of confrontational attitude towards China "does not disable China but merely antagonises her."

He also stressed the divergence of Asian views on the matter, saying, "Asian sentiment does not like much that China has done but it is strongly critical of American attitude during this great crisis"[77]. India was aware that the Chinese response to this sort of militaristic attitude would be to retaliate, and Nehru referred to a message from China, received by the Indian Embassy in Peking that said, "war and truce go ill together"[78]. Nehru differentiated between the American people who is his view "undoubtedly want peace" and the Pentagon, for whom "the settlement in Korea immediately brings up the question of Formosa and Chinese recognition in the UN"[79]. India, Burma, Indonesia, and other Asian countries did not support the US resolution, which they thought isolated China even further and would lead to a deadlock, as the UN could not possibly enter into negotiations with a state that it had branded aggressor. Nehru lamented this development, saying that Indian efforts were concentrated on bringing the two parties together to reach a truce[80]. He repeatedly warned against adopting an attitude towards China in haste, saying in January 1951, "There has been an aggression in Korea, but the Chinese Government took no action at all until the 38th parallel had been crossed. They told us very frankly that they would consider this a threat to their security in Manchuria. Remember that all invasions of China have taken place through Korea and the Chinese were concerned about their big industries in the north"[81]. This situation continued until the middle of the year, when Nehru wrote to Rau saying that there was no positive proposal India could make at the time[82], but he was most concerned about the prospect of a full-fledged war[83]. Nehru continued to exercise his position within the Commonwealth, pleading to them in January 1951 at the Commonwealth Prime Ministers' Conference that it was important for the Commonwealth to follow a policy independent of the US and that not doing so would involve them in war[84].

In the same week, President Truman relieved General MacArthur of all his duties, finding him unable to back UN-US policies, and replaced him with Lieutenant General Mathew B. Ridgway[85]. This proved to be a fortuitous turn of events, as Gen. Ridgeway proved willing to end the war, and made proposals to Kim Il-Sung and the Commander of the Chinese Communist forces General Peng Tuh-huai regarding "agreement on armistice terms"[86]. After some negotiation, the talks at Kaesong started in July 1951 and eventually moved to Panmunjom[87]. They proved to be more difficult than first anticipated, initially on the question of the ceasefire line, and later, on the question of the Prisoners of War (POWs). By mid-August, the talks were continuing "without producing any results" and "the question at issue [was] the ceasefire line", with the UN Commanders wanting "more or less, the present line, which in some places [went] beyond the 38th parallel", unacceptable to the Chinese and the North Koreans who wanted "to have the 38th parallel as the ceasefire line"[88]. However, North Korea suspended the talks on 23 August 1951 over the alleged violation of the neutral zone by American troops. By September, the ceasefire talks had practically ended, with little chance of resumption, although the US had made a proposal to that effect on 6 September 1951[89]. Therefore, the Indian effort at this moment was to "keep America out of an international conflict because her temper" was "both uncompromising and uninformed"[90]. Yet, Indian proposals at this time were evoking "little comment or enthusiasm"[91].

Anti-Indian bias was pervasive within the US at this juncture[92]. *The New York Times* wrote in August 1951 that "Nehru's attention was primarily turned on a local, national and intensely personal question Kashmir", that his statesmanship was not inspiring people and nations to do things but to leave them undone…"[93]. The British held a more charitable view that Nehru brought "to the surface, as no one else in Asia can, the suspicions of his continent"[94]. For their part, the Indians were deeply annoyed at the disregard with which the western bloc had treated their assessments and advice: "The advice of the GOI to halt at the 38th parallel and endeavour to seek a peaceful solution of the dispute was resented and went unheeded. Furthermore, India was accused to an equivocal stand on the matter and even of appeasement of the North Korean aggressors. Later, when China intervened, only grudgingly was recognition given to India's earlier warnings", said a diplomatic cable while rounding up the events of 1951[95]. There were no major initiatives from the Indian side, until the end of 1951, when Indian consular reports from the US detected a shift towards conciliation in the Korean War for two main reasons – the first was economic, with the fear of inflation looming large over the American public; the second was that the fear that the Korean War would turn into protracted conflict[96]. Despite these fears, American defence preparedness continued unabated, and the Chinese side also remained averse to negotiation especially after January 1952, when the UN admitted to having inadvertently bombed Kaesong because of human error[97].

For the rest of the year, the big issue was that of the repatriation of the POWs, which was effectively stalling the armistice negotiations[98]. The two sides disagreed on two fronts: the first was the number of prisoners on each side's list that differed considerably; the second was the principle of non-forcible or voluntary repatriation, where only those prisoners who were willing to return to their homelands would, advocated by the UN as against the Chinese demand for an exchange of prisoners on an "all-for-all" basis. This matter was further complicated when a screening by the UN Command revealed that only 73,000 out of 1,70,000 prisoners wanted to return home. The discrepancy of the American POWs on both lists became even more of a political issue, when it was learnt that the British POWs numbered the same on both lists, possibly due to British recognition of the PRC[99]. Then again, it was also suggested that perhaps the list "may have been deliberately "cooked" so as to give American [sic] that impression"[100]. In any case, when the Indian Embassy in Peking wrote to Nehru suggesting that a compromise number of 1,00,000 prisoners might be fixed so as to solve this issue, Nehru replied saying that there was no logic in fixing an arbitrary number[101].

During the middle months of 1952, the Chinese were offered three proposals, all of which they rejected. The first was a US-sponsored proposal asking China to accept the principle of non-forcible repatriation; India did not offer support for this proposal, and instead along with other Commonwealth partners – Britain and Canada – decided to put in its own proposal suggesting the creation of a commission that would take charge of all the POWs after the armistice had been signed to decide over time their final disposition. Krishna Menon also suggested a substantial role for the neutral countries – Sweden, Switzerland, Czechoslovakia and Poland were to be members with a fifth country that would serve as umpire. The US did not support the Indian position, even though the Commonwealth had supported it. US Secretary of State Dean Acheson offered the explanation that this would leave the prisoners' fates undecided and was therefore unacceptable to the US[102]. Menon, therefore, reworked his proposal incorporating American demands saying that willing prisoners would be repatriated immediately and that over the following 90 days, representatives of the belligerent countries would then be permitted to try to persuade non-repatriate prisoners to return home; if unwilling prisoners remained, their fate would be discussed at the political conference on Korea for a further 90 days; if still no decision could be reached the UN would decide their final disposition[103]. Acheson harboured suspicions on why the Indians were being so provocative[104] and dismissed the Indian plan out-of-hand, although American, and international opinion was considering it very seriously[105].

While Acheson was campaigning for his 21-power draft resolution, India submitted the new draft proposal on 19 November 1952[106], with Nehru insisting that India follow what he considered "the right path"[107], that of not appeasing either side. The Americans showed deep disdain for what they saw as the impatience of Nehru who had been so patient with China. They were also deeply concerned about the nexus between Britain, India and China, with France, New Zealand and Australia supporting them[108]. Acheson was to vote against the adoption of the resolution, but didn't as in a turn of events, the Soviet

Subimal Dutt Handing Over POWs
Indian Foreign Secretary Dutt (to the left) formally hands over 56 Korean and Chinese former POWs of the Korean War to the Brazilian Ambassador to India, Ildefonso Falco (in the centre), at the Brazilian Embassy in New Delhi the day before their departure to their adopted country. The ex-POWs, some of whom appear in the photo, had refused to return to either South or North Korea or Nationalist or Communist China. (Bettmann via Getty Images)

Foreign Minister Andrei Vyshinsky condemned the Indian resolution in absolute terms, accused Indians of adopting the American viewpoint on non-forcible repatriation, of being at best "dreamers and idealists" or at worst, "instruments of horrible American policy"[109]. The Soviet attack on the Indian proposal paved a way for America through the mess it found itself in, especially regarding allies in the western bloc. By suggesting that the differences between the Indian and American proposals were "linguistic rather than substantive"[110], Acheson was able to support the Indian proposal in the belief that it would not see the light of day, given Communist opposition. But the manipulation of the circumstances was evident to all, with Sir Anthony Eden, the British Foreign Minister making a statement on 22 November 1952 announcing Britain's backing of the Indian plan. The Americans responded to what they saw as a grouping together between the nations of the Commonwealth by defining the western hemisphere as being "as that part of the North and South American continents south of the Canadian border"[111]. But the importance of the Indian resolution was not lost on Chester Bowles, the American Ambassador in New Delhi, who said Nehru had gone an "extraordinarily long distance" in opposition to the Russians and Chinese on an "issue of crucial importance"[112].

Nehru was dismayed by American criticism, but guarded against taking sides, thus becoming "arenas of warfare"[113]. Rather, he saw an opportunity "for the United Nations to justify itself and help to recover the atmosphere of peace."[114] As for India's role in bringing about a peaceful solution, he spoke soberly, saying, "If our good faith in trying for a peaceful settlement is not appreciated, then, of course, it becomes difficult for us to take any step"[115]. The Americans were using Nehru as a conduit to China, discussing in earlier months how "it might have some effect on the Communists", "it could do little harm" "and if the approach is made and fails, it would help bring home to Nehru Communist intransigence and accelerate the process of his education in regard to the East-West struggle"[116]. On the other hand, India was in a precarious position vis-à-vis China – Nehru wrote to the Indian Ambassador in Peking expressing concern at "the repeated reference to Indian Resolution on Korea as being the parent of evil"[117]. He thought Krishna Menon had placed too much emphasis on the Commonwealth, thus inevitably distancing India from China, a position achieved and consolidated from the early years, which Nehru was unwilling to squander[118]. Nehru was also aware that China's own position on the proposal had changed in an understated but definite way, possibly under Soviet influence. A day before the resolution was being put to vote, he wrote to Sir G.S. Bajpai, "We have got rather entangled in this matter and it is not very easy to disentangle ourselves. We have little choice left at this stage except to go ahead with it, although it is clear that China does not accept it. We were certainly given the impression, without any commitment, that China was not opposed to it. Later, possibly due to Soviet pressure they expressed themselves strongly against it"[119]. Although the resolution was passed on 3 December 1952 in the absence of Soviet support[120], the Chinese rejected its terms shortly after[121]. However, once the resolution had been adopted, Nehru gained confidence in the Indian move, deciding that the "warlike trend [was] checked by our resolution"[122] and that it was clear that "China was much influenced by Soviet pressure in this matter. We have maintained an attitude of friendliness with China in spite of what they have said. But, with the friendliness is also a firmness. They do not appreciate weakness and we intend showing none"[123].

At this juncture, there were a number of factors that had directly influenced the Indian engagement with the Korean War and the armistice negotiations. The first was the incumbency of Dwight D. Eisenhower, who had won the Presidential race in 1952 by campaigning on the promise to fight "Communism, Korea and Corruption", otherwise known as the K1C2 formula. Eisenhower was a five-star general and had been the Supreme Commander of the North Atlantic Treaty Organization (NATO) in the past. He had won by a landslide victory against Adlai Stevenson, who had adopted a non-interventionist attitude, whereas Eisenhower had promised to personally go to Korea to end the war. Nehru saw his election to office as having "rather weighted the scales against peace"[124], particularly given Eisenhower's military background and the memory of MacArthur's approach towards the Korean problem. Therefore, he pushed ahead vigorously trying to achieve a political resolution to the deadlock on the question of the POWs, so as to prevent escalation on the military front[125]. The second factor to India's advantage was the number of influential Indians at the helm of affairs in the UN. Through 1952, Vijaya Lakshmi Pandit continued to be the Head of the Indian delegation to the UN, but in 1953, was elected as the first woman President of the UNGA at its 62nd session[126]. Rajeshwar Dayal had replaced B.N. Rau as India's Permanent Representative to the UN, and formerly India's High Commissioner to the UK, Krishna Menon arrived in New York with the special assignment of handling the Korean problem[127]. At first, no initiative seemed possible from the Indian camp as the belligerents seemed unwilling to compromise on any front[128]. Nevertheless, these changes prepared a strong Indian contingent to deal with the imminent Soviet peace offensive.

The third factor was the death of Stalin in March 1953, which brought to the fore the Soviet desire to ease Cold War tensions and changed the Soviet stand on the Korean War[129]. When Indian Ambassador to the Soviet Union, K.P.S. Menon had had an audience with Stalin right before Stalin's death, Menon had discussed the Korean question with the leader, but in the face of little to no response, had left with the impression that Stalin "might never have heard of [the Indian] Korean resolution at all"[130]. It was thus the peace offensive announced at Stalin's funeral that set things in motion, with the new Soviet statement addressing the question of the Korean War[131]. The Chinese, who realized that they would make no substantial progress on either Taiwan or their membership of the UN as long as those issues continued to be tied down with the problem of Korea, mirrored this attitude[132]. They then made two overtures – the first was to accept an offer from the UN to discuss the fate of sick and wounded prisoners; the second was Zhou Enlai's radio announcement on 30 March 1953, which was clearly based on the Indian Resolution in that it recognized "non-repatriated prisoners", and proposed they be taken to a neutral country for six months, in which time they could be persuaded to return to their homelands, or their collective fate would be decided by the post-armistice political conference on Korea[133].

Nehru saw these developments as amounting to a large concession from the Communists and instructed Menon to pursue a draft resolution to that effect. The Polish delegation at this time proposed an immediate cease-fire and the implementation of Zhou Enlai's proposal[134]. India then submitted a more moderate version of that proposal, which the US followed up with its own draft resolution noting the recent agreement on the exchange of sick and wounded prisoners, expressing its support for an early armistice, and adjourning the General Assembly until an armistice had been signed or developments required discussion. The Indian and American draft resolutions were merged, and the resultant resolution was sponsored by Brazil and was passed with unanimous support[135]. The passing of this resolution marked a historic turning point on Korea, as it was the first time a resolution had been unanimously passed and because it left the fate of Korea in the hands of the negotiators at Panmunjom, thus vastly reducing the effect of great power politics as played out in a US-dominated UN system[136]. The Indian contribution to this effort was so fundamental that for the first time, it was acknowledged by both sides[137]. Nehru was jubilant, but cautious, and saw India's role as the triumph of non-aligned politics, saying, "The turn that international events have taken has brought India into the picture and cast a heavy responsibility upon her. The independent policy that we have pursued and our constant attempts to remain friendly with all countries have borne fruit. The Great Powers look upon us with respect and realize that what we say will be listened to by many. Hence, they have to listen to it also... In the Korean deadlock, attempts are made on both sides to utilize India's services to help resolve it"[138]. Soon after, the Communist side proposed the setting up of the Neutral Nations Repatriation Commission (NNRC) consisting of Czechoslovakia, Poland, Sweden and Switzerland and an umpire nation as members[139]. The Korean Armistice Agreement was finally signed on 27 July 1953, in what Nehru called "the outbreak of peace"[140]. Under the provisions of the agreement, there came to be established two commissions – the Neutral Nations Supervisory Commission (NNSC) and the NNRC, which was formed under the chairmanship of Indian Lt. Gen. K.S. Thimayya, with Indian diplomat B.N. Chakravarty as Alternate Chairman.

In late June 1953, when both sides had all but reached a peaceful settlement, Rhee unilaterally released 25,000 anti-Communist North Korean POWs, almost derailing the entire process. Nehru was aghast and reiterated that it was "this deliberate shutting of eyes to the reality of the new Chinese Republic that has led to many subsequent disasters"[141]. Rhee and South Korean Foreign Minister Pyun retorted by making vicious statements casting doubts on India's neutrality, which they continued to make over the next year. India had been associated so closely with the objective of securing a truce that Nehru decided to participate in the NNRC despite Rhee's attacks. In this assessment, he was particularly motivated by discussions he had had with the US Secretary of State, who had warned him early on in May that "if the armistice negotiations collapsed, the United States would probably make a stronger rather than a lesser military exertion, and that this might well extend the area of conflict"[142]. Nehru's response was to think in terms of the POWs, who would be left in the hands of the UNGA if the armistice failed, leading to a problematic situation because China was not yet a member of the UN[143]. He was also certain that China would on no account "submit to coercion or threat"[144]. Yet again, he thought Indian involvement would provide an avenue for compromise and conciliation but was anxious to keep India out of any place where India was not wanted[145]. He was especially keen to avoid any military commitments on India's part, emphasizing that "India's defence forces [had] been organized essentially for home defence and not for service in distant theatres of war"[146]. Nevertheless, India sent a brigade-sized contingent called the Custodian Force of India (CFI), which was to – under the aegis of the NNRC – hold prisoners and facilitate their repatriation led by Maj. Gen. Thorat[147]. Nehru continued to speak of India's special role as a balancing factor, "a neutral among neutrals", as also the Chairman and Executive Agent of the Commission[148].

Following the signing of the armistice agreement, the issue of India's membership of the NNRC became intertwined with Indian participation in the political conference to decide the fate of Korea. In the run up to the armistice, India's participation in both processes was being debated within the US administration. Early reports from Gen. Clark, the Commander-in-Chief of the United Nations Command, writing to the US Joint Chiefs of Staff, indicated that India's participation in the NNRC was considered undesirable, as Indian neutrality was not "as well defined as in the case of Mexico"[149]. Gen. Clark noted his reservations saying that India was neither objective nor completely neutral[150]. Yet, Robert Murphy, Assistant Secretary of State and Political Adviser for the Armistice Negotiations, was of the belief that an armistice would only be obtained if the US adhered "as closely as possible to the Indian General Assembly resolution"[151]. Nehru was aware of these conflicting perspectives on India's place in the process, remarking that American statements were often contradictory and that "there appears to be no constant foreign policy in the US. Even between President Eisenhower and Secretary Dulles, there does not appear to be community of thought"[152].

But he was even more concerned when the US administration questioned the neutrality of the NNRC and by the end of the year, Nehru was regretting India's membership of the NNRC. Krishna Menon insisted that there would have been no armistice without India's involvement, but Nehru disagreed, saying it was really up to the belligerents to reach a compromise, a situation in which India had a very limited role to play; he also considered it "beneath India's dignity to go to another Asian country" where India was "not wanted, and where the head of the country would not let us land on its soil"[153]. Meanwhile, the other members of the NNRC were also finding it difficult to cooperate with Rhee, whose statements were getting increasingly bellicose and who had denounced the CFI as "policemen turned robbers"[154] and had threatened to move troops into the DMZ to halt "illegal screening of anti-Communist prisoners by Indian custodial troops" while repeatedly describing the Indian interviews and screening as "anti-Communist prisoners sent to their death by pro-Communist Indian forces"[155]. Rhee had written to the United Nations Command with a thinly veiled threat speaking of "a clash of a serious nature between the Communist or pro-Communist Indians and the anti-Communist Koreans"[156].

In light of these statements, India was anxious for the safety of Indian troops and Rajeshwar Dayal reported to the UN Secretary

General Dag Hammarskjöld India's intention to withdraw troops if they were unable to function in impartial circumstances[157]. As Nehru put it, "Indian troops are not going to Korea to fight anybody"[158]. Hammarskjöld wrote to Vijaya Lakshmi Pandit urging that "Thimmayya [sic] should not under any circumstances leave Panmunjom" and that "the Commission should remain in being whatever happens"[159]. Krishna Menon and Rajeshwar Dayal met with Arthur Dean, the US President's Envoy on Korea, and repeated this sentiment, but Dean saw the meeting as an Indian attempt at gaining a seat at the political conference on Korea[160]. Indeed, India's difficulties in functioning on the NNRC became increasingly intertwined with the question of participation at the political conference on Korea. President Rhee was exerting pressure on the Americans to exclude India from the talks insisting that "the democratic side must speak with a single voice[161]. Henry Cabot Lodge, US Ambassador to the UN told Vijaya Lakshmi Pandit that America would be *less opposed* to Indian membership in the Political Conference on Korea if Krishna Menon were replaced with Lt. Gen. Thimayya, a suggestion Nehru considered an affront to the Indian delegation and an ill-advised political move. He reacted by saying there had been "too many generals in the past concerned with Korean matters and too little political control"[162]. The Canadian High Commissioner to India, Escott Reid wrote to Canadian Prime Minister Lester B. Pearson saying it was highly unlikely that India would send a general to a Korean political conference"[163].

US Secretary of State Dulles thought India should be excluded from the conference given India had deliberately chosen to be neutral, even acting as the Chairman of the NNRC, and that this exclusion could be offset by American support for Vijaya Lakshmi Pandit for President of the UNGA, a policy Eisenhower agreed to[164]. By American estimation, this position ran contrary to the general mood of the Assembly; it was likely that Britain and Canada would propose Indian participation, but India had said it would not "agitate or canvass for membership"[165]. Likewise, Britain, Canada, Australia and New Zealand did sponsor a proposal, but the US persisted in a campaign against Indian participation, possibly because of a threat by Rhee to boycott the conference if India attended[166]. US Ambassador to India, George V. Allen urged Nehru to voluntarily withdraw from participation in the conference, saying the US's "genuine objective, as that of India, was to achieve success of conference, whether our views as to how this might best be achieved were similar or not"[167].

UN Meeting in Session
The UN Security Council voting on whether South Korea should gain entry to the world organization. All hands are raised in favour of the vote, except that of A. A. Sobolev (third from right), the Soviet Delegate, who later vetoed the entry of South Korea. (Bettmann via Getty Images)

UNSC Meets about Korea
The UNSC meets regarding the invasion of South Korea by northern Communist forces. The Soviet Union's delegation boycotted this meeting. 1 January 1950. (Hulton-Deutsch Collection/Corbis Historical via Getty Images)

Nehru took strong objection to American disdain of India's role saying, "A strong policy these days…apparently means going about looking ferocious and telling everybody we will punish them if they don't behave as we like. That may be good at a public meeting, but it represents great immaturity. Mature nations, as I think we are, do not behave this way"[168]. Nehru then spoke of America's unilateralism as the beginning of the end of the UN; he said, "It would be perverse if any country tried to destroy the United Nations. That country would suffer more than the organization if it left or sought to disrupt it.

One can't run away from problems. The UN, with all its failings, is a great world organization with the seeds of the hope of peace"[169]. Ten days later, this statement was followed up by Krishna Menon who presented a statement in the general debate at the UN General Assembly, where he spoke of two issues mainly – the first was that of the admission of China into the UN, especially in the context of the Korean War; he declared, "We do not look upon the United Nations as an exclusive body"; second, he spoke of India's participation in the political conference on Korea under the heading 'Asian Representation' and spoke about the lack of representation of Asia[170]. Subtly but surely, India had presented the question as one of Asian representation, and as a question of the credibility of the UN. Although Nehru had said to Allen that he was confident the US Government was not trying to "do GOI down", he wrote to Vijaya Lakshmi Pandit that "nothing would please the US more than to have an opportunity of tripping India up"[171].

Nehru was also quite certain that the American attempt to appear "reasonable and open to conviction" was a superficial one and so, India continued to disregard South Korean or American criticism of Indian policies[172]. Instead, Nehru made frequent statements regarding the political necessities of the Korean situation that warranted India's troop presence in a foreign country, through foreign policy pronouncements[173], as also in statements to the troops themselves[174]. He also personally corresponded with Lt. Gen. Thimayya until the CFI was shipped out from Korea in five stages[175]. In early 1954, Lt. Gen. Thimayya submitted his report to the UN General Assembly[176]. By mid-March, the Indian troops had left Korea, and had brought back with them 88 POWs who had elected to go to India[177]. The Indian Ambulance Unit that had served in Korea since December 1950 was awarded the highest commendations, with the unit Commander Lt. Col. Rangaraj being awarded the Maha Vir Chakra[178].

Eisenhower wrote to Nehru to thank him for Lt. Gen. Thimayya's and Maj. Gen. Thorat's alleviation of POWs' feelings of anxiety and offered his highest commendations for the troops and officers of the Indian Army[179]. Krishna Menon took a critical view of the General saying, "Thimayya appeared to take too much the American view" and also took a less than charitable view of the success of the NNRC saying that "ultimately...[the NNRC] didn't complete its tasks because a whole lot of prisoners went to Formosa, which they shouldn't have done"[180]. India's role in Korea had come to an end, with no opportunity to participate in the political conference[181], but nevertheless with an emphasis on the use of political means to achieve political ends[182].

"Delicate, Difficult, Embarrassing..."[183]

The Korean War represented a significant moment in the development of a non-aligned critique of two wars – the Korean War and the Cold War. In aiming for the resolution of the war, Nehru constantly drew attention to the military nature of the governments involved. In defining non-alignment, Nehru had said, "When we say our policy is one of non-alignment, obviously we mean non-alignment with military blocs"[184]. In reading such statements, the emphasis has always been on the question of blocs, but it is worthwhile to note that the emphasis was equally on the *military* nature of those blocs. Therefore, said Nehru, "...the slightest deviation from our policy of non-alignment and avoidance of military pacts would be a disaster beyond repair"[185]. Nehru went on to identify the governments involved in the Korean War as "more or less military governments", and highlighted the distinction between political objectives on the one hand and military objectives on the other - "even eminent statesmen get mixed up in solving the problem between realising the objective they are aiming at and victory in war. The two are not necessarily synonymous and past history shows that they are not"[186]. Therefore, Nehru was cautious about overstating the importance of the armistice agreement because he realized that the armistice had only ended the Korean War, but that peace would not be completely secured until the future of Korea and its people had been decided. As Krishna Menon said in a statement at the General Assembly, "the fact remains that this armistice is an uneasy one; and it is our concern to convert the armistice into a permanent peace"[187]. In order to secure the conditions for such peace to prevail, Nehru applied India's strength to the question of the POWs, which he saw as significant in bringing to a close the first formal confrontation between the US and China by political means.

Nehru attempted to disconnect the international relations of Asia, and of India, from the political imagination of the time that had become saturated with ideas of war. By repeatedly making statements emphasizing the poverty of Cold War political discourse, he critiqued the centrality of war in it. As Vijaya Lakshmi Pandit put it, "India's chosen role demands that she exerts herself in whatever capacity offers itself in the interests of peace. Her neutrality itself implies involvement in its cause[188]. India's involvement through the United Nations Temporary Commission On Korea (UNTCOK), the United Nations Commission On Korea (UNCOK), the 60 Parachute Field Ambulance (60 PFA), the Custodian Force of India (CFI) and the Neutral Nations Repatriation Commission (NNRC) all point to India's substantial contribution as part of this political project of restoring normal conditions in Korea, especially given that these were all unarmed forces. In Krishna Menon's words, "an unarmed army is today dealing with a situation in a way which is not only glorious from their point of view, but full of lessons for others who have to resolve political problems"[189]. Nehru located India, China, Korea and Japan within a political framework when he said "The mind of Asia immediately turns to wherever it is being suppressed"[190]. By historicizing the nation-state outside of its national boundaries, he made possible a move from a securitized discourse of nationalism to a politicized discourse of internationalism. He attempted to structure Asia's international relations outside the framework of war. Nehru said, "...this new Asia has a special duty cast upon her and ought not to allow herself to be pushed into wrong courses by the folly or the ambition of others"[191]. By attempting this move, Nehru also sought to distance Asia from the West's ordering of the state; he said, "Asia is a more distant continent; it is a troublesome place; it is a mysterious place; it is an unknown place. So, their outlook becomes governed much more by Europe's problems than by Asia's problems"[192]. Nehru's estimation of the West's approach to problems in Asia is borne out by statements made during the Korean War itself, such as one by Eisenhower where he said that the war should be "Asians against Asians" with American "support for freedom"[193]. Nehru understood that Asia and Europe were two strands within which history could be understood but that the interface between them was deeply political; in the event of any disagreement, he was wary of the West's propensity to "press a political solution through military means"[194].

Nehru also said, "Our object is to stop the drift towards war and not to put either China or the USA in the wrong"[195]. In pursuit of peace, India did not want inadvertently to aggravate adversaries and encourage war mongering amongst them saying that it was "bad politics at any time to try to humiliate even an enemy. To do so at the cost of war would be tragedy"[196]. The Indian approach was that peace could not be promoted by relying on power; on the contrary, the emphasis on power might become a threat to peace[197]. Indeed, Appadorai argues that this approach was "supplementary to the one based on power" because those who adopt it emphasize negotiation such as in the truces in Korea and Indochina[198]. This was in direct contradiction to the American position, particularly promoted by the likes of Dean Acheson who had spoken of "negotiating from situations of strength"[199]. Nehru criticised this attitude in plain terms, saying, "The Americans can apparently only think in military terms now and forget that human beings have to be handled differently"[200]. India's involvement in the Korean War made non-alignment slightly more credible and affected Indian relations with the Western bloc. India-US relations improved in contrast to US relations with Russia and China. The western bloc continued to suspect "probably a good deal of *oriental manoeuvring* between Chinese Communist and Soviets, especially in regard to Korea"[201]. However, the attitude towards India softened particularly under the influence of progressive diplomats such as Chester Bowles who adopted a different view towards India and at the height of the Korean War, claiming that "the success or failure of the effort being made in India and other Asian countries to create an alternative to Communism in Asia may mark one of those historic turning points which determine the flow of events for many generations"[202]. Even Dulles who had once said of non-alignment, "Those who are not with us, are against us"[203], tempered his stand with remarking, "India is neutralist in the sense that it has not joined up in any of the collective security organization...We don't quarrel with the Indian decision. India is not neutral in the sense that it is indifferent to the threat of communism..."[204].

Nehru's relations with China were also more tempered as he witnessed upfront Chinese foreign policy decision-making during the Korean War[205]. A Peking Radio broadcast that criticized "India's posing as voice of Asia", shocked Nehru and he sought to respond in no uncertain terms. When Nehru faced criticism in the Indian Parliament on grounds of abandoning India's non-aligned position by being too fervent in his support for China; he responded by saying that he was on his country's side and no one else's. Yet, he sought to integrate both the Soviet Union and China into the UN, saying that without their inclusion, the UN "inevitably drift towards being an agent for war or preparations for war"[206]. Stalinist Russia also warmed up to the idea of non-aligned India somewhat, a prospect that they only fully explored in the years after the death of Stalin[207]. Most importantly, India sought to build a relationship with Korea by recognizing and repeatedly emphasizing Korean sovereignty. In 1950, just at the start of the war, Indian officials serving on the UNTCOK had reported to New Delhi the divergence of views between the Indian and western positions, saying that the western bloc believed that "the people of Korea have no experience of the liberal and democratic processes" while the Indians did "not share this view as we feel that if the United Nations is called upon to make some vast sacrifices, they must be for the vindication of certain principles and for the establishment of a decent new order"[208]. They continued to report on this matter, "Many others, however, feel that India does not fully realize the nature of the North Korean regime and the menace of communism"[209]. Once the war was well in full swing, Indian Embassy reports from the US wrote to New Delhi about the American attitude towards Koreans as being "comparatively ill-equipped and under-nourished 'oriental' hordes"[210]. On the contrary, the Indian Parliament had unanimously voted in favour of the Government of India's support to the UN Security Council's actions for peace in Korea, while noting in the words of Nehru, "The future of Korea must be decided entirely by the Koreans themselves"[211]. Nehru unequivocally refused to treat Korea as a site of war but reminded domestic as well as international audiences of Korea's past as a nation and its future as a nation-state[212]. This view was accompanied by a sober assessment of India's role in bringing the war to a close, emphasizing the political as also dispassionate means India had used. In responding to a question regarding the success of India's policy, he said, "Perhaps the quiet and undramatic policy that we

Agreeing on a Major Issue for the First Time
The UN voted today that the Chinese Government be invited to participate in the council's debate on the American charge that its troops are fighting in Korea. Lake Success, NY, 8 November 1950. From left to right – Jacob Malik, Soviet delegate, Sir Gladwyn Jebb of Great Britain, and Warren K. Austin, American delegate.

have been pursuing on behalf of India has borne some fruit" and added that India's job had been "delicate, difficult, embarrassing...."[213].

Thus, India's non-aligned position allowed it to successfully use the UN as a vehicle for mediatory diplomacy but also at each step in the process, to draw attention to the narratives that had to be overcome in order for peace to be achieved. Nehru made important distinctions between war and peace, politics and security and means and ends in order to shape this discourse. Even though the events of the Korean War lasted over four years, the consistency in the discourse is remarkable[214].

K.P.S. Menon had referred in his report to the pithy observation that "the 38th parallel has become part of the long border line between the American and Soviet spheres around the globe"[215]; non-aligned India remained outside both those spheres and sought to dismantle their influence on international politics. In the following few years, Nehru reacted equally strongly towards the crises in Indochina and the Suez Canal. However, the discourse took a different turn in response to the Hungarian Revolution. That shift in direction is discussed in the following chapter.

4

The Fog of War

India, the Suez Canal Crisis and the Hungarian Revolution, 1956

In this chapter, I discuss the centrality of the state to non-alignment and its theorization within a non-aligned political vision. I present an account of the Suez Canal Crisis and the Hungarian Revolution, India's responses to both events, and I discuss the two events in conjunction, as the historical circumstances of political practice. Nehruvian non-alignment was concerned with the state in two ways – first, the state was the vehicle of politics, one that made moves towards or away from war possible; second, the non-aligned position was one of critically considering the system of states as the location of the balance of power. Previously, I have suggested that non-alignment was built on a critique of the received notion of the "nation-state" and on the conceptualization of the "international". In what might be called Nehru's theory of the state, the emphasis was on understanding the state as a unit of the international and in animating that relationship in a way that reimagined and remade the state. This conceptualization was in part a response to the structure of the state system in the Cold War period, and so, non-alignment was conceptualized as a turning away from that deeply securitized structure and instead, focused on remaking the state as an arena of politics. This movement was to some extent evident in India's approach to the problem of the Korean War.

Although the nation-state as a concept was critiqued and remade through its interface with the international, this theorization had at least two shortcomings. First, non-alignment assumed continuity between nationalism and sovereignty with the state in the foreground. In fact, these processes constituted a two-part process, which was concerned with the establishment of the state and with its consolidation. For Nehru, the relation between nationalism and the state was quite evidently one where the former led to the latter. In anticolonial movements, the arrival of modernity was often equated with the establishment of the state and Nehru certainly applied that model to India. However, this theorization didn't account for movements that aimed to displace the state. By drawing a straight line from nationalist aspirations to the establishment of the state, and to the consolidation of its sovereignty, non-alignment precluded the possibility that these three trajectories might come into conflict with one another. By neglecting these possibilities, non-alignment neglected a deeper theorization of the state, which limited the scope for effective non-aligned political practice. Instead, understandings of both nationalism and sovereignty relied too heavily on their provenance in anticolonial thought. So, nationalism in non-alignment was primarily anticolonial nationalism and sovereignty was the bulwark of the postcolonial state against the forces of imperialism, old and new.

By thinking the state in these terms, Nehru broke away from Gandhi whose political thought was premised on an exhaustive theoretical engagement with nationalism and the state, especially when it rejected them as essentially self-destructive. Nehru's insistence that it was possible to rescue the state from itself was built on the assumption that the state could act as a conduit for moral force. This moral force, as discussed in the opening chapters, was to be secured through the development of the international as an arena for politics. Yet, the second shortcoming of this theorization of the state was the conflation in non-alignment between the existent system of states, the concept of the international and internationalism as the force of an idea. This overlap is evident in Nehru's reading of the politics of the Soviet Union as primarily anticolonial and subsequently internationalist. Although the origins of socialist thought were anticolonial and the expansion of that thought into the socialist system of states was internationalist, the methods and objectives of that movement were drastically different from those of non-aligned India.

The anti-imperial character of Marxist struggle deeply influenced Nehru[1], and on attending the tenth anniversary celebrations of the Bolshevik Revolution in Moscow in 1927, he was quite clearly impressed by Russia's domestic advancement, remarking that "Russia, an outcaste like ourselves from nations and much and often erring in many respects, stands today as the greatest opponent of imperialism"[2]. Tagore had once remarked that Russia had raised the seat for the dispossessed[3]. Similarly, Nehru seemed in his assessment of Soviet Russia so convinced of the anticolonial discourse within Marxism that he evaded the question of methods to some extent, remarking that even though the purges of the 1930s had left the political leadership in India disillusioned about Soviet Russia, it was wise to "not mix up social and economic philosophy and communist methods"[4]. Thus, Nehru selectively analysed the politics of Soviet Russia. Although Nehru differentiated between Russian nationalism and world socialism, both directed from Moscow, he explained away the inconsistencies that arose as those two processes became fused with each other[5]. As the Indian response to the Hungarian Revolution shows us, this proved to be a blind spot in his approach to world politics.

As I will discuss further, the mutual visits of leaders from both countries to each other's in 1955 and Soviet Russia's not unenthusiastic response to the Afro-Asian Conference held at Bandung the same year might have led Nehru to believe that the socialist bloc was making a move from the socialist international to a post-ideological concept of the international as put forward by non-aligned India. If they had participated in this post-ideological process, the Soviets would have had to eschew the use of force against reformist nationalists within the Warsaw Pact countries. Indeed, it is clear that Nehru believed that neither would the Soviets send troops to Hungary, nor would Eden and others put troops in Egypt, against the wishes of the local populations. On both accounts, Nehru was proven wrong. It is interesting to note that both estimates stemmed from his belief that the time for colonialism of any kind was past. In this view, he was probably influenced by the wave of decolonization that was running through Asia and Africa at the time. Evidently, he was also more concerned with the exigencies of the Cold War, as India had experienced in the recently concluded armistice negotiations of the Korean War. By throwing these assumptions within non-alignment into question, the Suez Canal Crisis and the Hungarian Revolution produced an intense historical moment that challenged the configuration of non-alignment as a critique of war.

Indeed, Nehru's theory of the state was based on the assumption that the state could negotiate its presence in the international system in political terms and that although dissent was an integral part of that politics, the use of force wasn't, and in the future, could to some extent be replaced with diplomacy. Therefore, the Suez Canal Crisis invoked a predictable response from the Indian state, and particularly from Nehru, who denounced British and French aggression. Yet, India's defence of Egypt was played out in many parts that did not all reflect the critique of securitized politics so evident in the Korean case. For instance, Nehru advised Nasser against an appeal to the UN until the last phase of the crisis but when eventually the UN did get involved, India sent troops to the emergency force it constituted, in what was India's first deployment of troops abroad. Thus, in itself, India's response to the Suez Canal Crisis marks a move away from the early days of non-alignment when Nehru relied exclusively on Indian diplomacy and emphasized the necessity of the UN.

India's response to the Hungarian Revolution indicated a move even further away from the critical position of the early 1950s. Nehru's statements from the initial days of the revolution were met with accusations of "Bulganisation". Eventually, the reactions became even more ambiguous as Nehru vacillated between criticizing the use of force by the Soviets and pleading ignorance about conditions in Budapest[6]. Various memoirs of diplomats from the time are across the board puzzled by Nehru's lackadaisical reaction to the Hungarian Revolution. Unlike the Korean War, where India's approach to the crisis has received limited attention, the events of 1956 have been discussed somewhat more widely, particularly because the Hungarian Revolution is regarded as the first failure of Nehru's non-alignment, lending a severe blow to his prestige in the international arena, eventually damaged by the events of the Sino-Indian War of 1962. Some commentators have called the Suez Canal Crisis "the first international test of non-alignment"[7] and focus on the contrast between Hungary and Nehru's response to the Suez Canal Crisis, which as expected was unequivocal.

Instead, the approach that I've taken is to discuss the two events in the continuities they represent, as parts of a single historical moment. Crucially, in both Egypt and Hungary, Nehru used narratives of sovereignty in contradictory ways. During the Suez Canal Crisis, Nehru invoked Egypt's sovereignty constantly, even while explaining India's actions in the later stages of the conflict. In the case of Hungary, on the other hand, both parties justified their actions in the name of protecting Hungarian sovereignty; this presented non-aligned India with an unprecedented challenge, one that New Delhi responded to belatedly and inadequately. Therefore, I suggest in this chapter that 1956 can be read as a moment where it is evident that the theorization of the state within non-alignment was weak, and that it didn't account for systemic shocks such as those strongly felt in the wake of the Hungarian Revolution. As the critique of war was conducted in the perspective of the state, this weakness in theorizing the state reflected on the critique of war too. I study some of these practical limitations of this approach that can be observed in both the Suez Canal Crisis and the Hungarian Revolution, and in their simultaneous occurrence. In studying India's non-aligned approach to these crises more closely, it might be possible to anticipate the limits of the politics imagined within non-alignment.

The Suez Canal Crisis

Gamal Abdel Nasser came to power in Egypt in November 1954. The British, under Anthony Eden's leadership saw this development as inimical to their interests and saw Nasser, as "a threat to be addressed, not appeased"[8], an "Asiatic Mussolini"[9] and constantly compared him to Hitler[10]. The French, under the leadership of Guy Mollet, saw Nasser's Arab nationalism as a threat to their interests in Africa, particularly in Algeria[11]. India, on the other hand, saw in "the wise leadership of President Nasser" an opportunity to establish wider and friendlier relations with West Asia[12]. In February 1955, Turkey had signed a defence pact with Pakistan, a treaty that subsequently expanded to also include Iran, Iraq and the United Kingdom and which came to be known as the Baghdad Pact. Nehru, then on a visit to Cairo, made a statement saying, "We must think not in terms of war but prepare for peace. If the world is foolish enough to have war, I wonder what good alliances can be"[13]. On 16 February 1955, Egypt and India issued a joint communiqué denouncing military alliances[14]. Subsequently, in the run-up to, during and after the Bandung Conference, India's ties with Egypt were consolidated in a series of moves. When Nehru stopped in Cairo on his return from Europe, India and Egypt issued a statement lauding the "existence of an identity of views on major international issues"[15].

Egypt seemed to have accepted these Indian overtures because amongst other reasons, India hadn't called Neguib's rule a coup d'etat[16]. On 6 April 1955, India and Egypt had signed a Treaty of Friendship and Cooperation, which emphasized "a spirit of brotherliness" in the diplomatic relations between the states[17]. Later that month, Nasser made two stops at New Delhi to meet Nehru – one on the way to Bandung and then again on his return. At their first meeting on 12 April 1955, Nasser spoke to Nehru at length about the Arab-Israeli conflict, particularly that the "Gaza strip was totally indefensible" and that "ever since Ben Gurion's come back, Israel had become more and more aggressive"[18]. On his return trip, Nasser referred once again to "the difficulties in the Arab countries", and talked about a defence pact between Syria, Egypt and Saudi Arabia[19]. Nehru did not find this idea useful and sought to remind Nasser that in "the unfortunate event of a war with Israel, the burden would fall on Egypt. Saudi Arabia did not even have a common frontier with Israel. Syria would do little"[20]. It is evident that Nehru tried to steer Nasser away from the idea of defence pacts and towards the non-aligned countries, possibly because he thought of the group led by Nasser as "a small military group, with the support of the army... a good group, honest and seeking the welfare of Egypt" and of Nasser as "a good man and trying his best to face and overcome these evils"[21].

In this assessment, Nehru was influenced by his own observations of the negotiations over the Suez Canal, to which he referred periodically as an issue of international significance[22]. He had also been receiving news from Apa Pant about the centrality of Egypt to the entire African continent either by virtue of its location and through the practice of Islam that gave Egypt a special bond with the countries of the Mediterranean and with Equatorial and West Africa[23]. Pant reminded Nehru that until very recently "Egypt had her face turned towards Europe and European civilization" but that through the revolution Egypt had "burst into the consciousness of Africa"[24]. When Ali Yavar Jung took over from Apa Pant in 1955, he wrote to Nehru warning him of rising anti-Indian sentiment in West Asia; Nehru identified this line of propaganda as the idea that India was "pro-communist", and that India was "trying to develop into a strong dominant power"[25]. Nehru sought to neutralize this anti-Indian sentiment and to build closer ties with West Asia by encouraging Egypt to accept non-alignment and by following a resolute policy towards Israel, one that specifically denied any connection between the questions of Israel-Palestine and that of the ill treatment of Jews by Hitler[26]. Nehru also noted that there was "a great deal of sympathy in Europe and America for the Jews" but "that had nothing to do with the present situation"[27]. Nehru had even conceded, albeit reluctantly to the Arab demand to not include Israel in the Bandung Conference[28]. All in all, by the end of 1955, Nehru had distanced himself from the Western position on Israel, had consolidated India's efforts to encourage secular Arab nationalism in West Asia and had recognized Nasser as a significant partner in the process[29].

At Bandung, Nehru had sought to further integrate Egypt with the other Third World nations, including Yugoslavia. Thus, when

Tito invited Nehru and Nasser to his retreat in Brioni on the Adriatic Sea, the three undertook a series of discussions and announced a set of "principles that should govern international relations" on 18 July 1956[30]. The United States had paid close attention to the Bandung Conference and was now witnessing the founding of the NAM, particularly the part of the joint statement "expressly disassociating Egypt from any dependence on the West"[31]. Although Egypt and the US had entered into talks in November 1955 on American financing for the Aswan Dam to be constructed on the Nile, the US Secretary of State John Foster Dulles withdrew any offer of assistance on 19 July 1955, possibly in response to the statement issued by the three non-aligned leaders the previous day, but also as a cumulative effect of other happenings in Egypt, such as the finalization of an arms deal with communist Czechoslovakia in 1955 and Egypt's recognition of communist China in May 1956[32]. Additionally, the Indian Ambassador Ali Yavar Jung was certain that the American offer had been a mere counterfoil to an earlier Soviet offer for assistance, but once the Soviets withdrew their offer in June 1956, the Americans were looking for a pretext to withdraw theirs too[33].

At the end of the meeting of the non-aligned leaders, Nehru and Nasser flew back to Cairo on the same day; en route from Brioni to Cairo, Nasser showed Nehru the text of Dulles's speech announcing the withdrawal of assistance for building the Aswan Dam, in which the Americans had pointed to doubts about Egypt's economic climate[34], to which Nehru said, "These people, how arrogant they are"[35]. When they arrived in Cairo, Nehru and Nasser continued to hold talks for the next couple of days before Nehru left for India on the afternoon of 21 July 1956. During these Nehru-Nasser talks in Cairo, Nasser informed Nehru that he had decided to give up the Aswan Dam project[36], and was encouraged in this line of thought by Nehru, particularly as Nehru thought the Arab-Israeli tension was dissipating as at Brioni, the leaders had received an informal message from Ben-Gurion saying that Israel had erred in leaning on the Western powers and had realized that "they were of Asia and must look to Asia"[37].

Nasser first reacted to the withdrawal of American assistance in forceful rhetoric, "May you choke with rage...We Egyptians will not allow any colonizer or despot to dominate us...We shall yield neither to force nor to the dollar"[38]. Following this, on 26 July 1956, at the third anniversary celebrations of the Egyptian Revolution at Alexandria Square in Cairo, Nasser announced the nationalization of the Suez Canal, adding, "We shall rely on our own strength, our own muscle, our own funds"[39]. Jung wrote to Nehru saying this was a calculated response intended to reclaim credibility in Egypt's economic strength and assuage Egyptian and Arab public opinion[40]. Nehru responded by saying that the manner in which the British and the Americans had behaved was "very discourteous and almost contemptuous"[41] but also relayed his surprise to Nasser, "I learnt of your decision about Suez Canal. As this had not been mentioned by you in the course of our talks at Brioni and Cairo, I thought that decision must have been taken after I left Cairo"[42]. It was learnt later that Nasser had taken the decision after Nehru's departure, on the evening of 21 July[43].

There had been no discussion about the canal at the Commonwealth Prime Ministers' Conference held in the first half of the year; Nehru was keen on avoiding the impression that the matter had been discussed at Brioni or that Nasser's actions had Nehru's backing[44]. Thus, Nehru sought to distance India from Nasser's decision by emphasizing that he had no inkling of it and that in the event of a flare-up, India would remain non-aligned. Nehru wrote to Vijaya Lakshmi Pandit saying that there was "no reference whatever to Suez Canal during talks with Marshal Tito and Nasser at Brioni or later during my talks with Egyptians Ministers in Cairo"[45]. Nehru also wrote to the Great Powers, the Colombo Powers and Tito to say he had no prior intimation of this plan[46]. Tito replied saying the issue "although very serious is not so dramatic" and it was "possible to act towards both sides with a quietening effect"[47]. Nehru later wrote to Tito to say that Yugoslavia must not seem too partial in their support of the Egyptian position and Tito replied saying the press had been reigned in[48]. Nehru also sent detailed instructions to Ali Yavar Jung to say "we as an Asian country…should not appear to line up with Egypt and other countries sympathetic to Egypt just as we will not line up against Egypt with powers hostile to her"[49]. He also disagreed with the anti-western stand taken by Rajagopalachari who had written saying "The question here is not the Cold War but the freedom of Asiatic States to self-rule", further suggesting a declaration by all the Bandung countries clearly expressing their support for Egypt[50].

In a subsequent cable, Nehru conveyed to Vijaya Lakshmi Pandit the reassurance he had received from Nasser that the nationalization "does not in any way or to any extent affect the international commitment of Egypt"[51] but also that in his view "the Egyptian Government [was] undertaking more than it can manage and [was] being pushed by some extreme elements."[52] Vijaya Lakshmi Pandit replied alerting Nehru to the British Commonwealth Secretary Douglas-Home's talk of "the impossibility of allowing a gangster to remain in complete control" of the Suez Canal and "emphasized that Egypt could, if this action was not firmly curbed, destroy Western prestige and cripple UK economy in a matter of weeks"[53]. As expected, the British and the French had taken a less than charitable view of the situation. French Minister of Foreign Affairs Christian Pineau called the nationalization an "act of plunder"; British Prime Minister Anthony Eden spoke of "precautionary measures of a military nature"; British Foreign Secretary Selwyn Lloyd went to the extent of saying that "the Government would be failing in its duties if it did not take precautionary measures"; French Prime Minister Guy Mollet denounced Nasser as a "would-be dictator", "imitator of Hitler" and said the allies would "launch an energetic and severe riposte" to Nasser's actions[54].

In these circumstances, Nehru made the point that India's objective was to "prevent hostilities and to have a peaceful settlement which would ensure the use of the Canal as before", adding that any "restriction of traffic through the canal or blockade or imposition of higher tolls would have harmful results and might even prejudice the progress of the Second Five Year Plan"[55]. In a detailed statement that he presented to the Lok Sabha on 31 July 1956, Nehru repeated his stand that during his visit to Egypt and to Brioni, there had been no talk of the nationalization of the canal or any other aspect of Anglo-Egyptian relations. Most importantly, he in no uncertain measure distinguished India's position on the matter saying, "The way Egypt took hold of the Suez Canal was not our way. We follow a different way, but who am I to criticise others? If they had followed a different way, so many difficulties would not have arisen, but they had a right to follow their own methods"[56]. Subsequently, Nasser and Nehru exchanged a multitude of messages discussing a solution to this issue – Nasser complained that the threat of force was being employed against Egypt because they were "comparatively weak and an oriental people"[57] but he also spoke of his willingness for a conciliatory approach. Douglas-Home had asked Vijaya Lakshmi Pandit if India would agree to and enforce implementation of international control of the canal[58]. Nehru replied saying that it should not be difficult for Suez to remain an international waterway as Nasser had assured it but that in any circumstance, the use of force was wrong[59].

Immediately after the nationalization of the canal, Eisenhower had suggested to Eden a conference of the canal users to be held in London, therefore called the London Conference[60]. Eden accepted the idea but wanted to limit the numbers of attendees, but Eisenhower insisted that the conference be as inclusive as possible, in order to placate those supporting Egypt[61]. Nehru supported this view and encouraged the British to invite Yugoslavia, Burma, Poland and Saudi Arabia, although they weren't eventually included[62]. When Nasser showed resistance, Nehru first proposed a conference of "interested international parties" hosted by Egypt[63]. Yet, Nasser was opposed to the idea of the conference overall and wanted to take the issue to the UN[64]. In fact, he wrote to Nehru proposing a plan saying Egypt would boycott the London Conference and instead, ask for all waterways to be placed under the UN, negotiate a fresh treaty guaranteeing the security of the Suez Canal and freedom of navigation and that this treaty would be registered with the UN[65]. Nehru strongly advised against taking the issue to the UN, saying, "In the present state of the world, the alignment of forces there may not be favourable. Further, it can also lead to the interpretation of a prior acceptance of international control. It is wiser to be cautious about bringing in the UN just now"[66]. Thereafter, Nehru tried through Ali Yavar Jung to convince Nasser to at least jointly hold a conference with Britain in order to show that Egypt was "not adopting a *non possumus* attitude but made a constructive approach"[67]. Ali Yavar Jung, having pressed the case, reported to Nehru that the Egyptian Cabinet was "against association with Britain"[68]. In these circumstances, Nehru convinced Nasser to not boycott the conference entirely and send some manner of representation, which Nasser agreed to, eventually sending the head of the Egyptian General Intelligence Directorate, Ali Sabri along with V.K. Krishna Menon, the Indian representative to the London Conference[69].

Nehru then corresponded with Vijaya Lakshmi Pandit to ensure that India's attendance of the conference would not be tantamount to committing to the principles set out in the three-power communiqué[70]. Nehru wrote to Eden saying India would only attend if assured of it and that the whole approach to the conference could have been different, that Egypt should have been invited to host the conference and included in it[71]. Nehru also wrote to Nasser reiterating India's non-aligned position that did not "support any unilateral action or any group of nations"[72]. Nehru repeatedly wrote to the British saying that Egypt was likely to attend the conference and participate in negotiations in the absence of prior conditions or commitments. He also wrote to Eden to ensure that no force would be used against Egypt while negotiations were being carried forth at the conference emphasizing that "If however, force and coercive tactics are used, then the consequences all over Asia and in North Africa will be far-reaching"[73]. Eden replied saying, "We have no intention whatsoever of trying to coerce the conference by military threat or action"[74]. Nehru then wrote to Vijaya Lakshmi Pandit relaying Eden's message that the London Conference had nothing to do with the Aswan Dam and was only concerned with putting the Suez Canal under an international authority[75], that this was "not satisfactory", but that India had decided to attend the Conference all the same[76]. Although Nehru was at first of the opinion that "Egypt should have been consulted and invited to sponsor the conference"[77], he later thought that Indian "attendance could prove a check on the policy of intimidation". This was particularly crucial, as Eisenhower had decided against attending in person, as "Nehru would probably not be there personally, but only Krishna Menon"[78]. Zhou Enlai sent a message to Nehru through R.K. Nehru, the Indian Ambassador in China to say that India was in a "key position" and that being a Commonwealth country, India could exercise influence on Britain[79]. The Soviets sent a message to Nehru through K.P.S. Menon, the Indian Ambassador in the USSR to say that the "stand taken by India was absolutely correct" and would have the support of the Soviet Government[80]. Nehru considered the Suez Canal Conference "the most important conference that Independent India would be attending"[81].

On 8 August, Nehru made a statement in the Lok Sabha announcing that India would attend the London Conference, Krishna Menon would go as leader of the Indian delegation and that threats of force did not "belong to this age" and therefore that India had declined participation "in any arrangements for war preparations or sanctions or any step which challenged the sovereign rights of Egypt"[82]. He also expressed his growing anxiety stressing that India was "a principal user of this waterway" and not a "disinterested party" and that indeed, India was "passionately interested in averting a conflict"[83]. On the same day, Eden yet again called Nasser a dictator in a public broadcast saying, "With dictators, you always have to pay a higher price later on for their appetites grow with food." Nehru dismayed at this belligerence, said it was "in bad taste and was in addition, bad politics"[84]. In response to Nehru's complaints, Eden replied saying he was disappointed "at the manner in which the balance has been struck in India between Egypt and the Western Powers" and "it would seem hardly surprising that we should be concerned at a man with this record having his thumb on our windpipe"[85]. Dulles also wrote first to Menon, who relayed the message to Nehru that "the question of Suez was not only one of legal rights but of distrust of Nasser because of his gigantic ambitions and his attitude and policies"[86]. As expected, Nasser retorted on 12 August denouncing Anglo-French military preparations[87] and proposing a conference of all Constantinople Convention signatories and 45 countries that had been using the Suez Canal in 1955[88]. Nehru tried to temper this conflict by immediately writing to Ali Yavar Jung asking him to convey to Nasser, "our [Indian] policy under Gandhiji's leadership was to be firm on principles but at the same time conciliatory in approach"[89].

A parallel crisis erupted in India at this time with sections of public opinion led by C Rajagopalachari demanding India's withdrawal from the Commonwealth, calling it an "odious hypocrisy" and "not a reality", but an "instrument of aggression"[90]. Nehru stemmed these debates saying they were "from every point of view very undesirable"[91], placing emphasis on India's role in mediating between the conflicting parties[92]. Nehru wrote, "This is by far the most difficult and dangerous situation in international affairs we have faced since independence. I do not think we can do very much, but it is just possible that we might stop the rot. Probably we shall end by displeasing our friends on both sides"[93]. Evidently, Nehru was much alarmed by the aggressive attitudes adopted by both sides and was acutely aware that India's non-aligned position exposed it to the possibility of isolation in the event of a conflagration. He was also aware of how crucial the success of the London Conference was, remarking on 12 August 1956 that the "next week or ten days will indicate which way the world goes, towards conflict or away from it"[94]. He revisited this anxiety in his Independence Day speech delivered on 15 August 1956 saying, "the conference must not fail"[95]. To Nehru, the Suez Canal Crisis was a strong indication of the "progressive elimination of British and French influence in Asia and Africa"[96].

In these circumstances, the London Conference was held from 16–23 August 1956. Nehru's instructions to Krishna Menon were that the Indian position must be respectful of Egypt's sovereign rights and seek guarantees of uninterrupted navigation through the Canal for all nations in accordance with the 1888 Convention. Menon had stopped in Cairo en route to London, where he met Nasser and reported back to Nehru saying that he was "unyielding on issues such as international control"[97]. Menon also said he had argued the case for Egyptian sovereignty in talks with the Great Powers but had been embarrassed by the Soviets taking a similar line[98]. But Nehru had kept a line of communication open with the Americans, by encouraging G.L. Mehta, the Indian Ambassador to the US to talk to Secretary of State John Foster Dulles[99]. Nehru was certain that the Americans would not allow the British and the French to use force against

Egypt, and so he pressed Krishna Menon to take the middle path at the conference and not antagonize either side. At the Conference, two proposals came into prominence – the first was the Menon Proposal that recommended a consultative body of user interests - deliberative, consultative, liaison functions, suitable international

Nehru at 10 Downing Street
Indian Prime Minister Jawaharlal Nehru and British Prime Minister Anthony Eden leave 10 Downing Street after talks. London, 15 December 1956. (Keystone-France/Gamma-Rapho via Getty Images)

status with annual reports transmitted to the UN by Egypt. Eden thought the Indian delegation was speaking on behalf of Egypt, and so rejected the proposal; Nasser also rejected its terms as it included some form of international management of the canal. The alternative was a US-led draft proposing that a convention would be negotiated with Egypt providing for the creation of a Suez Canal Board for operating, maintaining and developing the Canal. This proposal – informally known as the Dulles Plan – received the support of 18 states in all and it was decided that representatives from Australia, Iran, Ethiopia, Sweden and the US would arrive in Cairo under the

Suez Crisis Talks
Madame Vijaya Lakshmi Pandit, the High Commissioner for India, arrives with V.K. Krishna Menon at Lancaster House for the Suez Conference. London, 16 August 1956. (Manchester Mirror/Mirrorpix via Getty Images)

chairmanship of Robert Menzies, the Australian Prime Minister to explain the proposals to Nasser. The proposal also said that disputes were to be settled by an Arbitral Commission, with safeguards against violations[100].

Meanwhile, Menon wrote to Jung and Nehru saying that the Indian proposals had "proved ineffective" and complaining that Nasser had to budge, as the Dulles Plan already "held the field" and the pivot would shift to the US if India did not come up with a suitable plan[101]. Jung wrote back saying that Nasser wanted to meet with Menon before meeting Menzies[102]. Nehru wrote to Jung saying this might appear as an attempt at Indian interference in the US-led initiative[103], but asked Menon to stop in Cairo on his return from London, but only after Menzies had departed[104]. Nehru also asked Menon to come up with a more "constructive scheme"[105]. When it came to the counting of hands, India, Indonesia, Sri Lanka and the Soviet Union disagreed with the provisions of the Dulles Plan. Yet, the 18 powers that had supported it decided to send the representatives to Cairo anyway. Menon threatened to walk out of the Conference, but Nehru dissuaded him, saying that would mean giving the conference too much importance[106]. Simultaneously, the British High Commissioner to India Malcolm MacDonald met with Nehru to convince him to support the Dulles Plan and the Menzies Mission. Nehru refused to press Nasser on the Dulles Plan, said Nasser couldn't undo the nationalization, that the London Conference had not made any negotiated settlement possible and that it was impossible to impose a solution on Egypt[107].

The Menzies Mission arrived in Cairo from 3–9 September 1956 to convince Nasser of the need for international management of the canal. Nehru supported the spirit of the mission saying, "Any attempt at reconciliation deserves Indian support"[108]. Nasser rejected these proposals, wrote to Nehru asking for his support to take the matter to the UN Security Council and for his influence in negotiating the

London Conference
Twenty-two nations assemble for the Suez Conference held in London in 1956. (Hulton-Deutsch Collection/Corbis Historical via Getty Images)

terms of the freedom of navigation to canal users. Nehru replied to Nasser resisting the involvement of the UN, instead advising Nasser to focus on the general terms of any offer, but not on specific proposals[109]. Nehru also wrote to Eisenhower and Eden asking them to reconsider their plans in light of the Egyptian position[110]. Yet, on 9 September,

Dulles proposed the creation of a Suez Canal Users Association (SCUA), an international consortium of the world's leading maritime nations. On 12 September, Eden announced his support for the SCUA and said that Britain and France along with the US would go ahead with the proposal despite Egypt's protests, adding much to Nehru's consternation that "Governments must be free to take whatever steps are open to them…"[111]. Nehru criticized these actions in a Lok Sabha speech made on 13 September 1956, saying "the action proposed is not the result of agreement, cooperation or consent, but is to be taken unilaterally, and thus is in the nature of an imposed decision" and implored both Eden and Eisenhower to accept the Egyptian proposal and not withdraw pilots from the Suez Canal, an act that "appeared to close the door to further negotiations"[112]. India then sent Indian pilots via the port authorities to work in the Suez, but Nehru categorically refused to supply Egypt with arms fearing that it might compromise India's non-aligned position: "For us to supply arms to the Egyptian government at this stage would naturally be greatly resented by the United Kingdom and other Western governments and make them feel that we are supporting Egypt one hundred per cent in peace and war. Our capacity for playing a mediatory role would disappear"[113]. Instead, Nehru now advised Nasser to approach the UN Security Council. In this, he was supported by the Soviets[114].

On 14 September, Nehru sent out simultaneous correspondence to Eden, Lloyd and Dulles, asking the former two for an emergency meeting of the Commonwealth Prime Ministers and the latter to exercise American influence to stop British troops from landing in Egypt. Dulles replied, saying that "while the US would not support any disregard of Egypt's rights, it was not clear what precisely these rights were"[115]. Nehru also seemed to privately believe that Britain wouldn't put troops anywhere and in this he seemed to still rely on his assessment of Eden from the latter's visit to India in 1955 and his tempering

UN Observers Arrive in Sinai
UN observers arrive in Egypt on 15 November 1956 during the Suez Crisis. An Anglo-French intervention has been launched after Egypt's President Nasser nationalized Suez Canal on 26 July 1956. End-of-December diplomatic action by the USA and the USSR forced Britain and France to withdraw and Israel to relinquish Sinai, which they invaded in October. (AFP via Getty Images)

influence at the Geneva Conference on Indochina[116]. Indeed, the community of thought between Eden and Nehru had moved Pineau to remark that he considered Eden "une sorts de Nehru brittanique, en plus fragile"[117]. Britain and France took the matter to the Security Council on 23 September 1956. Egypt filed a counter-complaint on 24 September 1956 and was informed by Secretary General Dag Hammarskjöld that the matter would be heard on 5 October 1956. Nehru, who was sceptical of progress through the UN said, "Our own experience of the Security Council has not been happy"[118]. Yet, he

Nehru in London
Prime Minister Nehru with his sister, the Indian High Commissioner to the UK, Madame Vijaya Lakshmi Pandit, outside India House, London, while he was attending the Commonwealth Prime Ministers Conference. London, 23 June 1956. (Central Press/Stringer via Getty Images)

expected to stretch out the situation for as long as possible, evading conflict. Yugoslavia, who was a member of the UNSC succeeded in getting an adjournment, citing Menon's continued efforts in Cairo and London towards achieving a settlement. Nehru, meanwhile, continued to urge Eisenhower, Eden and the Prime Ministers of Sri Lanka and

Leaders of the Non-Aligned Movement
From left to right – Egyptian President Gamal Abdel Nasser, Indian Prime Minister Jawaharlal Nehru and Yugoslavian President Josip Broz Tito meet on the Brioni Islands, 1956. (Archive Photos/Stringer via Getty Images)

Indonesia to consider the Egyptian proposals[119]. G.L. Mehta wrote to Nehru saying that in his conversations with Dulles, the latter had said he did not understand the Egyptian proposals, and that the American proposal for the SCUA was the "only available alternative to war"[120].

Nehru then wrote strongly worded letters to Eden, Lloyd and Dulles, repeating that the "repercussions on Asia as a whole of the use of force or steps that appear or are in effect suppression of Egyptian authority without consent are very grave"[121].

Menon then introduced his new formula that was a modified version of his earlier proposal and suggested Egypt enter into an agreement for cooperation with a Users' Association and regular joint sessions of the Egyptian Board and the Users' Association could be held to discuss all matters concerning the canal, with UN advisors supervising the three main sectors of operation[122]. Both Eden and Lloyd expressed their dissatisfaction at this plan[123] but Menon told Nehru that only "methodological problems" remained and that it was only necessary to convince Nasser[124]. However, the British High Commissioner Malcolm MacDonald disabused Nehru of this notion by saying this plan was unacceptable to the British as it left Egypt with "unfettered control of the Suez"[125]. Nehru in his reply to Eden continued to emphasize negotiation[126]. The Foreign Ministers of Britain, France and Egypt then began private talks in New York, at which Krishna Menon was present in a mediatory role[127]. Nehru thought the Suez Canal Crisis had passed over; in a speech in Calcutta on 21 October, he highlighted India's role in bringing it to a close. The Foreign Ministers meeting in New York then decided to meet for a second round of talks in Geneva on 29 October 1956. But before those talks could take place, on 29 October, Israel launched attacks on Egyptian soil[128].

In response, Britain and France first issued an ultimatum to Israel and Egypt "to stop all warlike action by land, sea and air forthwith and to withdraw their military forces to a distance of 10 miles from the Suez Canal"[129]. They also asked Egypt to allow Anglo-French forces to be stationed at Port Said, Ismailia and Suez, a demand Egypt declined. British and French forces then began attacking Egyptian airfields on 31 October. Nehru was shocked and aggravated by this "dastardly action" and undertook several measures in order to effectively mediate. First, Nehru assured Nasser of India's full support to Egypt and called the actions of the British and the French "a reversal of history"[130]; second, he asked Yugoslavia and other Bandung countries to join in the public condemnation of the aggressors, saying "the countries that were associated at Bandung have a special responsibility in this matter"[131] and that "no country in Asia or Africa, which has recently achieved freedom, can possibly tolerate this reversal[132]; third, he called on Hammarskjöld to ensure that the procedures of the UN were swifter than those of invasion and aggression against Egypt and that "argument that this invasion is meant to protect the Canal and to ensure free traffic has no force as the first result of this invasion is for this traffic to cease"[133]; fourth and most importantly, he turned to the US for support and intervention in the cause of peace, writing to Dulles, "the whole future of the relations between Europe and Asia hangs in the balance"[134].

The Soviets at this time first threatened intervention then proposed joint US-Soviet intervention and then wanted to send volunteers to Egypt. Nehru was against all these measures and chose to let the UN take up this matter now that it was involved. India's Permanent Representative to the UN, Arthur Lall, and Egyptian Permanent Representative to the UN, Omar Loutfi, went to see Henry Cabot Lodge to ask the US to interdict British-French-Israeli action against Egypt[135]. The UNSC met on 31 October, but both Soviet and American proposals were vetoed by Britain and France. The Americans were enraged by the actions of their allies and found themselves "in strange company fighting for peace"[136]. They also issued statements saying they had not been informed of any phase of these actions in advance and that there would be no US involvement in these hostilities[137]. Hammarskjöld sent a message to the British saying they were "completely flouting the UN Charter". Nehru's note to Eden lays out India's position clearly[138]: "For us in India and I believe in many other countries of Asia and elsewhere, this is a reversion to a previous and unfortunate period of history when decisions were imposed by force of arms by Western Powers on Asian countries. We had thought these methods were out of date and could not possibly be used in the modern age. The whole purpose of the UN is undermined, and the freedom of nations imperilled, if armed might is to decide issues between nations...unless these wrong courses are halted, the future appears to me to be dark indeed." MacDonald conveyed to the Foreign Office his impression that Nehru was "not unfriendly and expressed his views more in sorrow than in anger"[139].

After the initial setbacks at the UN Security Council, Arthur Lall and Omar Loutfi decided to take the matter up in the General Assembly, in the absence of the veto[140]. So, on 2 November 1956, the UN General Assembly met and passed a US-sponsored resolution under the Uniting for Peace formula that urged immediate ceasefire and asked all sides to withdraw behind the armistice lines[141]. The Americans and Canadians were now referring to the possibility of "the Eisenhower-Nehru formula"[142] and Eisenhower was ready and eager to meet with Nehru, "just the two of them because he thought they came closer [than anyone else] to commanding the respect of the world"[143]. Egypt agreed to accept the ceasefire on the condition that Israel did likewise. On 4 November 1956, Lall moved a 19-member Asian-African resolution saying that not all parties had agreed to the ceasefire or withdrawn their forces and urged full compliance. On the same day, a large majority passed a resolution moved by Canada, Colombia and Norway that provided for the first UN peacekeeping force that would supervise cessation of hostilities. This is how the United Nations Emergency Force I (UNEF I), to which India was a prominent contributor, came into existence[144]. On 5 November 1956, Egypt accepted the ceasefire and Menon arrived in New York to apply renewed pressure on Britain and France. The Germans also conveyed to Nehru through G.L. Mehta that they thought the aggression had been unnecessary[145]. Bulganin wrote to Nehru saying the "voice of India against the aggression could play an outstanding part"[146]. In his response, Nehru wondered whether it was possible "to rescue peace from the fog of war"[147].

Bulganin had also written letters to Eden, Mollet and Ben Guiron saying the Soviets were "determined to crush the aggression by use of force and to restore peace"; these also came into public view on the same day. This combination of factors led to Eden announcing ceasefire on 6 November 1956. Nehru and Eisenhower exchanged sustained correspondence during this period[148]. Eisenhower had impressed upon Nehru the "need to exert the greatest possible restraint lest this situation radically deteriorate"[149]. Nehru responded in kind saying, "any step which might expand the sphere of military operations and lead to world war would be a crime against humanity and must be avoided"[150]. Nehru knew that the Egyptian military resistance was dwindling and that "Nasser proposed to lay down his life fighting"[151]. The onus was now on India to send troops to the UNEF because the resolution had stipulated against drawing troops from any of the five permanent members[152]. The Canadians had offered to send troops but had a hard time convincing Nasser that Egyptian people could "distinguish between The Queen's Own from West Surrey and The Queen's Own from Calgary"[153]. This was further complicated by Canada's membership of the NATO. Pearson and Hammarskjöld both requested India for troops, but Nehru waited for the Egyptian Government's unqualified invitation for India's participation[154]. Nehru hesitated at first, expressing to Krishna Menon that India was "always reluctant to send Indian troops abroad"[155]. Yet, R.G. Rajwade, the Indian Charge D'Affairs in Cairo, wrote to Nehru saying Nasser had refused to reopen the waterway as long as British and French occupation of Port Said continued and that Nasser "would not accept anything limiting his sovereignty"[156]. On 9 November, Israel and Britain said they would withdraw their troops once the UNEF had arrived and was ready to discharge its task[157]. Thus, the composition of the UNEF took on an urgent character. The British asked India "to come in heavily and assist in bringing about a speedy settlement"[158]. The Indian Contingent for the Suez left on 15 November 1956; in his farewell speech, Nehru reminded them to act "with credit to India and her gallant army"[159].

Nehru also emphasized the conditions on which India had agreed to send troops to the UNEF in a speech to the Lok Sabha on 19 November 1956. He said, "I want to make it perfectly clear on what conditions we sent these forces to join the United Nations Force. First of all, we made it clear that it was only if the Government of Egypt agreed that we would send them; secondly, they were not to be considered in any sense a continuing force continuing the activities of the Anglo-French forces, but an entirely separate thing; thirdly, that the Anglo-French forces should be withdrawn; fourthly, that the United Nations Force should function to protect the old armistice line between Israel and Egypt; and finally, that it would be a temporary affair. We are not prepared to agree to our forces or any force remaining there indefinitely. It was on these conditions, which were accepted, that these forces were sent there"[160]. Both France and the United Kingdom suggested an assessment of Indian peacekeeping forces, which was rubbished in arguments at the UN with Krishna Menon arguing, "France and the United Kingdom have no right to tell us: 'We will decide, when your forces come in, whether they are big enough and whether they can take over'"[161]. The UNEF was placed first along the Suez Canal sector and then along the demarcation line in the Gaza area and subsequently on the Egyptian side of the international frontier in the Sinai Peninsula. The force was commanded by two Indians in both its phases, UNEF-I and UNEF-II,

Lt. Gen. P.S. Gyani commanded it between December 1959 and January 1964 and later, Maj. Gen. Indar Jit Rikhye took over between January 1966 and June 1967[162]. The force consisted of troops from eight countries – India, Indonesia, Colombia, Yugoslavia and the four Scandinavian countries, and was therefore mostly either non-aligned or neutral in character. At the request of the Canadians, Nehru pressed for Canadian force contribution to the UNEF citing Canadian protests in the UN, cancellation of an aircraft deal with Israel, and saying that Norway and Denmark were also in the NATO[163]. Nasser first agreed to a Canadian ambulance corps and air supplies, but Nehru pressed for a contingent to be placed with the UNEF, to which Nasser finally agreed[164].

An issue on which Nasser did not agree to Nehru's requests was the question of the deportation of British, French, and Jewish people from Egypt[165]. Nehru was disappointed and expected Nasser "to create a feeling of generosity which again results in a change in one's own favour"[166]. He was also aware that the British and French now just wanted to avoid further humiliation[167]. He summed up his assessment of the situation in his fortnightly letter to the Chief Ministers: "The … Anglo-French action in Egypt… was supposed to lead to a re-establishment of British influence over Western Asia and of French influence in Northern Africa and especially Algeria. In the result, it is President Nasser who has come out of it with greater strength and far greater prestige, and both the UK and France have suffered tremendously in their prestige, apart from the great losses that they sustained"[168]. India's relations with the US that had suffered as a result of the high visibility of the Bandung Conference regained some vitality. When Dulles had visited India in March 1956, Nehru had said "The most that we can expect out of his visit here is that he has got some idea into his rather closed head as to what we feel about various things"[169]. Likewise, in June of the same year, Dulles had criticized non-alignment as "immoral and short-sighted"[170]. In fact, during the early stages of the crisis, Indian Embassy reports from the US suggested that "the Americans seem to be prepared to support the UK to the very end if need be"[171] and that "no sympathy can be foreseen for the Egyptian point of view"[172]. But the unilateral and covert action taken by the British and French had alienated the Americans and they found themselves holding the same view as India's. When in December that year, Nehru met Dulles during a visit to the US, they agreed that the failure to consult other powers, but also "the use of force as an instrument of national policy" had constituted their primary objections to the aggression against Egypt[173]. The Soviet policy, on the other hand, had pushed the case for intervention captured in Bulganin's stance of "we have got rockets"[174]. Nehru found it rather difficult to align the Indian position with that of the Soviet line of thinking. Indeed, that influenced, and was influenced by the simultaneous events of the Hungarian Revolution.

The Hungarian Revolution

Relations between New Delhi and Moscow in the first decade after Indian independence can be divided into a Stalinist and post-Stalinist period[175]. Up to Stalin's death in 1953, the view from Moscow was to consider India an imperial outpost, and the Gandhi-Nehru political lineage a dynastic one. In the Indian view, it was considered significant to cultivate Soviet support of independent India, especially in international affairs. Yet, Indian political leadership was held back by a refusal to communism on the whole, and anxiety that the activities of Indian communists were being directed from Moscow[176]. However, with India's involvement in the diffusion of the Korean War's POW crisis, the Soviets turned their attention to India in a new light. This policy fell in line with increased Soviet engagement of the Third World as it began in 1952[177]. After an initial period of dismissiveness, by Khrushchev's own admission, Stalin and the others began to change their mind after the initial declaration from Bandung[178]. By 1954, K.P.S. Menon, the Indian Ambassador in Moscow was of the view that the situation was "extremely favourable to us" because Stalin's successors were to "discard his dim view of India"[179], particularly as newly decolonized states were swinging towards American support[180] but India had declared itself non-aligned[181].

This opening up of relations also extended to the Soviet Union's attitude towards Yugoslavia. This was a particularly important relationship for India at this juncture. Nehru relied to some extent on Tito's consul for his interactions with the Soviet Union. Tito, on the other hand, relied on Nehru's good offices to cultivate a stronger relationship with China. Both India and Yugoslavia entered a period of cooperation at this time, with mutual state visits. When Vijaya Lakshmi Pandit travelled to Belgrade in 1954 to discuss with Marshal Tito, amongst other issues, the expansionist character of Soviet communism, Tito said expansionism was inherent to communism, but that it was the US that posed a real threat. Nehru knew that Tito had been expelled from the Cominform in 1948 and had developed relations with the West, but he was particularly impressed that Tito had done so without compromising his particular strand of socialism. Yugoslavia, under Tito, had signed up neither to the Marshall Plan nor to the Warsaw Pact. Thus, Nehru saw in Tito a useful European partner in international politics[182].

In 1955, Khrushchev reached out to both Tito and Nehru to reverse somewhat Stalin's policy towards those outside the socialist bloc. Indeed, 1955 turned out to be a crucial year for many reasons, with two international conferences held on both sides of the North-South divide. Nehru attended the Afro-Asian Conference at Bandung, Indonesia, and played a significant part in the drafting of the Bandung

Declaration that emphasized peaceful coexistence, keeping out of the two camps and the social and economic progress of the newly decolonized countries. The Russians saw Bandung as a positive step, steering Asian and African nations away from the Western bloc. Editorials in Pravda during the conference said, "the peoples of Asia and Africa are on the eve of an important political event" and one in Izvestia summing up the conference said, "Bandoong was a sign of our age"[183]. The Pravda summed up the Soviet official response, which was as follows: "The people of the Soviet Union have complete understanding for the struggle of the Asian and African countries against all forms of colonial rule, for political and economic interdependence"[184].

Nehru travelled to Moscow in June 1955 and was impressed by the "intense urge for peace" he witnessed[185]. On this visit, Nehru and Khrushchev discussed a host of issues that had hindered India-Russia relations, including the place of Indian communists, and Soviet support on the problems of Goa and Kashmir[186]. The international climate was suitable for peace, a view cemented by the meeting of the leaders of the two blocs in July 1955 at the Four Power Conference in Geneva. The favourable view of Bandung taken by the Soviets continued after this conference too, with Moscow issuing statements saying, "You are following your own road"[187]. Nehru welcomed this assessment but did not invite the Soviet Union into this Asian-African collective, unlike other leaders who swept away by this unexpected show of solidarity from the Soviets declared that Russia had always been "more Asian than European"[188]. Later that year, the two Russian leaders travelled through South Asia, spending a significant amount of time in India. Nehru thought Bulganin's and Khrushchev's trip to India was a "historic event…because of its political aspect and the possible consequences" that would follow from it[189]. Khrushchev liked Nehru's anticolonialism and socialist disposition and expressed Soviet support for economic and military cooperation with the Third

World in general, and India in particular[190]. In public speeches, the Soviet leaders went as far as calling India "an ally"[191]. Nehru's regard for Eisenhower led him to distance India from this language of alliances, emphasizing that Indo-Soviet cooperation was not directed against any other country[192]. It is interesting to note that the growing relationship was cast in contradictory terms in Moscow and in Delhi. While Nehru attempted to hold on to the gains India had made in Indo-US relations, Khrushchev justified these moves to the CPSU as a strategic balancing of American interest in the Third World and sought to remind his audience of the Leninist prediction that the East would emerge as a "new, powerful factor in international relations"[193].

On the eve of 1956, the Indian establishment seemed to believe that in the event of an emergency, "the Russians would give us anything"[194]. Then came Khrushchev's CPSU speech of February 1956, in which he made references to further democratization in the Soviet Union's relations with its satellite states, and to the new doctrine of "peaceful co-existence"[195]. Nehru was careful to distinguish the Soviet concept from Indian Panchsheel, which he saw as more positively constituted. Nehru also thought "even the communist version of socialism and the way to achieve it, which have been rigid dogmas, are in the process of undergoing some change"[196]. In particular, Poland and Hungary were showing reformist tendencies in the wake of democratized narratives emerging from the Soviet Union[197]. The Stalinist leader Matyas Rakosi, who had ruled Hungary with an iron hand, fled; Imre Nagy, a former Prime Minister, was rehabilitated to the Communist Party on 13 October 1956.[198] The workers and students in Hungary had been putting forth various demands for reform. The main events of the revolution lasted for a little over two weeks, beginning 23 October 1956, when a student delegation led a protest to the offices of Radio Free Europe against the Hungarian People's Republic and Soviet influence on Hungary[199]. During the protest, the Hungarian Security

Force, the AVH fired upon the demonstrators and killed a student. This proved to ignite the uprising, which also then included workers. On 26 October, Nagy supported the uprising's demand that Soviet forces be all withdrawn from Hungary by 1 January 1957[200]. It is at this time, on 25 October 1956, that Nehru made his first public statement regarding the uprisings in Poland and Hungary, which he referred to as a "nationalist upsurge" and "a feeling that they themselves are going to fashion their policies and not necessarily others." This is a crucial statement because it indicates Nehru's reading of the revolution as being of a "nationalist" persuasion. Indeed, he did not want to "interfere in any way even by expressing an opinion on the internal affairs of these countries"[201]. The Indian stand on the issue began to draw criticism at this stage, both domestic and international, in response to a remark by Krishna Menon that the riots could be compared to the situations in Bombay and Ahmedabad[202].

The Soviets then installed Janos Kadar as the First Secretary of the Communist Party in Hungary, and started firing at protestors in Budapest's main squares, causing heavy fighting that lasted between 26 and 30 October. On 27 October, Britain, France and the US called for an emergency meeting of the UNSC to discuss the situation in Hungary, at which time the Soviets continued to increase troop deployment into Budapest[203]. On 28 October, international condemnation and pressure was reported from the meeting of the Security Council. However, the Soviet Ambassador the UN, Arkady Sobolev made a statement saying the Hungarian revolt was an "uprising of criminal Fascist elements" against the legitimate Hungarian Government[204]. In support, Janos Kadar made another statement saying the "counter-revolution had been crushed"[205]. The UNSC voted against the Soviets by 9 to 1, with Yugoslavia abstaining on the grounds of non-interference in Hungarian affairs, but opposition to the use of force. Nehru refused to align himself with this initiative of the US[206]. The discontent against the Soviets in Hungary continued to grow as the newspaper *Seczebad* said on 29 October that Hungarians felt "deeply wounded and insulted" when the Soviets had alleged that British and American imperialists had instigated the uprising[207].

On 30 October, called "the most hopeful day in the Hungarian revolution"[208], Imre Nagy announced the set-up of a new coalition in Budapest, appealed to the Soviets to withdraw their troops and announced free elections. Janos Kadar agreed to all of the above, citing a Soviet statement that the troops of one Warsaw Pact country would be in the other only with the approval of the host country[209]. The Soviets then announced on 30 October that they would agree to talks with Imre Nagy regarding the withdrawal of their troops from Budapest. Nehru continued to remain silent on the matter, focussing his condemnation on the Suez situation instead, although concerns were being expressed on what looked like his partisan approach to these situations of international crisis playing out in parallel[210]. The Americans, certain that Nehru was in the wrong and in time would come to that realization, began to discuss Nehru's imminent pro-West sentiment that "we would want to nurture and promote", while finding him a "face-saving device"[211].

In Delhi, the Suez Crisis took precedence over the situation in Hungary, which to Nehru seemed opaque and, in any case, to be resolving itself[212]. India didn't have a full ambassador in Budapest at the time of the events[213], but M.M. Rahman, the Charge D'Affaires continued to send detailed reports, which reached New Delhi belatedly[214]. In the absence of full information, Nehru delayed taking a stand condemnatory of Soviet action[215]. The Government of India was clearly "firm in its belief that when the Soviets announced withdrawal of their troops, they in fact intended to withdraw completely"[216]. In fact, Nehru seemed completely taken aback by this return to Stalinist policies that went against the grain of what the new Soviet line seemed to be, especially as Soviet actions in Hungary ran contradictory to the Soviet denunciation of the crisis in Egypt[217]. The Indian policy on this issue was to stress the futility of condemnation and the complicated nature of the situation, although Nehru did refer to the situation as a "civil conflict"[218]. On the contrary, as Hungary and the Soviet Union began to hold talks on Hungary's withdrawal from the Warsaw Pact, the Americans hailed these developments as the "dawn of a new day" in Eastern Europe[219].

However, the Soviet assessment of the situation changed once the news of the tripartite aggression against Egypt filtered through the rest of the world[220]. Khrushchev announced that the "English and the French are in a real mess over Egypt"[221]. Combined with fears that the Hungarian situation would cause ripples elsewhere in the Soviet Union, they decided not to withdraw the troops but to address the broader crisis in the relations with people's democracies of the Soviet Union and to discuss the movement and status of Soviet troops[222]. Clearly deciding that political solutions wouldn't work, the Soviets sent armoured forces back to Budapest in greatly strengthened numbers. On noticing this turn of the tide, Nagy protested to the Soviet representative in Budapest, informed him that Hungary was leaving the Warsaw Pact and turned to the UN to appeal for help to Hungary in protecting its neutrality[223]. The following day, Janos Kadar went over to Moscow as reports started flowing in from Hungary saying the border with Austria had been cordoned off by Soviet troops who had arrived in reinforced and large numbers.

At this point, Nehru was yet to make a statement condemning Soviet suppression of the Hungarian uprising, much to the consternation of the West[224] and disappointment of his own diplomatic corps[225]. Nehru responded by asking K.P.S. Menon to convey to the Soviet leadership that their actions were unacceptable. On 3 November 1956, Kadar returned to Budapest with even more reinforcements[226]. Meanwhile,

Zhou Enlai met with the Hungarian Ambassador to China, Agoston Szkladan, to ask if Hungary wanted to withdraw from socialism, to which the latter said that the vast majority did not agree with Nagy's policies[227]. Isolated as such by Soviet interference in Budapest, Nagy fled and sought asylum in the Yugoslav Embassy. On 4 November, Nagy appealed for help from inside the Yugoslav Embassy as Soviet troops moved to crush the revolution in Budapest, succeeded and installed a new government under the leadership of Janos Kadar, who they had previously installed as the First Secretary of the Communist Party of Hungary. Nehru, now increasingly outraged by events, sent another telegram to Moscow to say that Soviet suppression had to stop, "not only because they appear to be violation of Panchsheel which so many countries have loudly proclaimed but also because they have an adverse effect on Egyptian situation"[228]. Nehru's instructions to Arthur Lall were to support the right of Hungarian people "to decide for themselves without external intervention or pressure" but in the absence of "full facts", to avoid condemnation of the Soviet Union[229].

When the UNGA met on 4 November for an Emergency Session, the house passed a US-sponsored resolution condemning the use of Soviet military forces in Hungary, and requesting the Secretary General to investigate and observe the military situation through his representatives[230]. India abstained, much to the shock of Western countries, in particular the Canadians who failed to see why India would take such a strong view against the actions in Egypt but not in Hungary[231]. Subimal Dutt, who was then Indian Foreign Secretary, writes in his account of events that although the instructions had been sent to Arthur Lall, he had not yet received them when voting on the resolution began, and as Krishna Menon had not yet arrived in New York, Lall considered it best to abstain, given heavy condemnation of the Soviets in the resolution[232]. Nehru explained this vote to

G.L. Mehta, the Indian Ambassador in the US saying, "it seemed to us unwise to interfere when a settlement like Poland appeared likely"[233]. Mohan Singh Mehta, the Indian Ambassador in Austria had conveyed to the MEA information received from Budapest that "1000 Soviet tanks, phosphorus and incendiaries" were being used to suppress the rebellion, to which the Foreign Secretary replied saying that Nehru had conveyed his grave concern to the Soviet Government through the Indian Ambassador in Moscow[234].

On the same day, the Chinese came out in support of the Soviets, with Mao Zedong seeing no reason for troop withdrawal and Zhou Enlai reminding the Soviets that Americans had their troops in different countries too[235]. It became clear now that Nehru's support was essential in bringing the situation in Hungary to any sort of peaceful resolution as "no one else could speak for the whole of Asia"[236] and because the Hungarians were themselves "asking India to intervene and our Prime Minister to come out and bring peace"[237]. The Americans considered enlisting Nehru's support in the problem of Hungary but thought that Nehru was either supportive of the Soviets or did not have a fully considered policy on the matter yet[238]. This changed somewhat with Nehru's speech at the UNESCO General Conference held on 5 November 1956. Nehru took the opportunity to speak out against the situations in Egypt and Hungary, but also made pointed criticism directed at the Soviet Union by referring to countries that subscribed to the Panchsheel saying, "those five principles are also mere words without meaning to some countries who claim the right of deciding problems by superior might"[239]. Naturally, this charge could not have been levelled at France, Britain or Israel[240].

Thus, for the first time since the beginning of the revolution, Nehru decried in no uncertain terms the actions of the Soviets[241]. Jayaprakash Narayan had called upon Nehru to "speak out" or "be held guilty of abetting enslavement of a brave people by a new imperialism more dangerous than the old because it masquerades as revolutionary"[242]. Once Nehru made this statement, the Americans, particularly Eisenhower began to court his support[243]. The US and India were already cooperating on the resolution of the Suez Canal Crisis[244]. It was now left for Eisenhower to convince Nehru to extend that cooperation to Hungary as well[245]. This he did by referring to Nehru's speech in his first direct communication with Nehru over Hungary on 6 November 1956 saying that it was their duty "to make it clear that leaders of free and democratic countries cannot remain silent in the face of such terrifying pressures upon our fellow beings"[246]. The US administration had decided that if they wanted to accomplish something they had to "get Nehru a little fired up"[247]. The consensus between the US and Canada seemed to have been that given Eisenhower's fierce opposition of the French-British action in Egypt despite them being US allies, an American account of the situation in Hungary would seem impartial to Nehru[248]. Given that US Ambassador to India John Sherman Cooper had left India in April 1956 and Ellsworth Bunker had not yet been appointed to succeed him, the position of Escott Reid, the Canadian High Commissioner to India became significantly more crucial to these exchanges[249].

On 6 November, Bulganin also sent messages regarding the situation in Suez to Eisenhower, Eden, Mollet and Nehru. The correspondence between Nehru and Bulganin at this juncture convinced Nehru to some extent of the Soviet line and he began to refer to the situation in Hungary as a "civil conflict" with "mutual killings"[250]. Nehru also replied to Eisenhower's message conveying to him a summary of Bulganin's report about the situation in Hungary and agreeing nevertheless that "armed intervention of any country in another is highly objectionable and that people in every country must be free to choose their own governments without interference of others"[251]. On the day that Nehru sent this letter, Soviet troops took over the city of Budapest and installed a new government under the leadership of Janos Kadar. During this period, the Americans were convinced that Nehru had been brainwashed by the Soviets, especially as Nehru referred to the situation in Hungary as being "obscure"[252]. Eisenhower was convinced that "Nehru seemed to be falling for the Moscow line – buying their entire bill of goods"[253].

After what was being referred to as Nehru's Bulganisation, the West dove into a state of panic. This crisis of confidence was further complicated by India's voting on the three resolutions of 8 and 9 November at the UN General Assembly[254]. India voted against the first resolution sponsored by Italy, Ireland, Pakistan, Peru and Cuba, which came to be known as the Five Power Resolution, because it called for elections to be held in Hungary under the auspices of the UN[255]. On a second resolution sponsored by the US condemning Soviet actions in Hungary, India abstained[256]. India voted in support of a third resolution sponsored by Austria, calling for increased aid to Hungary[257]. The West was shocked that India had been the only non-communist country to abstain in the vote on the US-sponsored resolution. However, India had voted against UN-supervised elections in Hungary as this was different from a "fact-finding team" which Nehru opposed on the grounds that if today they were allowed in Hungary, tomorrow they would want to go into Kashmir[258]. Indeed, Nehru considered this proposal "not only unconstitutional but dangerous precedent for other countries" but sought to explain that the procedure of voting meant that even though India criticized Soviet actions, India had to vote on the operative part of the resolution, which concerned itself foremost with UN-supervised elections[259]. Nehru was anguished by the distortion of India's actions and thought that by way of exaggerating India's stand on the situation in Hungary, certain countries were attempting to shift attention away from the Suez Canal Crisis[260].

Nevertheless, there was widespread criticism of the Indian vote in many countries, and not least in India, where Jayaprakash Narayan criticized Nehru's double standards in a public meeting on 11 November in Bombay[261]. The AICC too criticized the government's actions considerably, and although Nehru publicly sought to explain away India's votes in the General Assembly, he privately chided Menon for his votes against the resolutions, where India could have merely abstained[262]. Nehru was also concerned about the response of the Hungarian people towards India's attitude in the UN[263]. Menon responded to Nehru's concern and criticism by saying that to "do more would be to put ourselves in a sheer opportunist and somewhat dishonest position"[264] and that what India had done "and should continue to do is to refuse to be made an instrument of power politics of either side and as things are here become part of Western propaganda and action to bring about a regime of choice by using the United Nations"[265]. Krishna Menon maintained this stand even in later years, insisting that the Indian position was "that countries in the UN cannot be regarded as colonies"[266] and that the UN cannot hold elections anywhere and that he resented the implication that this was about Kashmir[267].

On 11 November, things began to change as Tito made a statement saying that the second Soviet intervention was necessary to avoid counter-revolution and avert another World War[268]. Nehru, who had been led by Tito's appraisals of the situation in Budapest to a large extent, now began to diverge from that viewpoint and strengthened his criticism of the Soviets. On 13 November, Nehru said in a speech that he was critical of all military alliances as "instruments of increased war mentality", implicitly also pointing to the Warsaw Pact, which in turn strengthened Nagy's position of wanting to withdraw from the pact and declare Hungary's neutrality[269]. On 14 November, the Colombo Powers' Conference was held in Delhi.

Nehru tried to explain the rationale behind India's voting, placing emphasis on India's non-condemnatory diplomacy at the UN[270]. In the following two days, in correspondence to and from the Foreign Secretary, it was discussed whether it would be better for India to propose its own resolution in consultation with Asian and African countries, so India didn't have to vote against any resolution because of its condemnatory clauses – the draft Indian resolution prepared by the MEA did not name any specific country[271]. On 16 November, Nehru made a speech in the Lok Sabha on the situation in Hungary declaring, "There was no immediate aggression in Hungary in the sense of something militarily happening as there was in the case of Egypt. It was really a continuing intervention of Soviet armies in Hungary based on the Warsaw Pact. The fact is that as subsequent events have shown, the Soviet armies were there against the wishes of the Hungarian people"[272].

Thereafter, on 17 November in a note to the Foreign Secretary, Nehru outlined India's position, focussing on other issues such as deportations and observer teams[273]. The main issue at this point was the proposed visit to assess the situation in Budapest of the UN Secretary General Dag Hammarskjöld and his team of observers. This visit had been proposed in the resolutions of 9 November but Janos Kadar, now the head of the government in Hungary had not agreed to it. India had made various attempts at mediation, but Kadar only agreed to allow the Secretary General to visit but not a team of UN observers and had agreed to meet with representatives of the UN in Rome to discuss the situation in Hungary and proposed aid packages[274]. The same day, reports started coming into Delhi from Budapest about the continued forced deportation of Hungarian youths[275]. As the Soviets and Kadar had failed to comply with the General Assembly resolutions of 4 and 9 November asking for deportations to stop, on 19 November, Cuba moved a resolution in the General Assembly yet again asking for these deportations to stop; Nehru asked Lall to make India's position clear but to abstain during the vote; this resolution was adopted on 21 November[276].

These developments at the UN coincided with a foreign policy debate held in the Indian Parliament on 19 and 20 November, particularly focused on the situations in Egypt and Hungary[277]. First, Nehru explained in detail the procedure of the voting on the 9 November resolutions at the UN, explaining that votes had been cast on each of the nine individual paragraphs, of which the first five were preambular and the rest were operative. Nehru explained that India had abstained on the first five that dealt with condemnation of Soviet actions but voted for the operative parts of the resolutions. He also explained to the house that India was "trying to get the Soviet forces withdrawn from Hungary. What was proposed in the resolution would come in the way of withdrawal and an attempt thereafter to intervene with armed forces would have led to a major conflict"[278]. Thus, Nehru defended Krishna Menon's vote by saying that it was "entirely in consonance with our general policy and instructions"[279]. Nehru also went on to say that this resolution would have allowed future intervention in other countries on the pretext of elections[280]. Yet, he criticized Soviet actions unequivocally by saying, "I have no doubt in my mind that [the] uprising in Hungary was popular and widespread and had the backing of vast majority of people there, including Hungarian army and even Communists"[281]. Nehru came under fire from leading Indian socialists such as J.B. Kripalani, Ashok Mehta and H.V. Kamath who accused him of having applied a double standard[282]. Nevertheless, the two-day debate in parliament was received well in the West, who called Nehru's clear criticism of the Soviets an "open defiance"[283], even though Nehru argued that "the Soviet Government appeared unwilling to take any risk on the Hungarian border" in light of the "aggression in Egypt"[284]. All in all, these two days marked the beginning of the "de-Bulganisation" of Nehru[285].

At about the same time, relations between Yugoslavia and the Soviet Union became more strained. Nagy had been seeking asylum in the Yugoslav Embassy and Tito had made a public speech criticising the first Soviet intervention (of October) but declaring the inevitability of the second one (of November). Tito had also declared Belgrade's version as the "only road to socialism", which Pravda said, "radically contradicts the Marxist-Leninist tenet that each country can have its own methods, forms and tempo of transition to Socialism"[286]. Pravda also accused Tito of creating factions within the Soviets by dividing them between Stalinists and non-Stalinists – K.P.S. Menon had already apprised Nehru of this rising tension between Moscow and Tito since Molotov had taken over as Director of Ideology[287]. Nehru himself disagreed with Tito's assessment saying that "the first one is a catastrophe; the second one is an evil"[288] and so relied less and less on his consul in the days to come[289]. Nehru and Krishna Menon agreed that India would maintain its position of non-interference in Hungarian internal matters and that it was "for the people of Hungary to decide what government they should have"[290].

On 21 November, the General Assembly had adopted a resolution urging Hungary to permit the entry of UN observers. Additionally, India co-sponsored a resolution along with Indonesia and Ceylon asking for the Secretary General to be allowed to visit Budapest[291]. On 22 November 1956, Nehru wrote to Bulganin, Kadar and Tito urging them all to accept the clauses of the Indian resolution[292]. Nehru urged Bulganin to let the Hungarian Government accept observers "in view of the grave allegations made which have powerfully influenced world opinion", reassuring him that this would "in no way affect the sovereignty of Hungary"[293]. Nehru also dispatched J.N. Khosla as his Special Representative to Budapest, which had so far only been served by Rahman, asking Khosla to urge Kadar to accept the Secretary General's visit as to not do so "would confirm reports about deportations and other recent happenings in Hungary"[294] along with possible "non-recognition of Hungarian representative"[295]. Khosla did meet with Kadar, who felt the Russians would not like observers "without previously having sorted out at least some of the mess their troops have created and without dispersing bulk of over 500 tanks that still guard the streets, bridges and public buildings in Budapest"[296]. In his reply to Nehru, Kadar expressed the view that Soviet troops had "prevented open and unbridled fascist reaction" and that "the Soviet Union has given assistance"[297].

Although Tito had initially replied to Nehru saying Kadar was "an honest but helpless man"[298], the rift between Yugoslavia and the Soviet Union began to grow after a secret meeting was held in Brioni between Khrushchev and Tito. The Soviets had tried to convince Tito of the need to suppress the counter-revolution for the safeguarding of socialism, but Tito tried to negotiate the safety of Nagy. Khrushchev, however, demanded the extradition of Nagy, threatening that Yugoslavia would be considered counter-revolutionary in the absence of acquiescence to these demands. Tito however refused to withdraw the asylum granted to Nagy and was displeased that Khrushchev had tried to make Tito complicit in the Soviet action in Hungary by asking for a secret meeting at Brioni[299]. Soon afterwards, Nagy left the Yugoslavian Embassy in Budapest, was detained, arrested by Soviet forces, and deported to Romania. Nehru wrote to Tito saying Nagy's arrest "was utterly wrong and a breach of international conventions"[300]. Tito agreed that this was "most deplorable" and that it had happened despite assurances to the contrary from Kadar[301]. Nehru agreed to support Yugoslavia's protests in the UN against the Soviet abduction of Nagy. Sensing a loss of Indian support, the Soviets sent the Ambassador in Delhi to call upon Nehru to remind him of Soviet support to the question of Kashmir at the UN, in a form of "gentle blackmail"[302]. Yet, Indian efforts at diplomatic solutions continued as Nehru wrote to Menon saying, "If war comes, it will come in spite of us"[303]. Tito having turned against the Soviets[304], and with Rahman's incessant reports detailing the injustices imposed on the Hungarian population[305], Nehru began to advise restraint all around, saying "we should try to avoid giving needless offence or aggravating a situation that is bad enough"[306].

In the next phase of diplomatic activity at the UN, two resolutions were passed on 4 and 12 December 1956. The first resolutions demanded the withdrawal of Soviet troops from Hungary; the second resolution declared that the presence of Soviet troops was violating the political independence of Hungary. Nehru and Krishna Menon widely debated India's position on the resolutions in the UN that were demanding withdrawal of Soviet troops from Hungary[307]. Eventually, when India abstained on both resolutions, Menon explained it in the General Assembly on 10 December saying, India's "objection was to the use of Soviet forces in the Hungarian internal affairs" and that what had "happened in Hungary was a national uprising"[308]. Nehru then defended Menon's vote in a statement made to the Rajya Sabha on 13 December, saying that India did not want to call for the withdrawal of Soviet forces from Hungary or from the East European states but wanted them to stop interfering in the internal affairs of Hungary, for which there was no justification[309]. Menon believed that even though India was abstaining on the resolutions, "that this is an occasion when, independent of the resolution, we should express ourselves fully and critically about the Soviet Union."[310] Nehru agreed with Menon saying that although the justification provided by the Soviets could be seen from their point of view, it was "certainly contrary to Panchsheel"[311]. Yet, they both also agreed that the resolutions being presented in the General Assembly were meant to "draw everyone on one side or the other in the cold war by putting them in the position that you are for or against the Hungarian people" and that "a yes vote for the resolution as it stands is impossible with any sense of responsibility"[312]. In his statement in the Rajya Sabha, Nehru described the revolution in Hungary in relation to India's own independence movement using the language of "civil disobedience" and "passive resistance"[313].

"Between War and Peace, between the Atom and the Buddha"[314]

Nehru met with Zhou Enlai twice in December 1956. In both meetings, the leaders discussed the situation in Eastern Europe in detail. Zhou Enlai agreed that the situation in Hungary was difficult but supported the Soviet viewpoint[315]. He also accused the Western powers of carrying out "subversive activities" and tried to convince Nehru that in Hungary "the government was weak and could not control the situation and therefore asked the USSR to come in under the Warsaw Treaty and that is the only way out of it"[316]. Nehru desisted this interpretation on all accounts, saying the Indian position was that Hungary had seen "a national uprising of the workers, students and the youth" and that it was organized "to get rid of foreign domination, namely that of the Soviet Union"[317]. He also added that "a great majority of Hungarians do not oppose Socialism, but they want their own people to run the Government"[318]. Nehru also pressed Zhou Enlai to support the UN Secretary General's visit to Budapest, to which the latter reluctantly agreed in the end[319]. During the second round of talks, Nehru posed a question to Zhou Enlai asking, "Is it compulsory socialism?"[320]. This is a telling remark because it is directed at the crux of the matter – the difference between an ideological approach to politics and a non-aligned approach, which Nehru saw as necessarily post-ideological. A significant element of non-alignment from the Indian point of view was that by being non-aligned, states were lending themselves to political action. The states that were choosing to act from ideological bases were, also acting politically, but were always operating within a sphere circumscribed by their ideologies. As there existed multiple and conflicting ideologies, the political actions of these states caused them to come into conflict with other states, in the furtherance of their own ideological motives, and in defence of them. For Nehru, certain elements of socialism held great appeal, and he was keen to implement them in India. But the idea that socialism might be "compulsory" took away from its appeal to a great extent. Like Menon had said, "we don't by definition go there; affinity may take us there; that is the essence of non-alignment."[321] The essence of non-alignment was the exercise of sovereignty in the realm of political action.

The crises of 1956 are crucial to the study of non-alignment for this very reason. Nehru's responses have been widely criticized as exposing the indefensibility of the Indian position. Studies of the Suez Canal Crisis and the Hungarian Revolution discuss the imbalance in the Indian approach to both events. The analysis is that India took a staunchly anti-British/French/Israeli stand but not an equally forceful anti-Soviet stand, and that therefore, India was not equally condemnatory of both actions. The measure of India's non-aligned position, therefore, is whether the Indian response to both highly securitized situations was similar. In other words, the measure of India's non-aligned position is the extent to which India remained neutral between parties to the conflict, not to which extent India made political solutions possible once the conflict had heightened. In the case of Suez, India was clearly able to take both these steps. In the case of Hungary, the emphasis has been on India's neutrality, which has been called into question and thus, the second phase of the approach where Indian diplomacy at the UN put a brake on bellicose resolutions has been somewhat ignored. As discussed earlier, the Nehruvian conceptualization of non-alignment lacked a complex theorization of the state. This directly affected the understanding of the state as an international actor, especially as different states had different ideas of what constituted the international. This explains the delayed Indian response to the Soviet action in Hungary[322]. It can be argued, therefore, that the delay was caused not by India abandoning the non-aligned position, but because of it. As Nehru repeatedly stressed, the Indian reaction was contingent on "full facts" – arguably, these involved not only what events were taking place in Hungary, but also what had led the Soviets to fall back into the Stalinist pattern of relations within the socialist bloc.

The initial reaction rooted in non-alignment certainly proved inadequate, yet, in latter phases, Indian diplomacy at the UN functioned in much the same way as it did in the case of the Suez Canal Crisis, or before that, in the case of the Korean War. Indeed, it is significant to note India's stand against condemnation as a diplomatic tactic. The Government of India strongly believed that condemnation closed the door on negotiation, and that once the door was shut, there would be no room for political action left, thus causing a highly securitized situation. In this aspect, the parallels between Suez and Hungary are clear – in the resolution of 24 November 1956, which asked the three powers to withdraw from Egypt, the phrase "note with grave concern" was substituted with "note with regret", largely as a result of India's diplomacy to that end working alongside Norway and the United States[323]. Immediately after the start of the Emergency Session of the General Assembly, Arthur Lall spoke with indignation, but using the language of protest, not condemnation, saying that in India's view "a mockery was being made of the Charter, and the organs of the United Nations were being affronted by aggression and invasion"[324]. Menon continued in this vein, saying "without any superlative…we regard the action of Israel as an invasion of Egyptian territory, and the introduction of the forces of the United Kingdom and France as an aggression without qualification"[325]. On Hungary, while abstaining on a resolution, Krishna Menon squarely blamed the condemnatory clauses in it saying, "We believe that resolutions that involve condemnation, which in their logical consequences, would be followed up by a declaration of who is the aggressor and who is not, and would thereby stultify the UN are not the elements that would assist in a solution"[326]. When the clauses were replaced with a more conciliatory approach in a version of the draft put forward by the Asian bloc, it was defeated at voting, to which Menon said, "a constructive step is impossible, if at the same time, a contrary step has been taken"[327]. Nevertheless, Menon continued to make speeches asking for the UN to "place the responsibility squarely where it lies"[328] but that "a remedy to the Hungarian situation cannot be found in throwing political stones at people who one does not like"[329]. Indeed, Krishna Menon made various statements saying India was "not neutral where human freedom is concerned"[330], but that India couldn't "in any circumstances disregard the sovereign rights of members", although India recognized "the right of the Hungarian people to choose the form of Government they desired"[331] but "that the way to bring settlements of international problems was not to give ultimatums to other governments"[332].

In fact, Arthur Lall set out India's position with regards to both crises in no uncertain terms saying India "avoided as a negative approach to the situation... any condemnation of those who acted in clear violation of the Charter and the UN" but that India had acted "not because we were in any doubt about what had occurred" but "because of our firm conviction that to let indignation dictate the Assembly's approaches would have been detrimental to the situation and might well have caused a stiffening of attitudes and a prolongation and even a worsening of that situation"[333]. Indian representatives at the UN were making these statements partly as explanations for Indian votes on resolutions but also in response to thinly veiled allegations that India was not in reality, non-aligned, and that neither was a majority of the

Afro-Asian group. The delegate from New Zealand remarked that while it was "expected that Member States outside the Soviet orbit would have been prepared to give equal priority, as suggested by the United States, to the two crises: to speak and act at least as sternly as they have shown themselves all too ready to speak and act against the UK and France…certain countries had shown no such disposition"[334]. The neutral countries also found fault with countries "which on other occasions had stressed emphatically the principle of non-intervention in the internal affairs of other States [but] have seen no reason...to demonstrate this attitude of theirs with regard to recent events in Hungary"[335]. Even the delegate of the nationalist Chinese delegation remarked, "several Asian delegations, delegations which ordinarily are in the forefront as regards all matters concerning human rights and self-determination found it necessary to abstain from the vote on that important occasion" and went on to ask, "whether these delegations of Asia and Africa mean to tell us that the principles of the Charter are good only for Asia and Africa, and not for Europe"[336].

In making this last observation, the delegate had touched upon an important aspect of non-alignment – not only that it had failed to account for populist movements that displaced the state, but it had also a limited understanding of self-determination in the European context. Both Suez and Hungary had forced Nehru to rethink non-alignment outside of the Asian context – this required a recalibration of political thought that had so far drawn only from a limited context. In the case of Suez, the terms of engagement were still known, as these were democracies engaging in colonial action against an increasingly nationalist, and non-aligned, state. In the case of Hungary, it was doubly confounding, as Nehru had no sustained views on communism. In February 1950, Nehru said, "India does think that international Communism is aggressive, partly because of communist philosophy and partly because communism is very much Slavism"[337]. By April

1950, he was saying that "more and more" the Soviet Union was following a nationalistic expansionist policy[338]. Yet, it isn't clear what his understanding was of the relation between competing nationalisms, or indeed between nationalism and communism. As suggested above, it seems in the Indian view, nationalism was foremost anticolonial in nature, and as organized socialism had shared the same provenance, there was to some extent an equation of the two.

In a statement from 1951, Nehru had spoken as he always did of "the rising tide of nationalism not only in our own country but also in various other parts of Asia and Africa", which he had identified as "those remaining areas of the world where the natural urge of nationalism has not yet been satisfied"[339]. In this statement, as in many others, Nehru failed to address the question of European nationalism. In March 1956, he had told Dulles that the Soviet desire to increase their domain had diminished[340]. This points to the renewed tics between India and the Soviet Union, and to Nehru's assessment of the post-Stalinist phase of Soviet foreign relations, but possibly also to his belief that the Soviets would now enter a new period of internationalism. This in turn could have resulted from his view of the limited uses of Marxism as a historical lens and of communism as a political one. Nehru was influenced by Marxism but by no means entirely convinced of it, and thinking that the Socialist bloc was now entering an inevitable phase of increased integration with the rest of the world, he decided to extend relations with the USSR bilaterally, but also at the UN, so as to facilitate wider involvement with the international community and end the isolation that in his view increased the mentality of the Cold War[341].

Therefore, although Nehru was hesitant for Nasser to take the matter of Suez to the UN, he was keen that the Secretary General should visit Budapest. In fact, it was the Americans who were considering whether it would even be useful for Hammarskjöld to go, that in the case of

Suez, he "was dealing with decent people subjected to political opinion pressures" but that in the case of the Soviet Union it might not be wise to lean on him[342]. On the contrary, the Communist bloc decided that Hungary could not be compared with the British and French invasion in Egypt[343] and that the non-aligned had vested interests[344]. Zhou Enlai asked Kadar to be weary of too much Indian influence, saying, "Don't fall into the Indians' trap. Don't hurry the elections" as he thought Indians wanted the "nature of power in Hungary to change". Indeed, Zhou took a rather strange view of Nehru telling Kadar in 1957 that one could either ignore Nehru or present to him carefully prepared cases and that Hungary's expulsion from UN on account of not holding democratic elections didn't matter as "China exists pretty well outside the UN, and then at least we could keep each other company"[345]. Thus, Nehru's efforts to extend the mark of the UN to the socialist bloc met with resistance from all sides.

However, for Indian diplomacy at this stage, the UN became an indispensable platform. Between the anticolonial momentum generated by the events of the Suez Canal Crisis and the anti-Cold War sentiments of the Hungarian Revolution, the UN became for India, the instrument and the "chief institutional theatre"[346] of other contests too – such as the ones between the First, Second and Third Worlds. During the Hungarian Revolution, the UN was the vehicle through which aggrieved parties thought Nehru would exercise his "moral authority", his "consequent attitude to justice"[347], and his "peace policy based on this moral position"[348]. This was in part due to Nehru's own stature as a statesman, long considered "the only Asiatic equivalent to Stalin"[349] and in part "due to the friendship of the people of India and the Soviet Union"[350]. This was when the Americans were still thinking of the situation in Hungary in Cold War terms, wanting to prevent "needless self-slaughter because we need that type of courage alive behind the Iron Curtain"[351].

The approach taken by Nehru once both the crises had abated somewhat was rather different. By the end of both crises, Nehru spoke of how all the aggressors - the Soviet Union, England and France (no mention of Israel) – were "trying desperately to find a way out without complete loss of dignity" and that preventing "them from finding a way out…might to a desperation and even war"[352]. He invoked Gandhi in saying he "always left a door open in this way, without ever sacrificing his principles", and thus urged the international community to make it easy for the Soviet Union to withdraw troops from Hungary; if not, "then process of withdrawal will be delayed, the crisis will continue and war may well result and come in the way of what we want to do"[353]. An important Indian contribution to diplomacy at the UN, and in the move towards more politicized processes, was the renunciation of condemnation as a tactic, not only because it did not achieve any results, but also because it was considered "unpolitical"; as Krishna Menon put it, "to think that the withdrawal of Soviet forces could be brought about merely as a result of what is called an organization of votes"[354]. Indeed, Nehru considered the two contradictory, saying, "Are we going to satisfy ourselves by a strong denunciation or condemnation, or are we to have some constructive approach to the problem"[355]. This understanding within the Indian delegation harked back to negotiations on the Korean armistice; it was that "a group of like-minded powers making up their minds beforehand in order to bargain with powers of unlike minds" was not politics, because a preconceived position was usually entrenched in a securitized discourse, so it was important for the UN to become an arena of contestation, not mere organization – "a palaver, a discussion, a conference in the real sense of the term"[356].

India's diplomatic efforts to end the impasse on Hungary were recognized by Hungarians whose future Prime Minister Arpad Goncz declared that during the revolution "the Indian Embassy in Budapest became the Embassy of the Revolution"[357]. Yet, at the time, nothing "caused so much misunderstanding…regarding India's foreign policy than her attitude towards the Hungarian Revolution"[358]. Nehru's objectivity was questioned from within the establishment by his own Foreign Secretary Subimal Dutt, in Parliament by socialists such as J.B. Kripalani, and by an international community of people who were disappointed in him[359]. Yet, a slightly more charitable reading of the situation suggested that Nehru thought a hot war was about to commence and decided to cool tempers and not allow American intervention in Hungary[360]. Indeed, with American support during the Suez Canal Crisis, and Soviet rapprochement of 1955, Nehru came very close to achieving what he saw for non-aligned India, "the idea that it would be one of few areas of great power agreement"[361]. The Soviets were also aware that the US having distanced itself from the Suez debacle and the Soviets suppressing Hungary had increased American prestige in the Third World[362]. Thus, vis-à-vis India, they adopted appeasement as a policy, initially by expressing unequivocal support, with Bulganin telling Nehru in 1957, "Neither Pakistan nor any other power can come in the way of our friendship"[363]. Eisenhower was of a similar opinion, writing to Eden that "the peoples of the Near East and of North Africa, and to some extent, all of Asia and all of Africa, would be consolidated against the West to some degree which, I fear, could not be overcome in a generation and perhaps, not even in a century, particularly having in mind the capacity of the Russians to make mischief"[364]. Ironically, in the immediate aftermath of the crises of 1956, both superpowers took a conciliatory attitude towards India, embarrassed by their own actions or those of their allies.

This inadvertent gain for India points to the two-fold nature of non-alignment – its potential uses for pursuing national interests and as an approach within international relations. On the first count, India stood neither to gain nor to lose – India's prestige was increased through support to Egypt but tarnished by India's perceived blindness to Hungary. On the question of international relations, both Suez and Hungary altered the critical path that non-alignment had taken so far, as India became involved in peacekeeping and the supply of arms in a conflict. Nehru wanted to exercise restraint on the British, the French and the Soviets by refusing to condemn them; it worked to some extent in the one instance, but definitely not in the other. Yet, the Indian assault on the balance of power politics that gave rise to these situations continued unabated. As Menon put it, "in the particular circumstances that obtain, there are different alliances ranged one against the other and a policy of balance of power which is rapidly pushing this world into a state of war"[365]. Nehru was equally keen to maintain India's position; he said, "I am very much concerned with maintaining the peace of the world, but I am equally concerned with our acting rightly and in conformity with the principles we have proclaimed"[366]. This continued long after the actual end of the Hungarian Revolution – the execution of Imre Nagy by the Soviets in 1958 angered Nehru deeply who thought it would be difficult for the Soviets "to outlive this black mark" and that it "was a cold-blooded act done no doubt after full consideration", one that "puts an end to the idea of real peace in our generation"[367]. He also criticized China saying that Chinese attitude was even worse especially as he knew Zhou Enlai had always held it against Tito that Yugoslavia had given Nagy asylum[368].

All through these crises, non-aligned India was critical of the use of superior might and the extension of colonialism and the Cold War into Egypt and Hungary. Nevertheless, by discouraging Nasser from taking the issue to the UN, and by belatedly addressing Soviet suppression of the revolt in Hungary, India became complicit in the new and continued aggression that marked both situations. Eventually, Indian diplomatic efforts recovered lost ground on the two problems, successfully using the UN as an instrument for political action in the case of Egypt and attempting the same in the case of Hungary. Yet, on Suez, India's contribution to the UNEF marked a new phase in Indian involvement with the UN through peacekeeping, further accentuated by India's considering arms supply to both Egypt and Hungary. These developments were new, and only three years earlier, in Korea, Nehru had declared that India would not send troops abroad, then that they would not be armed, then again that India would not send arms. By 1956, all these positions had been abandoned, making it a key moment when India became directly involved in wars, even if through peacekeeping. Indian involvement in armed peacekeeping or the use of force in foreign territories was now a question to be considered on an individual basis, not to be outright dismissed as contrary to non-alignment. Some conceptual weaknesses in non-alignment had also been exposed, and it was evident that certain aspects needed to be recast, particularly in relation to drawing overly only from the experiences of Asia. Indeed, this became the central question in the 1960s, with the eruption of the Congo Crisis.

5

"Bad Ethics and Worse Policy"

India and the Congo Crisis, 1960–1964

Many of the issues that sprung up during the Korean War, the Suez Canal Crisis and the Hungarian Revolution all came together in an intensified episode that unfolded over three years in the newly independent Congo. The case of the Congo Crisis is especially significant in understanding the limitations within non-alignment coupled with India's increased integration into the UN. Nehru's view of the crisis was shaped by his view of the twin forces of decolonization and the Cold War, which he believed to have led the Congo into the situation it was in. He was thus, also convinced that the international community would have to find a solution to the political instability in the Congo by confronting the realities of the decolonization of large swathes of the African continent and the looming threat of superpower intervention in these newly independent states. Consequently, Nehru also believed that it was only the UN, its neutrality strengthened by the presence of non-aligned nations from Asia and Africa, like India, that could successfully resolve this crisis. India had the additional advantage of being a former colony, of understanding the intricacies of building a postcolonial independent state and had not had territorial holdings of its own in Africa.

Thus, the Indian policy towards the Congo Crisis stemmed from the twofold belief that first, non-aligned diplomatic practice could successfully mediate in a crisis brought on by the incomplete decolonization of the Congo, which had pushed the new nation-state into being a site of Cold War competition; and second, that the effectiveness of the UN peacekeeping mission was dependent on the neutrality of contributor states and would be especially potent when troops were drawn from Asian and African non-aligned nations. The neutrality of the UN was the subject of contention and controversy from the very start of its mission in the Congo, with each bloc convinced that the UN was biased towards the other. To save the UN from such criticism, Secretary General Hammarskjöld requested Nehru for troops on the ground and diplomats in the field – both of these requests were acquiesced to. In fact, it is worth emphasizing that apart from the overall Indian contribution to the UN mission in the Congo, key Indians were closely involved with policymaking and often took decisive action, whether they were part of the UN mission, and thus representatives of the UN, or when they were representing the Government of India as part of the newly set up Indian embassy[1].

There are some excellent accounts from the period, four of which have been written by Indian diplomats who served in Léopoldville at the time[2] and a detailed account of the UN's involvement in balancing the diplomatic and military aspects of the crisis[3]. Secondary accounts are centered on Nehru's outlook on the issue[4]. The Congo Crisis seems to have been almost entirely written out of India's diplomatic history, but also only tangentially pursued in more international accounts. Literature on the Congo Crisis is enormous, which makes this gap even more glaring. Where there is a discussion of Indian personalities or indeed, even the Indian contingent of the UN peacekeeping force, there is no attempt to connect it with larger Indian motivations for being in the Congo. This account aims to fill this large gap in the literature on India's international relations. I discuss the questions pushed forward by the unfolding of the crisis, particularly in relation to India's approach to international politics.

The African Context

As discussed in the chapter on the Korean War, Nehru's understanding of Asian history, and his consequent emphasis on Asian modernity was quite precise and had developed over the course of his involvement in the Indian nationalist movement. Indeed, as discussed in the opening chapters, Nehru perceived Asia sociologically, as a region of the world with a large population, and therefore as essentially full of underdeveloped potential. To exploit that potential, Nehru's narratives of Asia were always laced with futurity, and he sought continuously to remind Asians and the rest of the world that Asia's greatness would become possible and evident in the time that was yet to come. In turn, these views informed his ideas of the Asian century, and so within non-alignment, ideas of Asia were always simultaneously geographical and temporal, and in both senses, deeply political.

These political ideas then informed non-alignment as an approach to the problems of the Korean War and that of the decolonization of Indochina, for these were specifically Asian problems, rooted in Asian contexts. By the 1950s, as crises such as that of the Suez Canal and the Hungarian Revolution erupted onto the international scene, non-alignment had to adapt to understand and respond to contexts other than the much more familiar Asian one. As discussed in the previous chapter, this proved to be somewhat of a challenge. Through the 1940s and 1950s, the theatre of politics had shifted and acquired an even more global character. Certainly, some of the themes were recurrent through these decades, and through these crises: anti-colonial nationalism, decolonization and the Cold War remained firmly in the foreground. But each process of decolonization had its historical specificities, each anticolonial movement was distinct, and the Cold War affected every situation differently, with an altering balance of power between the two superpowers. All these processes influenced and were influenced by the locations where they unfolded. By the 1960s, as decolonization increasingly spread to Africa, it became evident that to respond to these changes, Indian non-alignment would have to reinvent itself to a large extent. Non-aligned India's response to the crisis in the Congo is an excellent example of how this reinvention did and did not take place. India's approach to the crisis has two main characteristics – first, the silence within Indian non-alignment on the question of race, and second, the centrality of the UN to India's response to crises in Africa in general, and the Congo in particular. I will suggest that these two characteristics are fundamentally correlated and discuss how this correlation characterized the last phase of non-alignment in the Nehru years.

I have previously discussed at length the ideas of pan-Asianism that were prevalent in early-twentieth century Asia. Simultaneously, the cause of pan-Africanism had also begun to gain currency. The first Pan-African Congress had been held in London in 1900, and subsequent congresses were held in Paris, New York, Dar es Salaam and Kampala. Unsurprisingly, the congresses were most concerned with the decolonization of African countries and with the end of racial discrimination against black people around the world. Prominent advocates of African identity included intellectuals such a W.E.B. Du Bois and Frantz Fanon and leaders such as Haile Selassie of Ethiopia and Kwame Nkrumah of Ghana. The Pan-African Congresses led to the establishment of the Organization of African

Unity (OAU), set up in Addis Ababa in 1963[5]. Thus, 1900 to 1963 represents a long and significant period in the development of African identity along the lines of anticolonialism, anti-imperialism and the end of racial discrimination[6]. This period of intellectual ferment and the enunciation of an African identity coincided with decolonization in Asia and the emergence of Asian-African relations on the basis of these shared concerns[7]. These two movements developed in parallel, and some colonies gained independence before others, but were all brought together at the first Asian-African Conference held at Bandung, Indonesia in 1955[8]. Although the crosscurrents of Asia-Africa cooperation and solidarity were in force even before, Bandung held special significance as the high-water mark of solidarities forged on various lines. In India, Bandung was seen as a sort of "coloured United Nations", where the leaders of the Asian-African peoples "pledged themselves to use their full moral influence to guard against the danger of falling victim to the same evil [of racialism] in their struggle to eradicate it"[9].

Indeed, not only was Bandung the site of Asia-Africa relations but was also where the idea of the Third World developed beyond its local confines to its most visibly internationalist form[10]. The Third World, which had so far spread as an idea, morphed into an ideological movement at Bandung[11]. In the previous chapter, I have discussed the reactions of the superpowers to this movement. The Soviet Union began to accommodate the ideology of the Third World in the hope that its turn leftward would bring this vast collective of nations closer into the Soviet sphere of influence[12]. For this reason, the Americans were less than enthusiastic about this congregation, and because the question of race had occupied center stage at Bandung, especially amongst African nations[13]. With race being a significant issue within the US in the 1950s, the Americans looked at Bandung with some trepidation[14]. India actively participated in the conference, and Nehru in his speech was forthright in his disapproval of the idea of blocs, and of defense pacts based on those blocs[15]. Nehru also spoke of "the moral force of Asia and Africa", without once referring to the Third World[16]. In fact, Nehru had always spoken out against the idea of a third bloc, and so had Krishna Menon, who was also in attendance as part of the Indian delegation. Menon's chosen phrase instead was "an arena of peace" as he considered the third bloc "a foolish idea" as "a Third Bloc to be effective must have at least two and a half times the power of one bloc!"[17] It is important to note the Indian position on the possibility of a third bloc as an ideologically motivated formation because as I have discussed previously, Nehru's idea of being non-aligned was based on an idea of a post-ideological world. As host of the conference, President Sukarno of Indonesia referred in his opening speech of the need to mobilize "all the spiritual, all the moral, all the political strength of Asia and Africa"[18]. Clearly, for the Asian participants, the emphasis was on the collective strength of the voices of the peoples of Asia and Africa in world politics and not particularly on Asian or African representation at the conference.

Nehru addressed the question of race in broad sweep, usually in the context of Empire, but not as a subject in itself. Especially with respect to Africa, his silence on an issue so central to contemporary politics is interesting. After all, it was the experience of racialism in South Africa that had ignited Gandhian politics, which in turn had animated Indian anticolonialism. Indeed, Gandhi had deeply considered questions of race, of discrimination based on race and of the colonial subjugation of certain races. His response to that condition, and his refusal of violence pitted him against Frantz Fanon[19]. Race was an inescapable condition for Gandhi dealing with Africa under colonial rule, and he addressed it by advocating non-violent protest, a form of resistance he later brought to the public life of colonial India[20]. Thus, it is interesting to note Nehru's divergence from Gandhi's consideration of race as an essential element to understanding African anticolonialism. Yet, the absence of race as a trope in Nehru's writing can be traced to a slightly different source of political thought. As also discussed in the opening chapters, Nehru's ideas of the international, and of internationalism were influenced by Tagore's ideas of cosmopolitanism. Unlike Gandhi's ideas of anticolonial politics in which the state was abjured once independence had been achieved, Tagore's cosmopolitanism remained relevant even in the presence of the state, and in the period after successful decolonization. Nehru sought to place the state at the center of those processes, as the nurturing of links between peoples of different parts of the world, particularly in the colonies was an ongoing project, one that had had tremendous successes despite many difficulties.

As some colonies achieved independence before others, and others were negotiating the last stages of their freedom from colonial rule, these networks became even more important. Former colonies sought to support the colonies that remained and to institutionalize some of these relations that had previously had a somewhat subterranean quality to them, forged despite and within more visible imperial networks[21]. A significant development in the later stages of decolonization was the rise of coloured cosmopolitanism, which brought an added element of race relations to the existing anticolonial conversations taking place around the world[22]. Despite ideological differences that later surfaced within this loose collective, newly emergent states rejected overtly Western models of nationalist politics. Indeed, it is surprising how deeply invested many of these states were in an international sphere even before they gained independence. In fact, the 1950s and 1960s are precisely that period, in which organized peoples around the world were moving between being colonies, nation-states and members of the international system of states[23]. As they were negotiating these different identities, and the dangers of the Cold War, these states relied on each other at fora such as the Bandung Conference to reclaim and reinvent their identities and to base their politics off these. These movements relied rather heavily on the essentialist narratives of pan-Asianism or pan-Africanism but also on the divide between the East and the West, and on the denunciation of the West.

For Nehru, this was politically unacceptable. The suggestion that any idea be denounced merely on the basis of its geographical origins rode roughshod over Nehruvian non-alignment, which was specifically tailored to accommodate seemingly contradicting concepts no matter their provenance. Whether it was the Empire and the colonies, or the two blocs of the Cold War, Nehru's idea of India's role in international politics was to mediate between conflicting positions by belonging to neither. In Nehru's image of the Indian future, India would recover its identity not by subscribing to exclusivist ideas of race, region or religion, but by integrating into the international as a sovereign state. Thus, in non-alignment, the identity of India was always cast in a modernist mould. This idea had limited purchase in the African context, where reflections on race continued to dominate social and political discourse. Nehru was aware of these differences, such as existed not only between nations in Africa and Asia, but also between Asian nations. In the 1930s, he had pointed to the specific needs of the African nations saying, "the people of Africa deserve our special attention"[24]. At the Asian Relations Conference held in New Delhi in 1947, Nehru pressed this issue further and declared India understood "the value of freedom not only for ourselves but for all others" and that she "stood for the freedom of all people in Asia, Africa or elsewhere"[25]. This message was relayed through James Beauttah to the Kenyan African Union, and indeed to all of Africa. Thus, Africa remained at the forefront of India's calls for decolonization, and so, in the 1960s, when parts of Africa became independent of colonial rule, India applauded these developments.

Yet, Nehru distanced himself from the rest of African politics, particularly in its local forms. Nehru's interest in African politics was cursory and even though India shared good relations with many African states, India's main interest in African affairs stemmed from decolonization and from the large population of Indians in Africa, although this at times undercut Indian influence on decolonization diplomacy[26]. This situation was complicated by the resistance of the colonial powers exercising control in African states towards India; they considered "Indian penetration" dangerous and held the view that "wherever the Indian plants himself in Africa, he breeds immorality"[27]. In response to "the non-white conference" held at Bandung, the Belgians had spoken of their fears regarding "Asiatic penetration into the Congo"[28]. As discussed in the previous chapter, even when India sent troops to Suez in 1956, India did so reluctantly and under the aegis of the UN. Indeed, Nehru considered African affairs "beyond the area of his responsibility"[29].

Much of this changed with the swiftly deepening crisis in the Congo. A Belgian colony until it gained independence in June 1960, the Congo was a vast country rich in mineral resources. With independence, and no strong political power in control, the Congo fell back almost immediately into the hands of a meddling Belgian presence. This was further complicated by the secession of the Katanga region and a situation not dissimilar to civil war. Nehru wrote to his Chief Ministers barely a month after the Congo had become independent, saying "as a result of Belgium's policy in the past, is almost wholly lacking in educated and trained personnel" and that "before the Congo can look after its own affairs adequately, and there is always the danger of someone else trying to fill that vacuum", but he was more optimistic about the role of the UN, which he thought "brought a measure of balance" and "prevented the ambitions of some Powers to take advantage of the situation"[30].

India played a significant role in bringing the secession to an end and in bolstering UN efforts in the strife-torn country[31]. However, it is also important to note that the crisis in the Congo coincided with a parallel crisis in the UN. As the study of India's response to the Congo crisis will show, Nehru sought to approach African problems only when he was pressed to do so, and exclusively through the interface of the UN. Evidently, as in Korea and later in Egypt, one of the prime motivators for this approach was respect for the sovereignty of the country in question. Additionally, in the case of the Congo, Nehru considered India too far removed for a comprehensive appraisal of the situation on the ground or even a sense of how events were developing. Moreover, Nehru was certain that the Cold War would play out in Africa as it had in Asia (and as India had experienced during the Korean War). He also knew that the independence experiences of the Belgian Congo and of British India were very different from each other and that in dealing with the Belgians, the UN was dealing with an imperial power that was reluctant to give up its colony and had had no process that could be considered equivalent to the transfer of power in India[32]. A review of Belgian colonialism had explicitly said that the Belgians "never thought with the British in terms of African self-government as the ultimate goal of their administration nor have they thought with the French in terms of assimilation and the eventual merger with the metropolitan area"[33]. Subsequently, the continent was also easily susceptible to the forces of the Cold War. Indeed, an early estimation of the situation had said that "the African nations from the very moment of their birth have been in the frontline of the "big" game of Power Politics and Economics", having been considered "the hinterland of Europe", as European prosperity depended on Africa and West Asia[34].

The UN, thus, became an extremely crucial conduit in the relations between India and Africa in general, and the Congo in particular.

On one level, it was important for the Congo not only to retain Indian independence and sovereignty but also to integrate into the international system without coming under the influence of either of the two superpowers. On another level, it was crucial for the Congo (and indeed, other African nations) to develop not as nationalist and inward-looking states, but as fully participatory members of the international community. By removing the accent from race, and from relations based solely on race, Nehru seemed to be pushing forward the idea of heterogeneity as the basis for cosmopolitanism – the idea that it was important to look for "unity in diversity" rather than to highlight similarities amongst largely similar groups of people[35]. By relying so heavily on the UN, and not using the channels of Asia-Africa cooperation that had been opened at Bandung, Nehru made it very clear that the Indian approach to international cooperation was to cooperate with the seats of empire too, and with the US and the Soviet Union, not just with the other nations of Asia and Africa. So, in that sense, India's non-aligned policy took precedence over India's position as member of the NAM, and certainly did not stem from a simple neutralist position[36]. After all, even in Asia, Nehru had adopted this approach and had rescinded the idea that Asian relations would be built distinctly from those relations formed at the UN. This is a logical progression from Nehru's ideas of modernity and how Asia would shape its future based on an internationalist approach to world politics. By extending the Asian metaphor to Africa, Nehru sought to skirt the issue of race, which he clearly perceived as potentially divisive. Yet, by not clearly specifying what the limitations of race politics were, Nehru created a theoretical absence in non-alignment[37]. A reading of non-aligned politics now simply shows a lack of engagement with the question of race – whether that silence is borne out of ignorance or apathy is hard to tell. This is in stark contrast with Nehru's handling of Asian crises, as seen in the Indian approach to the Korean War.

The inconsistencies in non-alignment also come across in the case of European contexts, such as the one in Hungary. There was a lack of effort on the part of non-aligned Indian diplomacy to understand the racial politics of newly emergent African states.

Indeed, race was a significant component of politics in independent Congo – while some Congolese leaders such as Moïse Tshombe condescendingly referred to Africans other than themselves as "les noirs"[38], others such as Patrice Lumumba tried to use socialist methods to overcome race-based discrimination on the domestic and international fronts. In so doing, these leaders were looking to preempt "the exploitation of coloured races by coloured men"[39]. Thus, race constituted a prominent source from which African leaders drew inspiration for their politics. Indeed, political narratives in African colonies were often framed in the language of race. And so, African anticolonialism was at a remove from Indian anticolonialism that had very different emphases. In the case of Africa, there was a history of settler colonies, and a specific sort of violence borne out of that context. Nehru had no tailored response to the specificities of African problems, or indeed, more narrowly those of the Congo. His awareness of the differences between Asian and African contexts did not lead to a systematic treatment of particularly African conditions. Instead, to overcome these differences, Nehru sought to use the UN as a forum, and as a neutral actor in the Congo. The UN, itself in crisis over leadership, relied very heavily on the deployment of troops to bring peace to the Congo. Although Nehru caveated its contribution to these operations, India did participate in substantial measure to bring them to a victorious close. As a close look at India's involvement in the UN response to the Congo crisis will show, this gap in non-alignment reduced the possibilities for political action to a large degree. India had contributed troops to the UNEF in the

Suez too, but the troops sent to the Congo were armed, and mandated with the specific objective of carrying out an offensive and reclaiming territory. This necessarily involved the use of force, thus marking this phase as one in which Indian non-alignment lapsed into a substantial practice of security.

The Congo Crisis

The Congo gained independence from Belgian rule on 30 June 1960, when the First Republic was established with Joseph Kasavubu as President, and Patrice Lumumba as Prime Minister. Soon after the first constitution of the new republic was promulgated, a mutiny erupted on 5 July 1960 amongst the Congolese troops of the Force Publique (the Congolese Army) against their Europeans officers, leading to the Africanization of the army, its renaming as the Armée Nationale Congolaise (ANC) and the appointment of Victor Lundula as the Chief of Army Staff with Joseph-Désiré Mobutu as his deputy[40]. As the mutiny spread throughout the Congo, Belgian authorities sent paratroopers beginning on 9 July 1960, and continued to initiate military action, killing black civilians in the process and intensifying racial violence. Soon, another crisis erupted when Moïse Tshombe declared Katanga an independent state. Léopoldville was now faced with the two-pronged problem of Katangan secession as well as Belgian intervention in the affairs of the Congo[41]. Nehru wrote to Indian Chief Ministers barely a month after the Congo had become independent, saying that the Congo was "as a result of Belgium's policy in the past… almost wholly lacking in educated and trained personnel" and that "before the Congo can look after its own affairs adequately… there is always the danger of someone else trying to fill that vacuum", but he was more optimistic about the role of the UN, which he thought "brought a measure of balance" and "prevented the ambitions of some Powers to take advantage of the situation"[42].

On 12 July 1960, the Congolese Government asked the UN for military assistance and protection of its national territory against external aggression[43]. Accordingly, UNSC Resolution 143 (1960) led to the establishment of the United Nations Operation in the Congo (known by its abbreviation in French, ONUC), initially mandated with military and technical assistance to the Congolese Government[44]. The UN sent a peacekeeping force consisting mainly of troops from Sweden, Ireland, United Arab Republic, Ghana, Morocco, Mali and Indonesia, who arrived in the Congo on 15 July 1960 as a "temporary security force"[45]. Less than a week after the ONUC started its operations, Hammarskjöld approached India to send an official to act as military adviser for the operations[46]. The UN continued to pass resolutions reaffirming its commitment to ending the crisis in the Congo. On the other hand, the Secretary General had travelled to the Congo but met with resistance from Tshombe, who was heading a secessionist movement that would sever the province of Katanga from the rest of the country. On 8 August 1960, under the command of Albert Kalonji, the province of Kasai also seceded from the Congo. The Congo now had two secessions to deal with. Even so, the Security Council continued to commit to non-interference by UN forces in any "internal conflict, constitutional or otherwise"[47].

Responding to this perceived reluctance on the part of the Security Council to take any action, Prime Minister Lumumba accused Hammarskjöld of acting "in connivance with the rebel Government of Katanga and at the instigation of the Belgian Government", thereby interfering in the internal matters of the Congo and "retarding the restoration of order in the Republic, particularly in the province of Katanga"[48]. Lumumba and other Congolese seemed to not fully grasp that the UN was not a sovereign entity providing assistance to them, but a body where it was imperative for member-states to agree on each action or decision[49]. Thus, the main question at this point became precisely whether UN operations in the Congo could be allowed to use force against Katanga to end its secession. At the UNSC, the Congo and the Soviet Union voted in favour of a resolution proposing the use of force but the rest of UNSC members, including the US, preferred using political measures first. African states with troops in the ONUC attempted mediation between the two positions, as they did not want the UN to fail in its mission. It was quite clear that the Soviet Union and the United States had at this point diametrically opposite points of view on the role of UN's peacekeeping forces, with the USSR in favour of using any means necessary while the US remained against the use of force. The Congo was becoming a testing ground for this debate between the superpowers. Kwame Nkrumah of Ghana wrote to Lumumba to warn him of the Cold War coming into the Congo, which would "become a battlefield between East and West" and emphasized his concern that this could spell "disaster for all in Africa"[50]. However, Lumumba chose to impose martial law on the Congo anyway and declared that the province of Katanga must be taken by force or that the Congolese Government would attack it.

At this stage, India's role in the management of the crisis was confined to aid and assistance. In fact, India did not even have an embassy in Léopoldville at this point. Nehru had issued a statement saying that India recognized only one state of Congo, that the Belgian troops were the cause of the problem, that the Secretary General had acted with "vision and also wisdom" and that albeit complicated, the situation was also rather straightforward[51]. India had also sent 700 tonnes of wheat flour and 36 personnel from the Indian Air Force (IAF) for logistics support to the UN mission[52]. This, however, did not prevent the anti-Indian sentiment rising in the Congo with Indian personnel providing logistical support finding it hard to work there, given the "unfriendly and rough treatment by members of the Congolese Force Publique" towards them[53]. In response to this situation, Nehru was keen to underline the importance of the UN, and of India's support to the UN mission in the Congo by emphasizing his belief that in the absence of the UN, there was "the possibility of a great deal of internal conflict" in the country and "a possibility of intervention by other countries, big and small"[54]. Very soon after, the Indian commitment to the peace operation in the Congo was taken a step further. Nehru issued a statement in the Lok Sabha informing the house that India would send Brig. Indar Jit Rikhye as Military Adviser for the UN Mission in the Congo and Rajeshwar Dayal as Hammarskjöld's special representative, and Political Head of the ONUC[55]. Nehru outlined non-aligned India's role by saying that India's policy "was not an acrobatic feat of sitting on a spiked fence and balancing between the two sides; it had to be an effort to uproot the fence and throw it away"[56]. At this point, India's goal was to support the UN in whatever the UN's objectives might be. It might be noted that India's contribution at this point was limited only to the contribution of personnel in advisory roles, technical expertise and food aid.

The Deepening of the Crisis and Evolution of India's Congo Policy

Rajeshwar Dayal, an Indian diplomat, arrived in Léopoldville on 8 September 1960 to replace Andrew Cordier as Chief of the ONUC. Cordier had ordered the closing of radio stations and all airports, giving rise to a great deal of anti-UN sentiment amongst the Congolese[57]. Dayal's first order of business, thus, was to facilitate the re-opening of the radio stations and airports to reverse the damages caused to the public perception of the ONUC[58]. However, soon after his arrival, he found himself in the midst of an additional constitutional crisis when

Joseph-Désiré Mobutu orchestrated a coup, appointing himself Army Chief of Staff, placing Lumumba under house arrest, suspending parliament, while keeping Kasavubu as president[59]. The UNSC was in session when this coup took place, and thus it evoked a great deal of criticism of the UN's handling of the situation, particularly from

India at the UN
Prime Minister Nehru and Defence Minister Krishna Menon at the UNGA Session in New York, 1 October 1960. (AFP via Getty Images)

Khrushchev and Nehru
Prime Minister Jawaharlal Nehru talks with Soviet Premier Nikita Khrushchev in New York, 5 October 1960. (Bettmann via Getty Images)

Egypt, Ghana and the Soviet Union[60]. Amongst the non-aligned nations, Yugoslavia withdrew its diplomatic mission from the Congo and Nasser expressed Egypt's deep regret at the events. Nehru sent a letter to Hammarskjöld saying that the situation in the Congo seemed to be extremely unclear and wondering what the UN Force was doing if the constitutional processes could be so easily subverted[61]. Although Nehru was critical of the UN mission at this stage, he did not support the idea of providing direct military assistance to the Congolese, an idea put forth by Ghana's Nkrumah[62]. By opposing this initiative, India found itself in opposition to the majority of African and Arab states, many of whom shared its non-aligned outlook on international affairs[63]. From an Indian point of view, it thus became even more imperative that the UN mission in the Congo succeeded and did so quickly. Additionally, Indian troops suffered casualties when on 13 September, Belgian-led Katangese para-commandos and gendarmerie opened fire on them, killing one Indian soldier and wounding seven others[64]. Thus, when the UNGA convened in October 1960 for an emergency meeting on the situation in the Congo, the head of the Indian delegation to the UN, Krishna Menon, pleaded for "a greater sense of urgency and imperativeness"[65].

The Indian position at this time as outlined by Krishna Menon was to ask whether the UN would be taking military measures to quell the situation in the Congo or whether a political settlement was still considered possible. Although the Indian delegation had outlined two possibilities for further action by the UN at this stage, Nehru continued to press for a solution "by the people themselves"[66]. In part, this exhortation was brought on by Nehru's reluctance to commit troops or additional technicians to the Congo although India made no move to recall the Indian personnel already sent[67]. In a key statement, Nehru had categorically rejected the idea that the UN should use force to achieve a solution[68].

When in November 1960, Stanleyville also seceded, and along with Léopoldville, Kasai and Katanga, became a fourth centre of power in the Congo, non-aligned India became even more critical of superpower politics as played out in the Congo. The Soviets were pushing for the ousting of the Secretary General, and for the use of force by UN peacekeeping forces in the Congo. The Americans, while on board with trying diplomatic measures to end the crisis, were blinded by their anti-communist paranoia, their fear that the Congo would turn communist if Soviet influence was not somehow undermined, and so, in later months, became averse to the key personalities on the ground who they thought favoured the Soviet position. It appeared to the Indians that the UN was under attack both in New York as well as in Léopoldville. Even though the superpowers were acting to undercut each other's influence, they only seemed to weaken the UN in the process, with the Soviets launching an anti-Hammarskjöld campaign in New York and the Americans going after Hammarskjöld's envoy, Dayal in Léopoldville. Khrushchev's exhortations to "spit on the UN" and the introduction of the Troika Plan intended to replace the Secretary General's office with a triumvirate found absolutely no echo with the Indians[69]. Nehru categorically refused to indulge Khrushchev instead placing his faith entirely in both the Security Council and the Secretary General[70]. When in a few months' time, Alexei Kosygin, Deputy Premier of the USSR, met with Indian Vice President Sarvepalli Radhakrishnan and Prime Minister Nehru on a state tour of India, he repeated the Soviet idea of a *troika*, accusing Hammarskjöld of being "the one at fault for events in Congo" while Nehru tried in vain to bring how the UN functioned into the picture[71]. Nehru had no patience for the Soviet plan to reform the UN under the "three-headed god", a move he considered purely propagandist and counterproductive[72]. By the end of 1960, Soviet influence in the Congo had waned in comparison to that of the US, who then pursued a "vendetta" against Dayal[73].

Dayal had refused to grant official UN recognition to Mobutu's government, causing a great deal of friction between the UN represented by Dayal, and the US, represented by their Ambassador Clare Timberlake[74]. The Mobutu question acted as a wedge between the UN and the US all throughout the mission, creating numerous issues for Dayal as head of the ONUC[75]. Dayal's assessment, contained in his report of November 1960, was that "the Congo could only be ruled as one country if parliament was reopened, and representative government restored"[76]. The report "questioned Belgian good faith", "criticized Mobutu's military takeover", and envisaged a role for Lumumba in the running of the Congolese state, all of which were anathema to the Americans[77]. Dayal also wanted the ANC disarmed[78]. Thus, the report caused an "explosion" in Léopoldville, and was seen as "a diplomatic bombshell", which had caused a "blow to US policy"[79]. The US regarded Dayal as possessing some sort of "typical high-caste Indian arrogance", without understanding that for Dayal, Hammarskjöld's envoy, the UN's role was that of "an impartial arbiter"[80]. Instead, he was caught with the West's "parochial view of the situation" that resulted in a "dialogue des sourds" with the various Congolese factions[81]. He had become "a helpless witness to events which would cast a pall over the future of ONUC and had serious implications for his future role"[82]. For the next few months, the American policy was focused on "forcing Dayal out"[83], although future historians have called Dayal a "diplomat of unusual perspicacity" and "the sharpest observer in the Congo"[84]. Between Nehru's rejection of the *troika* plan and anti-Dayal sentiment on the rise, it was now evident that India's position ran counter to both the Soviet and the American approaches to the issue[85].

Hammarskjöld put great stock in Nehru's role in influencing the Afro-Asian front, which could enable or cripple the UN[86]. India's role was to politically ensure that "it was the United Nations rather than the great powers which would intervene in July 1960"[87]. Yet, over the next few months, the situation only worsened, and Nehru was alarmed that a "large number of African countries…infuriated by the turn of events [had] started withdrawing their forces from the Congo"[88]. Nehru clarified India's position with respect to its troops in the UN force saying India could not guarantee "that the question will not arise whether it is worthwhile keeping [Indian troops] there or not"[89]. By the end of the year 1960, gradually three provinces of the Congo had seceded, and India had been unable to influence policy at the UN in any way to bring the situation closer to resolution. Having provided all manner of aid, assistance and personnel, India was anxious to avoid overcommitting to the UN mission. Simultaneously, anti-Indian sentiment in the Congo had peaked at this time, with accusations against Dayal and Nehru personally, and attacks against Indian officers growing[90]. When foreign diplomats were targeted in the Congo, Nehru reassured the Indian parliament that no Indians had come under attack directly but referred to both "the personal sense of injury and indignation" felt in India at this turn of events, and the deeper significance of attacking non-aligned non-combatant troops working under the remit of a UN mission[91].

Sporadic violence continued the following year, and events took a rather dramatic turn when Patrice Lumumba was murdered on 17 January 1961[92]. Nehru was aghast, called it "murder probably by people who occupy high places"[93], denounced the death as an "international crime of the first magnitude"[94] and informed Hammarskjöld that in the absence of a revision of UN policy, India would have to reconsider its association with "the perpetrators of these crimes to continue in their gangster methods"[95]. Shocked that "Mobutu's forces [had] behaved scandalously", Nehru reminded Hammarskjöld that the regime had "neither a legal basis nor moral or political strength" and consequently no, "chance of practical effectiveness"[96]. Nehru reiterated India's policy that "a meeting of the Congo Parliament and support of a Congolese Government by it [was] the only solution", a position espoused by the UN, especially quite vociferously by Dayal[97]. In a second note to Hammarskjöld, Nehru made perhaps his most significant intervention to date, suggesting a "minimum policy" that could have the approval of both the West and the East, and that would make it possible for

Salaam, Nasser, Nkrumah, Thant and Nehru
Members of the 44-nation Afro-Asian Bloc attend a special meeting at the UN headquarters, New York, 4 October 1960. From left to right – Prime Minister Saeb Salaam of Lebanon, United Arab Republic President Gamal Abdel Nasser, President Kwame Nkrumah of Ghana, Burmese Ambassador to the UN, U Thant, and Indian Prime Minister Jawaharlal Nehru. (Bettmann via Getty Images)

the Afro-Asian bloc to be enlisted in a UN effort to bring the Congo crisis to a close[98]. Nehru rallied western governments, particularly those of the US and the UK to support this initiative[99]. He wrote to Harold Macmillan, the British Prime Minister, twice, reminding him that the "cold war [had] descended in full force upon the Congo"[100], that India and the UK seemed to be "proceeding on entirely different assumptions and different appraisals of the facts of the situation"[101] and that it might soon be "too late to have any policy at all"[102]. Nehru also

Talks on the Sidelines
Prime Minister Nehru and Yugoslav President Josip Broz Tito hold a meeting while the General Assembly is in session at the UN, New York, 28 September 1960. (AFP via Getty Images)

continued to stave off the Soviets and their demands for the removal from office of Hammarskjöld, which he considered "not fair or just" and "likely to lead not to any improvement in situation there but to greater conflicts"[103]. To Khrushchev's proposals on the dismantling of the UN, Nehru responded with his own proposals on why the UN must remain in its present form, reminding the Soviet premier that despite pursuing a different approach, India was not prepared to "sacrifice essential principles on vital issues such as Congo or Colonialism"[104].

Meanwhile, in the US, John F. Kennedy had taken office shortly after Lumumba's murder, prompting Indian hopes for a new American policy towards the Congo. Nehru wrote to the US Ambassador in New Delhi, Dean Rusk, agreeing to cooperate with the Americans, if a new approach were forthcoming (the Americans had suggested the formation of a broad-based government)[105]. Nehru talked about "cooperating with the US in order to find a solution to this difficult problem of the Congo"[106] and Kennedy agreed that the UN offered "the best if not the only possibility for the restoration of conditions of stability and order" in that crisis[107]. Yet, in fact, there was to be no significant departure from the policies of the Eisenhower administration, and the new government continued to partake in the paranoia that the Congo would turn over to the Communists if they attempted a more liberal approach[108]. In fact, the US continued to support the Mobutu government, much to the utter disappointment of Nehru, and his continued incredulity. Writing to Nasser, Nehru bemoaned "the odd situation" where the US and the UK continued to support people who had "practically declared war on the United Nations"[109]. Indeed, this obstruction of UN work also meant that western propaganda was "running down Dayal and Indian forces", making Dayal's position rather untenable[110]. Even though the Indian position and that of Indian nationals working under the aegis of the UN had been made difficult by western provocation, Nehru refused to respond to it, proclaiming that it was not "in keeping with the dignity of the Government of India to go about protesting and shouting at every provocation"[111].

During this time, anticipating resistance from Dayal for their pro-Mobutu policies, the Americans began to wage an open campaign against his presence in the Congo. At the UN, Adlai Stevenson, the US Ambassador to the UN, refused to engage with Dayal at all, suggesting instead that he take a "long vacation"[112]. When it came to light that Dayal enjoyed the continued support of Hammarskjöld and had been asked to continue his assignment in the Congo[113], the

Americans protested and asked the Secretary General to reconsider his decision in light of Kennedy's public support to the ONUC[114]. This put Hammarskjöld in an impossible position where he risked antagonizing either Kennedy or Nehru, and also put at stake the neutrality and prestige of the UN if he were to acquiesce to either's position[115]. Ironically, this dilemma was resolved when Mobutu "swore he would turn his soldiers on the UN force and threatened to assassinate Dayal"[116]. Dayal had already become too controversial a figure and was probably straining the UN's relationship with the Congolese by virtue of his being so widely disliked in that political landscape[117]. By becoming a possible target of assassination, he would also be endangering the mission, its personnel and the success of the operation[118]. Between Hammarskjöld and Dayal, it was thus decided that he would be recalled to New York for consultations at the UN and replaced in Léopoldville by the Sudanese diplomat Mekki Abbas[119]. This was a difficult decision to make for Hammarskjöld and to accept for Nehru, as both men had placed great faith in the abilities of Dayal[120]. Nehru had to repeatedly explain to the Indian parliament why Dayal's assignment had come to such an abrupt end[121]. Nehru, convinced that the western vilification of Dayal had been directed not only against his personality but also against his policies, feared the successful implementation of the February resolution of the UNSC that Dayal had had a central role in formulating. Dayal left Léopoldville a few weeks after Indians troops had arrived there[122]. With Dayal's departure, and a larger mandate available to the UN forces, the next phase of the UN mission in the Congo soon began[123].

UN Peacekeeping and the End of the Katanga Secession

In the aftermath of Lumumba's death, the Soviets had decided to stop recognizing Hammarskjöld as Secretary General, Egypt and Guinea recognized the new regime in Stanleyville and Guinea began to withdraw troops from the UN force. Nehru forewarned Hammarskjöld that if "African troops were withdrawn from the UN Command, India could not be expected to replace them"[124]. Nehru relayed to other non-aligned leaders such as U Nu, Nasser and Sukarno, his utter dismay at western support and encouragement of the Mobutu regime, and India's difficulties in committing to troop enhancement under the UN mandate as it existed[125]. Although Nehru was questioning India's contribution to the ONUC, he expressed his conviction that "the Operation must not be allowed to fail as it would destroy the United Nations and threaten peace in Africa"[126]. Hammarskjöld sent a personal appeal to Nehru asking him for a battalion of combat troops, to which Nehru responded provisionally saying he would send a brigade[127]. Convinced that in the absence of tangible support to the UN mission at this crucial juncture, it would fail, Nehru decided to send Indian troops, but "with the caveat that he would insist on their effective use"[128]. To that end, of strengthening the peacekeeping mission, at the UNSC, the Afro-Asian bloc began deliberations on a draft resolution to further the mandate of the UN in the Congo. While the bloc was looking to remove clauses related to non-interference by the UN in internal matters, it is Rajeshwar Dayal who suggested adding to the resolution instead, to address specifically the use of force by UN forces[129]. This draft resolution that India was working on in consultation with other Asian and African members was put forward and adopted as UNSC Resolution 161 (1961), allowing, amongst other measures, for India to send troops to the Congo mission[130].

The events of the first two months of 1961 had thus turned India in favour of the use of force in this peacekeeping mission. In fact, at the Lok Sabha, Nehru spoke of India's support for the UN mission even in the event that the mission was required "to use armed force and not merely look on while others use armed force for a wrong purpose"[131]. This acquiescence to the use of force was not unconditional[132]. Given Nehru's concern with the "political implications of sending [a] whole brigade"[133], the Indian position had also been clarified in communication with the Secretary General[134]. Specifically, Nehru was deeply worried that India "might even get involved in civil war between one side and the other, besides creating tensions between Asian and African forces"[135]. Hammarskjöld tried to placate these fears by communicating to Nehru that "the views and position of the Government of India with regard to the use of armed Indian troops in the Congo" would be carefully noted and under UNSC mandate, the troops could not "be used to further any partisan political ends"[136]. Recognizing the "military value of such force"[137], Nehru then informed the Secretary General on 3 March 1961 that troops were being dispatched to the Congo. With growing tensions on the Sino-Indian border that eventually resulted in the war of 1962, Krishna Menon (by this time, Minister of Defence) and others were less than enthusiastic to send troops to the Congo. However, Nehru's wish prevailed, and a brigade was sent[138]. The arrival of the Indian brigade is considered pivotal to the strengthening of the ONUC, as it made up one-third of the entire force of the UN and impacted the military outcomes of the mission[139]. Hammarskjöld praised this "great act of faith" saying it would "go down in history as a most remarkable and in many ways the decisive event"[140]. Nehru insisted the troops "went in to do a job of work" and stage a "small show of force"[141].

The first contingent of troops arrived in Léopoldville on 15 March 1961, as the Congolese Government threatened that "blood would flow"; Tshombe added from Katanga that he considered Indian involvement a declaration of war[142]. Tshombe and collaborators fundamentally mistrusted Indian involvement in the Congo[143]. By April, with at least four competing sovereignties, the Congo was experiencing complete administrative chaos[144]. Additionally, there was a refugee crisis in the North Kasai region (where Indian nurses had also been deployed)[145]. The first half of the year ended with India pledging 105,000 USD for the United Nations Fund for the Congo[146]. Simultaneously, India continued to seek assurances from the UN about the effective implementation of policy in the Congo[147]. The troops of the 99th Infantry Brigade sent from India to contribute to the ONUC were engaged in fighting in and around Léopoldville[148]. The brigade under Brig. K.A.S. Raja was sent by air and sea to Léopoldville from March to June 1961[149]. The secession of Katanga was tackled in phases lasting from August–September 1961 to January 1962 and the second from December 1962 to March 1963. The operations conducted were Rumpunch, Morthor and Grand Slam, aimed at freeing Elisabethville and Jadotville from the grip of the Katangese gendarmerie and were commanded by Brig. K.A.S. Raja, Brig. R.S. Noronha, and Maj. Gen. Dewan Prem Chand respectively[150]. The IAF also contributed substantially towards the success of the UN troops in the Congo, led by Wing Commander A.I.K. Suarez[151]. The B (1) 58 Canberra light bombers left India on 9 October 1961 for the Congo. Together with five Swedish J29 Tunnan fighter jets, four Ethiopian F86 Sabre jets, and Italian Fairchild C-119 transports, the Indian Canberras became what was dubbed the first "UN Air Force"[152]. Indian Canberras provided the UN with its only long-range air support force[153]. The Indian troops faced many difficulties in being transported to the Congo, and anxieties were rife in New Delhi and in New York about the sort of reception that they would receive in Léopoldville, with reports that they would be attacked on arrival by the ANC[154]. However, a later report from the UN confirmed, "Indian troops in Katanga [had] created an excellent impression on the local population and [had] won their admiration"[155].

During this first leg of operations, Hammarskjöld was killed in a controversial plane crash on 18 September 1961, while on travels to the Congo. Nehru maintained the view that the "Congo was still the symbol and the touchstone of the success of the United Nations"[156]. In contrast to Hammarskjöld's policy of reconciliation, and perhaps partly aggravated by his death, Secretary General U Thant's policy was more aggressive[157]. He announced in November 1961 that the UN would not hesitate to use force to end the secession and bring the conflict in the Congo to a close. UNSC Resolution 169 (1961) of 24 November 1961 spoke of this new policy, completely rejecting Katanga's claims to statehood and denouncing armed action against UN forces. The resolution authorized the Secretary General to use whatever means necessary to rid the Congo of all mercenary forces and paratroopers, and to prevent their return. Thereafter, the ONUC continued to engage with the Katangese forces, their main objective being the disarmament of the secessionist forces and the deportment of mercenaries, in line with the view that the only Katangese forces to attack UN forces were those led by non-African officers[158]. The Indian arm of the ONUC played the most significant role in these operations[159], leading Nehru rather uncharacteristically to exclaim, "Thank God for India!"[160]. U Thant continued to request member countries that had contributed troops to the mission to persuade other countries to send troops as well and commended the effort of the Indian contingent as "due special praise for the role they played"[161]. Brigadier K.A.S. Raja had also undertaken a reorganization in Katanga, removing most non-Indian forces making the ONUC "a largely Indian affair"[162]. On 13 November 1962, India's first Ambassador to the Congo, D.N. Chatterji, arrived in Léopoldville, tasked with providing an assessment for Nehru if in his judgement, "the Indian troops were not going to be employed to end the secession in Katanga, or if the military operations were to be undertaken again at 'half cock'". This was especially time-sensitive, so Nehru could "consider withdrawing the entire Indian Brigade from the UN Forces, especially in view of the threat to India from China"[163]. India's continuous troop contribution to the UN effort had been receiving widespread domestic criticism considering India's increasing troubles with China, but Nehru defended his policy saying national issues would not come in the way of "India's international commitments"[164].

In December 1962, Congolese Prime Minister Adoula appealed yet again to the UN to use force and end the secession in Katanga. In light of the intensified mandate of the mission in the Congo, the pressure on India to keep its troops in the Congo increased manifold, with both Justine Marie Bomboko, the Foreign Minister, and Isaac Kalonji, the President of the Senate, appealing to the Indian Ambassador, "not to withdraw your troops until the secession has terminated", given that "no other military contingents could adequately replace Indian troops"[165]. The main questions at this time were whether Tshombe's troops would be able to resist the UN offensive. In the absence of a clearly defined answer, it became increasingly difficult for India to justify the presence of its troops in the Congo, given the Sino-Indian border conflict[166]. However, the pressure from the international community was immense, with Robert Gardiner, the Chief of Operations of the UN Mission in the Congo, exclaiming to Chatterji, "They know the country; their military reputation is tremendous; how can they be replaced?"[167]. Indeed, the Indian troops had been known for their "qualities and discipline", which had made them "the backbone of the UN force", and "their removal would [have] cut UN forces by one-third"[168]. This worry that Indian troops might be repatriated seemed to have affected UN policy to a large extent, particularly due to the continued failure of negotiations with the gendarmerie[169]. Thus, immediately after Christmas 1962, following provocation from Tshombe's troops, the ONUC launched the second phase of the UN engagement in the Congo, which lasted until January 1963[170]. Maj. Gen. Dewan Prem Chand, UN Commander in Elisabethville convinced the Secretary General to approve an offensive operation, after failed attempts to secure a ceasefire[171]. This offensive was Operation Grand Slam that finally ended the Katangese secession on 14 January 1963, when Tshombe conceded defeat[172]. The operation used high-intensity combat, not even restricted to counter-insurgency measures, but using three-inch mortar, which are not considered small arms but high trajectory artillery[173].

Even though New Delhi considered the operation a success, many controversies broke out during and after Indian involvement in the mission. The Congolese Government, unhappy with Indian involvement in the first place, was also not happy that Indian troops would now be repatriated, complaining that this would leave the Congolese helpless. Most significantly, a controversy also broke out in the UN over rumoured unauthorized actions of Indian troops during the offensive. These rumours concerned the allegedly indiscriminate use of force by Indian members of the peacekeeping mission including an allegation on the floor of the General Assembly, of Indian troops firing at a Red Cross van, which provoked a cry of protest from India[174]. An even more serious controversy surfaced when it was alleged that the UN's ground forces, under the command of Maj. Gen. Prem Chand, had overstepped the UN mandate by crossing the Lufira River and taking the UN offensive into Kolwezi. U Thant blamed the lack of contiguity between the UN command and the ground forces on a breakdown in communications, although it has been suggested that Maj. Gen. Prem Chand shut down the radios and asked his men to march forward[175]. The Indian position with regards to this controversy was to defer to the position taken by the Secretary General, and official documents from the time do not address the controversy directly or state the position of the Government of India on the actions of Indian forces, or of

Maj. Gen. Prem Chand. Yet, these allegations are crucial because it is in protesting them that India began to debate and conceptualize a position on the use of force during UN peacekeeping operations. As D.N. Chatterji, the Indian Ambassador in the Congo, put it, it was unlikely that the troops could have functioned or achieved any results without such use of force. In fact, in the Indian understanding of the issue, without such enabling provisions, the mission would have amounted to "a fishing expedition"[176]. Indian military and diplomatic delegations to the mission both were of the view that tactical successes had been made possible by the UNSC Resolution 169 (1961), which had enabled troops to use all means necessary to end the secession and that casualties of Indian troops had been curtailed because the provision to use force allowed for retaliatory action[177].

Yet, assaults on Indian troops and personnel mounted feverishly, with Indian spokespersons in Léopoldville, New York and New Delhi having to explain their position repeatedly[178]. The earlier vilification of Dayal seemed to have been extended to the military leadership as well, including criticism of Brig. K.A.S. Raja[179] and Brig. Indar Jit Rikhye[180], even though they had worked to curtail the excesses of UN troops under their commands[181]. These controversies seem to have largely overlapped with a general Western attitude towards Indian leadership and the confidence they enjoyed with the UN Secretaries General, both Dag Hammarskjöld and U Thant and a Congolese disdain for Indians, including peacekeepers[182]. Albeit, following their success, the repatriation of the 99th Indian Infantry Brigade started on 1 March 1963 and was completed on 30 June 1964. In all, 39 units of the Indian Army participated in the Congo operations during 1961–64. As the ONUC was withdrawn in phases and the UN's military presence began to fade, foreign powers began to approach the Congo to establish broad-based bilateral relations with the state. India, the "sword arm of the UN in the Congo" withdrew from the scene completely, after assisting an international operation where none of its national interests were involved in the least measure[183].

The Congo Crisis was a litmus test for Indian peacekeeping that had thus far only participated in Korea (1950–1954), Indochina (1954–1970) and the Middle East (1956–1957) – all unarmed missions. Apart from being written out of India's diplomatic history, the operation has also been neglected in writing India's military history. As part of ONUC, two infantry brigades took part in the operations[184]. Even though India suffered the largest number of casualties (39) and did not achieve the expected restoration of relations with the Congo, on the tactical front, this proved to be a largely successful undertaking[185]. Captain Gurbachan Singh Salaria, who died in Katanga, was posthumously awarded the Param Vir Chakra, the only one ever to be awarded to an officer for peacekeeping duty[186]. Another officer to have lost his life in the Congo was Maj. Ajit Singh, also of the 1st Gurkha Rifles. The deployment also included two recipients of the Victoria Cross, Havildar Ghaje Ghale and Naik Agansing Rai of the 5th Gurkha Rifles, which is extremely unusual, given that Victoria Cross bearers are not placed in combat operations[187]. This illustrates the seriousness with which India approached the mission in the Congo, sending its best troops to the UN. The Gurkha troops in particular were widely thought of as "real soldiers" and a symbol that their movement into a city was taken as an indication that any disorder would not be tolerated[188]. Along with the UN Emergency Force I of the Suez Canal Crisis, the ONUC has thus proved to be the start of India's long tradition of contributing to UN peacekeeping.

From a political point of view, the peacekeeping mission in the Congo also extended the idea that had taken seed during UNEF that neutrality and non-intervention in domestic matters were a critical condition for the conduct of peacekeeping forces. For states such as Sweden, Canada or India, this proved to be especially significant in that it elevated their international status, allowing them to play a larger role in mediatory diplomacy, while allowing for the UN to appear less susceptible to the tug and pull of the Cold War[189]. The Congo Crisis provides an ideal case study to examine whether it is possible for nations with a stated policy of non-interference (non-aligned India), operating in foreign territories (the Congo) to remain outside the arena of internal as well as international politics as affecting the situation in that country (the Cold War, Belgian colonial control). One of the reasons that India was approached in the first place was its non-aligned status as well as a resulting position of significance within the Afro-Asian bloc. However, as the situation continued to unravel, anti-Indian sentiment was pervasive in the Congo, within the leadership, the ANC as well as the general populace. By the end of the mission, India was unpopular with the US, the Soviet Union, Ghana and Egypt for not forming a coalition with either of them.

From the military point of view, allegations of an excessive use of force by peacekeeping forces brought to light a more fundamental problem of whether the UN should engage in these sorts of peacekeeping missions at all, as "only a state [could] wage war"[190]. This represented a dilemma for India, who was willing to throw its weight behind the UN, but not through military measures, but once it had committed to supporting the UN, had to participate in missions that often took on a military character. Once the mission was launched, casualties had to be limited and effectiveness multiplied, which meant India would have to agree to and in fact, propose robust mandates. Nehru often emphasized that the Congo operation was a test case for the sustainability of the UN and should therefore not be allowed to fail[191]. Thus, Nehru personally put much stock in the UN, whose mandate in the Congo was initially unclear, and subsequently, almost completely reliant on the use of force, "the only recognized medicine to be administered by whichever side was in a position to do so"[192]. Nehru tried to draw a distinction between the initiation of and retaliation against military action, insisting that the UN had never been allowed the former, but were conceded the latter for effectiveness on ground[193].

On the question of political objectives vis-à-vis military operations, it is quite clear from the Congo experience that in the absence of a well-thought-out policy, the UN came to eventually rely on full-scale military operations. The policy of approaching the situation through incremental diplomatic measures backfired in such a way that eventually the military offensive became unavoidable. For contributors such as India, this conflation of political and military measures presented a unique dilemma where they could not argue for the use of force or against it but inaugurated a longstanding debate on whether peacekeeping could be passive at all[194]. It was quite clear that India anticipated the use of force as conditions deteriorated but resisted the option politically while preparing for it militarily. Although literature on the crisis often mischaracterizes India's peacekeeping policy being uncomplicatedly pro-force, the archive does not support that claim, and shows the complex ebb and flow of India's evolving position[195]. These observations lead to a final point about the ability of states such as India to shape the ways in which debates on peacekeeping took place during the earliest missions. In the 1950s and 1960s, the main Indian concern was two-pronged: to maintain a neutral stance involving the impartial use of force and to respect the host nation's sovereignty. As this study of Indian peacekeeping during the Congo crisis has demonstrated, it was often unclear in the course of peacekeeping missions whether these criteria had been met.

The question of peacekeeping raised and was intimately related to other questions that were crucial to India's evolving presence on the international scene. Even though Nehru was insistent that much of the UN's work in Africa was beyond the pale of India's limited capacity, Indian participation was slowly increased to a very substantial degree.

In the end, it was an empathetic understanding of the "tremendous revolutionary upheaval in Africa" that placed the Congo in the foreground of India's activities at the UN in the early 1960s[196]. India's Congo policy was informed in great part by Nehru's cognizance of the "continuing crisis in Africa", his belief that Africans, like Asians, were "just not interested in the cold war approaches", even though the west was still rooting for "a united Congo but not a Communist Congo"[197]. At the behest of Nehru, Indian diplomats chose to work with the Afro-Asian bloc at the UN, but also in direct diplomacy with other African states for want of a stronger policy on the Congo, and especially on Katanga[198]. Yet, Nehru refused to align the Afro-Asians with one side or another or work as "a rival to the United Nations", refusing to go to the King of Morocco's Casablanca Conference[199], and turning down Kwame Nkrumah's idea for a meeting in Accra to decide the future of the Congo[200]. Speaking at a seminar on the "problems of emergent Africa" organized at the height of the crisis in the Congo, Nehru was at his prescient best, warning the gathering, but speaking as he oft did, to the world at large, "...behind every subject relating to Africa, we will have this tremendous shadow of the Congo in its present day conditions with all kinds of other shadows, ghosts of the past, ghosts of today haunting it"[201]. He tied up the question of the Congo with the survival of the UN, and that of the UN with "the future of humanity"[202]. Nehru's direction of India's policy towards the Congo thus had far-reaching implications for Indian participation in peacekeeping operations, India-Africa relations and for India's diplomacy at the UN.

"The Blood of the Martyrs Is the Seed of the Church"[203]

When it emerged as a state newly independent from Belgian colonial rule, the Congo declared itself non-aligned. Thus, in their conduct with Léopoldville during the crisis, the Soviets, the Americans and indeed, other non-aligned powers such as India, Egypt and Ghana were dealing with a non-aligned state. But disagreements on how the crisis must be handled left opinion divided across these divisions. Indeed, at times, India found itself in agreement with the US rather than with Ghana or with the United Arab Republic (UAR). This was particularly true in light of the aggressive anti-imperialism of the latter two, with India deeply worried that Indian troops would have to face Arab troops in the Congo[204]. Nkrumah tried to court American cooperation since in his view their "ideas seem fundamentally so much the same"[205]. Thus, Nehru found himself at a distance from most of the other major non-aligned members of the UN, who were looking to adopt either the American or the Soviet view on the Congo. Instead, Nehru sought to use that position to temper between those of the US and the Soviet Union[206] and believed that non-aligned states would have to be non-aligned amongst themselves too, even if this caused discord between them. In fact, when the NAM was founded in Belgrade in September 1961, most tensions within members had been directly influenced by the crisis in the Congo[207]. When the second summit was held in Cairo in 1964, a controversy broke out over whether Kasavubu or Tshombe would attend, leading to great diplomatic embarrassment for the host country[208].

The American policy on the Congo meandered throughout[209]. While Eisenhower had adopted a passive outlook, Kennedy seemed more agitated, leading to a more enthusiastic handling of the crisis, yet one that "took many vital months" to gain speed[210], and was abruptly cut short by Kennedy's assassination in 1963. Even at the time when they were deeply engaged with the Congo, the Americans believed that Lumumbism represented a sort of "voodoo version of communism"[211]. This led to a rather jaundiced view of their interests in the resolution of the crisis[212]. In fact, the US kept track of the inroads that not only the Soviet Union, but also China was making into Africa and was convinced that Peking saw Africa "as the major field of the battle"[213]. Washington tried to impress upon the Indians "the stake which neutrals have in support of the genuine independence of other neutrals"[214], whilst advertising their own accomplishments in the Congo so "no literate adult east of the Suez" was left unaware of them[215]. In trying to convince Nehru of India's "stake" in assuring the independence of other newly decolonized nations, the Americans were preaching to the choir. In fact, Nehru's brief to Indian officials concerned with the crisis, whether it was Dayal, Rikhye or Chatterji, was to gain a "friend with an international outlook similar to our own"[216]. Chatterji notes that, in fact, "this had not happened"[217] and that a majority of Congolese, including Kasavubu had wondered why the Indians had had any interest in their situation at all, why they "did it, or whether it was worthwhile"[218]. Nehru had always wondered whether a "patched-up unity" could only lead to "bad ethics and worse policy" in a volatile situation – these fears were becoming manifest in Congolese politics[219].

Meanwhile, the assault on Indian troops and Indian personnel mounted feverishly, with Indian spokespersons in Léopoldville, New York and New Delhi having to defend these actions repeatedly[220]. The allegation on the floor of the UNGA that involved Indian troops allegedly firing at a Red Cross van, provoked a cry of protest from India, and prompted Krishna Menon to remind the assembly that "a Red Cross van does not become a Red Cross van because a cross is painted on it. It fired on and killed the Irish crew of a United Nations armoured car"[221]. He also pointed out that Belgian paratroopers had mounted the van with a bazooka and quoted from the officer-in-charge of UN operations to say that the Indian troops were "well led, well-disciplined and conducted themselves well"[222]. The explanation for India's involvement in the Congo crisis was captured in the view that India had sent troops because "the UN had got itself into a mess", because India was in principle "against the secession of Katanga" and because for India, the crisis in the Congo spoke of "the come-back of the Empire"[223]. New Delhi found it strange that they had had to defend the actions of Indian troops that they had been reluctant to send in the first place and that were not always deployed by the UN to the best advantage[224].

In fact, even when India's troop contribution had "shored up the UN position" to the point of saving it, the domestic risks of this commitment had been considerable[225]. When in 1962, India's own borders became temporarily indefensible, its contribution to the UN mission was not held back. Those closely associated with it have suggested that this was for Nehru "a personal act of faith in the UN"[226] and "impinged on two moral commitments of Nehru's - to the values of the UN and to the people of Africa"[227]. Nehru expressed it as India doing its "best to further the purposes of the United Nations"[228]. Menon was more forthright and admitted that for the UN it had been "an untried step", one perhaps it should not have taken as "only a state can wage war" and that in the event that "nobody else who had any troops was willing to send them", India had stepped up to the task[229]. In fact, it was the Indian view that Indian troops should by no means represent the "biggest numerical force in Congo" and that "that honour should belong to [the] African country"[230]. Indeed, Menon also held the view that India "should have stood behind the nationalist forces instead of weakening them" and that when the ONUC had "became a Western operation", it "caused splits in Asian and African opinion"[231].

In fact, it was this "growing resentment voiced by African countries over India's role in the Congo"[232] that tested non-alignment in this last phase of the Nehru years. As I have suggested earlier, non-alignment began to resemble a practice of security, albeit a critical one. When it had erupted onto the international scene, Nehru praised the Congolese anticolonial movement as an "astounding revolution"[233]. When eventually the state became Balkanized, India should have taken into account the fact that it was dealing with a new African state[234]. Further into the crisis, when Foreign Minister Bomboko declared that the Congo was "at war with the UN"[235], it should have alerted India to the deep discontent brewing in the Congo, against the UN, and against India who had become a very visible representative of that presence. Yet, when Indians such as Dayal publicly announced their estimation of Congolese state capacity, declaring the Congolese army was "rabble"[236], and further alienated India from the Congo and the Congo from non-alignment. This was in no way aided by the superpower rivalry that coloured this operation from the start, particularly their disagreement over "the increasingly powerful role assumed by the UN secretary-general"[237], which became symptomatic of the Cold War tensions, and their entry into Africa.

Yet, Nehru continued to place an accent, and his faith, not in the Congolese people or their state leaders, but in the UN, proclaiming that "the operation must not be allowed to fail and the UN must be fully supported"[238]. He thus put much stock in the UN, whose mandate in the Congo was initially unclear, and subsequently, almost completely reliant on the use of force, "the only recognized medicine to be administered by whichever side was in a position to do so"[239]. Nehru was fully aware that the Cold War had swept the UN in its wake, therefore sought to remake it to some extent, exclaiming to the General Assembly, "I have listened attentively and with respect many of the speeches here, and sometimes, I have felt as if I were being buffeted by the icy winds of the cold war. Coming from a warm country, I have shivered occasionally at these cold blasts"[240]. He sought to remind them that the UN was "not fully representative" and that "if there had been no United Nations today, our first task would have been to create something of that kind"[241]. Nehru recognized the "African problem as tremendous" and kept "the hope that Khrushchev will calm down"[242].

But the crisis increasingly took shape in a security context. Even though Nehru insisted that the "United Nations forces in the Congo have never been authorized to initiate any military action"[243], the problem in the years 1961–1962, at the height of the crisis, was primarily about the use of force. India's response to this problem, via India's contribution to the upkeep of the UN was to send troops, for military action albeit under the aegis of the UN. Dayal, who had been the only non-military UN personnel from India was also removed at a time when the UN moved into providing technical assistance. Justice Bidhu Bhusan Malik, an eminent jurist was eventually appointed by U Thant on a panel to draw up the Congolese constitution, but this took place at the deep end of the Indian presence in the Congo[244]. From 1961 itself, the Indian Embassy became estranged from the seat of government in Léopoldville. When D.N. Chatterji arrived at the end of 1962, he came primarily to oversee the usefulness and effectiveness of the Indian contingent as part of the ONUC. Thus, quite conspicuously, Indians in Léopoldville took on a rather securitized identity for the Congolese, who saw them as military men, before all else. The initial Indian contribution in terms of food aid, Indian medical assistance and logistics support became overshadowed by an entire brigade of the Indian Army and the IAF carrying out military manoeuvres in the country. This representation of India became even more entrenched when Nehru, unsure of who was in power after the death of Lumumba, kept correspondence with the Congolese Government to a minimum, and making the UN indispensable to that relationship. Seeing that relations between the Congo and the UN were fraught with distrust, this also coloured Congo's relations with India. This precarious situation suffered more setbacks as the Belgians, who had been anti-India from the very start, and the Americans, who put their bilateral interests before the Congo's national interests and the UN's international mandate, orchestrated much of Congolese policy. As Dayal put it, "the mouth was the mouth of Esau but the hand was the hand of Jacob"[245].

Nehru tied up the question of the Congo with the survival of the UN, and that of the UN with "the future of humanity[246]. But he chose to ignore the early advice of his own emissaries, who had suggested that with the coming decolonization of African states, Asia "shall have to understand fully this new dynamism vibrating to express itself in Africa"[247]. In the 1950s, the estimation was that Africa was "keeping an open mind about Asia"[248]. Many of these newly emergent forces lent themselves to solidarity by virtue of their shared goals, as was evident at Bandung. Africa looked to Asia and to leaders such as Nehru and Sukarno, particularly with respect to the sculpting of their foreign policies. Many African states adopted non-alignment immediately after independence, for it was marked by the imprimatur of the states of Asia who had successfully maneuvered Cold War politics by being more than neutral. At the time, it was possible for Asia, and particularly for India, to make "a special effort to know and to understand Africa"[249], and more particularly the centrality of race to the question of African politics. Nehru recognized the differences between Asian and African politics but sought to reconcile them by developing the UN as a theatre of politics. However, the UN as an international body, functioned on the basis of sameness, one that overrode the heterogeneity to be found within the politics of Asian-African countries. In the absence of a fully formed critique of African politics, then narrowed down to suit the specific contexts of each new state, and simultaneously address the looming question of race, non-aligned politics relied much too heavily on the apparatus of the UN, assuming over the time that role for itself. In so doing, the critique within it became subsumed by the practice of security it slid into. The distance between politics and security grew once more, and India found it difficult to close that gap in the years after 1964, when the last of Indian troops returned home, and by which time, Nehru was dead.

Epilogue

What power did non-alignment have as an idea? An idea might have had a public life in a national setting, but by seeing it as indivisible from the political philosophy of a nation-state, we are constrained in our analysis of it. This is a shame when ideas travelled, were experienced and evolved from those experiences across national lines, and when foundationally, the ideas were rooted in internationalism, as I suggest in this book is the case with non-alignment. More critical forms of International Relations theory and more global strands of twentieth-century history make it harder than ever before to cling to localized and parochial notions of Indian non-alignment. An alternate way of thinking about non-alignment is to consider its relation to world order as essentially non-conformist. This was achieved in many ways – first, thinkers of non-aligned politics defied the set ways in which they were expected to consume the political. Given that non-alignment has a postcolonial character, architects of non-alignment were often nation-builders, but they also had a lot to say about what kind of political energies would animate the world beyond their national borders. Take, for instance, the very twentieth-century acts of engagement and eventual disillusionment with socialism, nationalism, anticolonial agitation and organized internationalism. The non-aligned position is one of ambivalence to such isms, to questions of how political objectives may be secured, a position that I think bears deeper engagement. This position also results in attempts to build theory. This book has explored through a narrative of Indian non-alignment how relative and relational that theory-building was.

The anticolonial movements of the early- and mid-twentieth century had gained enough momentum to be taken seriously as fresh evidence that there was a lag between political discourses on the one hand and global movements on the other. This gap was further widened by the inability of a Eurocentric political discourse to acknowledge or remedy it. Dabashi says that Eurocentrism is now completely blasé, that of course Europe sees the world from its vantage point. But, already at the beginning of the last century, anticolonial leaders were alert to this lapse. Indeed, the anticolonial oeuvre read Europe and empire as cognate and sought to overcome Eurocentrism by dismantling empire. The questions of Europe and Empire were so closely tied together, that by dismantling Empire, the anticolonials were forcing Europe to acknowledge the multitude of existing vantage points, even if they continued to see things from their own. Although they succeeded to a certain extent, particularly through the vehicle of the UN, International Relations theory has not paid sufficient heed to the trials and triumphs of these moves. That has remained the reserve of social and political history.

One of the ways in which the anticolonials chose to override the Eurocentric character of the international space was by institutionalizing processes that were simultaneously nationalist and internationalist. Therefore, by paying selective attention to these historical forces, theories of International Relations produce partial and incomplete analyses of non-alignment. This is partly because the field of Global History has had limited interaction with the field of International Relations, even less so in the study of the Cold War. Studies that are interested in the "perspective that shifted south"[1], and so, are capable of discussing non-alignment in different contextual settings are only recently being written as the archives of ex-Soviet satellite states, the Soviet Union itself and those of countries such as India are becoming more accessible. This shift in perspective might also disrupt assumptions about the "character and location of political life"[2]. For instance, non-alignment was conceptualized in part as a response to Nehru's assumption that the Cold War would be located not solely in the United States or in the Soviet Union, but increasingly in the countries of Asia and Africa. The assumptions on which non-alignment was based were partly derived from sources outside the Cold War paradigm. But the theories that attempted to explain non-alignment were still trying to impose on it categories derived from political realism for the most part, and liberalism in some other cases.

As a radical political vision, non-alignment was riddled with risk. The task before Nehru was to reconcile the question of achieving, what he later called "a just society by just means"[3] on the national front with the twin objective of advancing India's position in the international setting. As a foreign policy, non-alignment was intended to secure India's strategic autonomy in case war came, while pushing ahead in the UN to prevent the conditions for such a war. Indian diplomacy brought two particular methods from India's anticolonial experiences – that of an emphasis on the means-ends question and equally, the force of morality in public life. Gandhi had successfully ousted the British by invoking them to apply their standards of morality to their rule in India. Nehru propagated this method at the UN by repeatedly calling into question the methods of the two blocs and their insistence of maintaining the Cold War, which he saw as anomalous – an uneasy stage before full-blown war. Thus, under Nehru's leadership, India imagined and constructed the UN as a space where the decentring of war could be made possible. Nehru's foreign policy establishment did not even like the idea of a defence policy, thinking there was none apart from a foreign policy.

From the Korean War to the Congo Crisis, the idea of the UN acquired more and more salient form, primarily through the expansion of its membership. Over that time, Indian commitment to the UN was also elevated in unprecedented measure. This came from Nehru's belief that the UN was the sphere in which politics could be sequestered from war. Thus, the evolution of the UN as an organization and that of non-alignment as an idea were processes braided together from the very start. In all the crises studied in this book, the UN was faced with defiance from states that had committed aggression. Nehru, and indeed leaders of other Asian-African states, had long believed that the UN represented their best (even if not ideal) hope for political action. Therefore, the crisis of the UN and the challenge to its authority drove them into diplomatic initiatives. As the book shows, new sites for political action were opened up especially through the diplomacy of Asian-African states, and frequently under the leadership of non-aligned India.

A particularly fascinating aspect of this period is Nehru's articulation of India's non-aligned stand in relation to different events or periods. It is interesting to see Nehru frame non-alignment in response to different globalities, modernities, forms of nationalism, forms of government, varieties of state systems, etc. In responding to these many differences, there is constant revision and re-articulation, the making and unmaking of non-alignment, with a somewhat stable core – one that begins to unravel in the latter part of the 1950s and the early 1960s. From the mid-1940s for a decade after, non-aligned India catalogued the deficiencies of world politics and constantly critiqued the positions adopted by the two blocs as partaking of a neo-colonial discourse. By appropriating and setting the agenda for the UN, India, under Nehru's leadership, offered an alternative imagination to the countries of Asia and Africa, and provided a new role for the neutrals – countries such as Sweden and Switzerland – in international diplomacy. If 1919 was the Wilsonian moment, 1955 was just as easily a Nehruvian moment.

This book is a resource for thinking of non-alignment as a source of political imagination. The fundamental objective of the study has been to write new history, one that gives us a powerful critique of the past of non-alignment. Past studies have often treated non-alignment as a historical anomaly, an idea with such shaky foundations that its collapse was inevitable in the absence of Nehru, or eventually along with the disintegration of the Soviet Union and the receding reach of communism. This charge is often accompanied by the claim that ideological rivalry persists, so the normative project taken up by non-alignment has been unsuccessful. Both these points of view are themselves embedded in realist or liberal retellings. On the contrary, I have taken a rather different approach, whose fundamental objective has been to show that politics is defensible against war and that such ramparts around politics were quite often built through non-western, non-Eurocentric processes.

This book has outlined the possibilities, limits and adaptability of non-aligned politics. With leaders of other non-aligned nations too, such as Sukarno, Nasser and Nkrumah, Nehru had differences of opinion – this divergence of views between these different forms of non-alignment has not received any methodical examination. Nehru, and others such as Vijaya Lakshmi Pandit and Krishna Menon, showed unease with certain aspects of the NAM, the changing contours of Asia–Africa cooperation and the concept of the Third World. The adjacency of these concepts meant that they were bandied together without clear distinctions, particularly in the 1950s. In turn, this meant that India stayed at somewhat of a remove from these forums even while participating in them, mostly by laying emphasis on the fact that Indian resources were constrained by domestic issues. Thus, by engaging with these audiences in a limited way, Nehru kept Indian non-alignment rather insulated from the exchanges between these political collectives. We see in later phases, his distance from formerly like-minded thinkers and leaders. This estrangement did nothing to revitalize non-alignment that would have perhaps benefitted from contestation over its meaning, and reflection from a wider variety of sources.

As such, the book brings back contention as a significant, indispensable tool for political action and thought. Historians have not been able to decide whether non-alignment was firmly in the present or sufficiently in the past. It might be difficult to find a policy in another national setting that is neither denied nor confirmed, yet so clearly at the centre of a nation's political life. Even though this book is decidedly not a manifesto of Indian exceptionalism, it has a certain redemptive quality because the climate of the time has certainly not been kind to non-alignment, which is simply seen as emerging from Nehru's thinly veiled liberalism, collapsing ineluctably into his later-day realism.

This book generates new accounts of episodes in India's international history, rejecting the unnecessary separation between India's national histories and the histories of wars fought elsewhere. After all, Indian nationalism was forged in those wars, in faraway theatres too, both before and after independence. This book also seriously situates India in the Cold War and certainly involves the writing of Indian narratives of the Cold War, but these are not intended to be new material for old thinking. More critical perspectives, both empirical and theoretical, are being called for in the writing of International Relations theory. This is not a burden Cold War history can refuse either. The ambition of the book is to widen the scope of both those disciplines. The internationalism of the enterprise is so integral to it, in fact, that it is shocking how an entire nation's international politics is not recognized as having anything to offer to the discipline of International Relations. *The Nehru Years* confronts that view.

In the introduction I have spoken of critique being foundational to non-alignment. A history of the non-aligned critique of world order is indispensable to understanding how disciplinary knowledge of International Relations is "produced within worldly institutions"[4]. While a history of the disciplinary knowledge production within International Relations offers an insight into how theoretical frameworks are often usurped by Eurocentric epistemological assumptions, this can be and is increasingly remedied by attempts to demythologise the discipline, particularly through historical texts. While diplomatic historians in the West are calling for foreign relations to be treated as a field, and not as a subset of national histories, to some extent, this is not a problem but an aspiration for writers of Indian diplomatic history who want to be able to see Cold War history as a subset of Indian history so that one might centre India in those larger histories and say, "we have a view from here too". This also helps historians of India's foreign relations move beyond a citationary politics that emphasizes solidarities amongst Asian and African states, instead choosing to complicate the narrative, and ask difficult questions about broken connections, animosity, the failure to sustain a shared political vision. After all, Indian non-alignment struggled to respond in any sustainable way to the "unstable politics of cross-racial affinity"[5], and indeed, even with other Asian political movements.

Yet, as this book has shown, thinkers from Asia and Africa were able to denaturalize the present they were in by rejecting someone else's past as constituting their history, extending a subaltern refusal to the colonial memory of the present. Instead, through strategies such as non-alignment, thinkers such as Nehru sought a meaningful relationship with their cosmopolitan pasts and a soon-to-be Asian future.

Notes

1. Introduction

1. Adom Getachew and Karuna Mantena, "Anticolonialism and the Decolonization of Political Theory," *Critical Times*, 4(3), (2021): 359–388.
2. For a discussion of the relation between nation and Empire, see Partha Chatterjee, "Empire and nation revisited: 50 years after Bandung," *Inter-Asia Cultural Studies*, 6(4), (2005): 487–496; Faisal Devji, "A minority of one," *Global Intellectual History*, (2021): 1–7.
3. For an essay on Nehru's rhetoric, see Swapna Kona Nayudu, "Nehru's Voice – An Essay on the 100 Volumes of Nehru's Selected Works", *Reviews in History*, 12 May 2023, accessible at https://reviews.history.ac.uk/review/2474

2. A Lonely Furrow

1 For a detailed exposition of this idea, see Sudipta Kaviraj, *The Imaginary Institution of India: Politics and Ideas*, (New York: Columbia University Press, 2010), 71. Kaviraj says that for Nehru, "history came to be a central idea".

2. These writings are most accessible through *The Selected Works of Jawaharlal Nehru (SWJN),* 2nd ser., vols. 1–48, eds. Sarvepalli Gopal, Ravinder Kumar, H.Y. Sharada Prasad, A.K. Damodaran, Mushirul Hasan, Mridula Mukherjee and Aditya Mukherjee, (New Delhi: Jawaharlal Nehru Memorial Fund) and G. Parthasarathi, ed. *Jawaharlal*

Nehru, Letters to Chief Ministers 1947-1964, vols. 1–5 (Delhi: Oxford University Press, 1986).

Priya Chacko, "The Internationalist Nationalist: Pursuing an Ethical Modernity with Jawaharlal Nehru," in *International Relations and Non-Western Thought: Imperialism, Colonialism and Investigations of Global Modernity*, ed. Robbie Shilliam (London & New York: Routledge, 2011), 179.

3. David Armitage, *Foundations of Modern International Thought* (Cambridge: Cambridge University Press, 2013), 24.
4. John Dunn, *Political Obligation in its Historical Context: Essays in Political Theory* (Cambridge: Cambridge University Press, 2002), 368.
5. Odd Arne Westad, epilogue to *The Cold War in the Third World*, ed. Robert J. McMahon (New York: Oxford University Press, 2013), 211–212.
6. Mehta refers to how the British rulers of India were "like men bound to keep time in two longitudes at once." Henry Maine, *The Effects of Observation of India on Modern European Thought Cambridge*, the Rede Lecture, 1875, quoted in Uday S. Mehta, *Liberalism and Empire: A Study in Nineteenth-Century British Liberal Thought* (Chicago: University of Chicago Press, 1999), 13.
7. This characteristic comes out quite strongly in Guha's discussion of Gandhi's choice of successors in Ramachandra Guha, *The Last Liberal and Other Essays* (New Delhi: Permanent Black, 2004).
8. Alasadair MacIntyre's concept, quoted in Pratap B. Mehta, "People of the Past," *Indian Express*, 15 August 2013, accessed 15 August 2013, http://archive.indianexpress.com/news/people-of-the-past/1155521/
9. Partha Chatterjee also discusses this "appropriation" but is of the view that Nehru used "the scientific method of Marxism" for purely nationalist purposes. Partha Chatterjee, "Nationalist Thought and the Colonial World," *The Partha Chatterjee Omnibus* (New Delhi: Oxford University Press, 2007), 140.
10. Jawaharlal Nehru, Constituent Assembly of India, Debates, vol. 1, 13

December 1946, accessed 25 October 2014, http://parliamentofindia.nic.in/ls/debates/debates.htm

11. For a narrative of India's political economy woven into its political history, see, Sunil Khilnani, *The Idea of India* (New York: Farrar, Straus & Giroux, 1999), 263.
12. For an interesting account of the League, see Vijay Prashad, *The Darker Nations: A People's History of the Third World* (New York: New Press, 2007), 364; for an interesting account of Nehru's interface with the Congress of Oppressed Nationalities, see Frank Moraes, *Jawaharlal Nehru: A Biography*, 2nd ed., (Mumbai: Jaico Publishing House, 2008), 107–123. Also see Michele L. Louro *Comrades against Imperialism: Nehru, India, and Interwar Internationalism*, (Cambridge: Cambridge University Press, 2018), 309.
13. Michele L. Louro, "The Making of the League against Imperialism, 1927", in *Comrades against Imperialism: Nehru, India, and Interwar Internationalism*, (Cambridge: Cambridge University Press, 2018), 65–102.
14. To see how that changed over the years he was in power, see Paul F. Power, "Indian Foreign Policy: The Age of Nehru," *The Review of Politics* 26, 2 (1964): 272.
15. Vijay Prashad, *Darker Nations*, 364.
16. For how nationalist histories of postcolonial states are written through histories of their anticolonial movements, see Erez Manela, *The Wilsonian Moment: Self Determination and the International Origins of Anticolonial Nationalism* (New York: Oxford University Press, 2007), xi.
17. Partha Chatterjee, "The Nation and its Fragments," *The Partha Chatterjee Omnibus* (New Delhi: Oxford University Press, 2007), 30.
18. Chatterjee suggests that this might have to do with the fact that they didn't consider themselves "culturally inferior/ill-equipped". See, Chatterjee, "Nationalist Thought and the Colonial World," 1.
19. Shruti Kapila, *Violent Fraternity: Indian Political Thought in the Global Age*, (Princeton: Princeton University Press, 2021).

20. Faisal Devji, ed., *The Impossible Indian: Gandhi and the Temptations of Violence*, (London: Hurst Publishers, 2012), 44.
21. P.N. Furbank, quoted in Sunil Khilnani, "Looking for Indira Gandhi," *Seminar*, 13 August 2004, saying this about political life, but it could have just as easily been applied to the domain in which those lives took place.
22. Sunil Khilnani, "Politics and National Identity" in *The Oxford Companion to Politics in India,* eds. Niraja G. Jayal & Pratap B. Mehta (New Delhi: Oxford University Press, 2010), 194.
23. Michael Collins, *Empire, Nationalism and the Postcolonial World: Rabindranath Tagore's Writings on History, Politics and Society* (Oxon: Routledge, 2012), 90–91.
24. Rabindranath Tagore's expression, Sugata Bose, "Post-Colonial Histories of South Asia: Some Reflections," *Journal of Contemporary History* 38, 1 (2003): 133–146.
25. Ramachandra Guha, ed. *Makers of Modern India* (Cambridge: Belknap of Harvard University Press, 2011) 197, 202.
26. Rao's phrase is "between peripheries", see Rahul Rao, "The Elusiveness of 'Non-Western Cosmopolitanism,'" in Sonika Gupta and Sudarsan Padmanabhan (eds), *Politics and Cosmopolitanism in a Global Age,* (New Delhi: Routledge India, 2015), 21–22.
27. Tanika Sarkar, quoted in Ramachandra Guha, *Patriots and Partisans: From Nehru to Hindutva and Beyond*, (New Delhi: Penguin, 2012), 1.
28. Rabindranath Tagore's phrase made memorable by Sunil Khilnani, *The Idea of India* (New York: Farrar, Straus & Giroux, 1999), 263.
29. Collins, *Empire, Nationalism and the Postcolonial World*, 72–73; 90–91.
30. Rabindranath Tagore, *Nationalism* (New Delhi: Penguin Books, 2009), 45; Guha, *Patriots and Partisans*, 189.
31. Rabindranath Tagore, quoted in Guha, *Patriots and Partisans*, 195.
32. Rabindranath Tagore, *Greater India*, trans. Surendranath Tagore (Madras: S. Ganesan, 1921), 101.
33. "Peace and Empire", Presidential Address at the Conference on Peace and Empire, Organized by the India League and the London Federation

of Peace Councils, Friends House, London, 15–16 July 1938, quoted in Jawaharlal Nehru, *The Unity of India, Collected Writings 1937-1940* (New York: John Day Company, 1942), 268–277.

34. Paul F. Power makes the point that "true internationalism is incompatible with alignment", but this formulation insufficiently explains the motivations of non-alignment towards internationalism. See Power, "The Age of Nehru," 272.
35. Bose, "Postcolonial Histories", 146.
36. For a study of this, see Karuna Mantena, "On Gandhi's Critique of the State: Sources, Contexts, Conjunctures," *Modern Intellectual History* 9, 3 (2012): 535–563.
37. Devji, *Impossible Indian*, 191.
38. Ibid., 5. Devji also discusses how this ideal community was not to be based on ethical relations, ibid.,111.
39. Ananya Vajpeyi, *Righteous Republic: The Political Foundations of Modern India* (Cambridge: Harvard University Press, 2012), xxi
40. Sudipta Kaviraj, ed., *Politics in India* (New Delhi: Oxford University Press, 1997), 57.
41. For a study of this, see Karuna Mantena, "On Gandhi's Critique of the State: Sources, Contexts, Conjunctures," *Modern Intellectual History* 9, 3 (2012): 535–563.
42. On "enlightened anarchy", Gandhi writes in January 1939 in *Sarvodaya*, quoted in Sugata Bose and Ayesha Jalal, eds. *Nationalism, Democracy, and Development: State and Politics in India*, (New Delhi: Oxford University Press, 1997), 187.
43. Akeel Bilgrami, "Gandhi, the Philosopher," *Economic and Political Weekly* 38, 39 (2003): 4159–4165.
44. Faisal Devji, "Morality in the Shadow of Politics," *Modern Intellectual History* 7, 2 (2010): 373–390.
45. Ibid., 6.
46. Michel Foucault, *Power/Knowledge: Selected Interviews and Other Writings, 1972-1977*, (New York: Random House, 1988), 121.

47. Uday S. Mehta, "Gandhi and the Common Logic of War of Peace," *Raritan* 30, 1 (2010): 134.
48. For an extensive treatment of the means-ends question in Gandhi's political thought, see Karuna Mantena, "Another Realism: The Politics of Gandhian Nonviolence," *American Political Science Review* 106, 2 (2012): 455–470, and also Karuna Mantena, "Gandhi and the Means-Ends Question in Politics", Paper Number 46, 2012, unpublished, accessed on 29 July 2013, https://www.sss.ias.edu/files/papers/paper46.pdf.
49. Uday S. Mehta, "Gandhi on Democracy, Politics and the Ethics of Everyday Life," *Modern Intellectual History* 7, 2 (2010): 356. The essay deals with the question of "security" understood in Gandhi's thought as a concept of corporeal safety within bounded territory.
50. For an exposition on why war is warranted by "the permanent idealism of politics and peace", see Uday S. Mehta, "Gandhi and the Common Logic of War," 136.
51. Tarak Barkawi and Shane Brighton, "Powers of War: Fighting, Knowledge, and Critique," *International Political Sociology* 5, 2 (2011): 133. The atom bomb presents a difficulty for Gandhi's theorization of violence and war. For a statement of this problem, see Devji, *Impossible Indian,* 149–162.
52. Mohandas K. Gandhi, *Collected Works of Mahatma Gandhi*, vol. 89–90, November 1929, quoted in Rajmohan Gandhi, *The Good Boatman* (New Delhi: Penguin Books India, 1997), 403.
53. Sudipta Kaviraj, "On the enchantment of the state: Indian thought on the role of the state in the narrative of modernity," *European Journal of Sociology* 46, 2 (2005): 289.
54. Kaviraj suggests that Gandhi "refused to deal in modernity's terms". See, Kaviraj, *Imaginary Institution of India*, 24.
55. Chatterjee, "Nationalist Thought and the Colonial World," 132.
56. Neville Maxwell, "Jawaharlal Nehru: Of Pride and Principle," *Foreign Affairs* 52, 3 (1974): 634.

57. Kaviraj, "Enchantment of the state", 289. Also, see, Rajni Kothari, "The Crisis of the Modern State and the Decline of Democracy," in *Transfer and Transformations: Political Institutions in the Commonwealth*, eds. Peter Lyon and James Manor (Leicester: Leicester University Press, 1983), 123.
58. Vajpeyi, *Righteous Republic*, 172.
59. Kaviraj, "Enchantment of the State," 285.
60. Sunil Khilnani, "Nehru's Faith," *Outlook Magazine*, 9 December 2002, accessed 28 July 2013, http://www.outlookindia.com/article/Nehrus-Faith/218248.
61. Thompson, George. "The New World of Asia." *Foreign Affairs* 48, 1 (1969): 125.
62. Akeel Bilgrami, quoted in Amartya Sen, "On Interpreting India's Past," in Bose and Jalal, *Nationalism, Democracy, and Development*, 27.
63. Sudipta Kaviraj, "On the Enchantment of the State: Indian Thought on the Role of the State in the Narrative of Modernity," *European Journal of Sociology* 46, 2 (2005): 263296, 288; Partha Chatterjee, "A Possible India," *The Partha Chatterjee Omnibus* (New Delhi: Oxford University Press, 2007), especially the section titled "The Nehru Era". Also see the "Moment of Arrival," in Chatterjee, "Nationalist Thought and the Colonial World", 131–148.
64. Tibor Mende, *Conversations with Mr. Nehru*, (London: Secker & Warburg, 1956), 140.
65. Ibid., 75–76.
66. Ibid., 49.
67. "The Importance of Asia" in *SWJN*, 2nd ser. vol. 8, ed. Sarvepalli Gopal, 291.
68. Ibid.
69. Edwardes suggests that there is a basic incongruence between Nehru's personality and the role he undertook. Michael Edwardes, "Illusion and Reality in India's Foreign Policy," *International Affairs* 41, 1 (1965): 48–58.

70. Jawaharlal Nehru, "The Unity of India," *Foreign Affairs* 16, 2 (38): 231–243.
71. Mende, *Conversations with Mr. Nehru*, 139.
72. "The Role of the United Nations – Address to the Third Session of the UNGA at Palais de Chillot", Paris, 3 November 1948, Ministry of External Affairs (MEA) File No. 42 (12)/48-PMS, *National Archives of India (NAI)*, New Delhi, India. Also *SWJN*, 2nd ser., vol. 8, 290–295.
73. Jawaharlal Nehru, "Changing India," *Foreign Affairs* 41, 3 (1963): 453–465.
74. Sunil Khilnani, "Politics and National Identity," in *The Oxford Companion to Politics in India*, eds. Pratap B. Mehta and Niraja G. Jayal (New Delhi: Oxford University Press, 2012), 195, says "a willingness to invent, and crucially, to temporize when it came to defining the terms of India's identity."
75. Edwardes, "Illusion and Reality", 51.
76. Michael Brecher, *India and World Politics: Krishna Menon's View of the World* (Toronto: Oxford University Press, 1968), 7.
77. Speech delivered by Nehru on Gandhi's death. For full text, see, "We must hold together", *The Hindu*, 30 January 2013, accessed 1 February 2013, http://www.thehindu.com/opinion/op-ed/we-must-hold-together/article4358063.ece.
78. Kaviraj, *Imaginary Institution of India*, 111, talks about the different registers in which Gandhi operated.
79. On how anticolonial Indians may not have realized how conservative internationalism was in the early twentieth century, see Florian Wagner (2022), *Colonial Internationalism and the Governmentality of Empire, 1893-1982*, Cambridge University Press, Cambridge, 9.
80. Winston Churchill's phrase, quoted in Appadorai, *Dilemma in Foreign Policy in the Modern World* (Delhi: Asia Publishing House, 1963), 6.
81. Odd A. Westad, *The Global Cold War: Third World Interventions and the Making of Our Times* (Cambridge: Cambridge University Press, 2007), 2.

82. Jawaharlal Nehru, "The Role of the United Nations – Address to the Third Session of the UNGA at Palais de Chillot, Paris, 3 November 1948, MEA File No. 42 (12)/48-PMS, in *SWJN*, 2nd ser., vol. 8, 290–295. "Peaceful co-existence" is understood here neither as Soviet policy towards the western world nor as Panchsheel specifically. Although Nehru said, "If these principles were recognized in the mutual relations of all countries, then indeed there would hardly be any conflict and certainly no war." See Jawaharlal Nehru, "The Colombo Powers' Peace Efforts," *Jawaharlal Nehru's Speeches*, vol. 3, March 1953–August 1957 (New Delhi: Government of India, Ministry of Information and Broadcasting, 1958), 253.
83. Jawaharlal Nehru, "Speech in Constituent Assembly, 8 March 1948," *India's Foreign Policy*: Selected Speeches, September 1946–April 1961, (New Delhi: Publications Division, Ministry of Information and Broadcasting, GOI, 1961), 35.
84. Braj K. Nehru, *Speaking of India* (Washington: Information Service of India, 1963), 104.
85. Extracts from Nehru's speech to the Constituent Assembly of India, 4 December 1947, partially reproduced in Angadipuram Appadorai, *Select Documents on India's Foreign Policy and Relations 1947–1972*, vol. 1 (Oxford: Oxford University Press, 1982), 10.
86. "Note to Jayaprakash Narayan," Nehru Papers, 14 May 1949, *Nehru Memorial Museum and Library (NMML)*, New Delhi, India.
87. Krishnaswamy Subrahmanyam, "Alternative Security Doctrines, *Security Dialogue* 21, 1 (1990): 72; Khilnani, "Politics and National Identity," 196.
88. Westad, *The Global Cold War*, 2. Triloki N. Kaul, "The Idealist and the Revolutionary," Nehru Memorial Lecture London, 1983, accessed 4 April 2014, https://www.cambridgetrust.org/assets/documents/Lecture_10.pdf.
89. Krishnan Srinivasan, *Diplomatic Channels* (New Delhi: Manohar Publishers, 2012), 93.

90. Mehta calls it "a plausible geographical demarcation of where the two strands operate"; Pratap B. Mehta, "Still Under Nehru's Shadow? The Absence of Foreign Policy Frameworks in India," *India Review* 8, 3 (2009): 211.
91. Jawaharlal Nehru, "A Foreign Policy for India," Article written in Montana, Switzerland, 13 September 1927, AICC File No 8, 1927, 1–27, *NMML*.
92. Akhil Gupta, "The Song of the Nonaligned World: Transnational Identities and the Reinscription of Space in Late Capitalism," *Cultural Anthropology* 7, 1 (1992): 63–79.
93. "Note to G.L. Mehta (Indian Ambassador at Washington)," Nehru Papers, 1 June 1955, *NMML*.
94. An Indian Official, "India as a World Power," *Foreign Affairs* 27, 4 (1949): 540–550.
95. Brecher, *India and World Politics*, 12–13.
96. Indian Constituent Assembly (Legislative), 8 March 1948. Indian Information, vol. 22, 15 April 1948, 412, accessed 25 October 2014, http://parliamentofindia.nic.in/ls/debates/debates.htm, (emphasis mine).

3. The Outbreak of Peace

1. It is surprising that India's involvement in the war has received such scant attention. Shiv Dayal's *India's Role in the Korean Question* remains the most comprehensive account of India's approach to questions raised by the Korean War and is focused on the dispute settlement under the aegis of the UN. For a contemporary account that takes a dim view of India's role, see Ross N. Berkes and Mohinder S. Bedi, *The Diplomacy of India: Indian Foreign Policy in the United Nations* (Stanford: Stanford University Press, 1958), 105–139. International histories that pay the most attention to India's role are William Stueck, *The Korean War: An International History* (Princeton: Princeton University Press, 1995), 496; Robert Barnes, *The US, the UN and the Korean War: Communism

in the Far East and the American Struggle for Hegemony in the Cold War (New York: I.B.Tauris, 2014), 366; Barnes "Between the Blocs: India, the United Nations, and Ending the Korean War," *Journal of Korean Studies* 18, 2 (2013): 263–286. For a study of the Korean War as an episode in India-US relations, see Dennis Kux, *India and the U.S.: Estranged Democracies, 1941-1991* (National Defense University Press: 1992), 72–78; Rudra Chaudhuri, *Forged in Crisis* (London: Hurst & Company, 2014), 49–80, and Srinath Raghavan, *The Most Dangerous Place – A History of the United States in South Asia*, (New Delhi: Penguin Allen Lane), June 2018, 136–137, 139.

2. Bruce Cumings, *The Korean War: A History*, (New York: Modern Library Chronicles/Penguin Random House), July 2012, 320.
3. See John Steadman, *The Myth of Asia* (New York: Simon and Schuster, 1960), 35; Carolien M. Stolte and Harald Fischer-Tiné, "Imagining Asia in India: Nationalism and Internationalism (ca. 1905–1940)," *Comparative Studies in Society and History* 54, 1 (2012): 65–92.
4. See Sven Saaler and Christopher W.A. Szpilman, eds. *Pan-Asianism: A Documentary History, 1920–Present*, (Plymouth: Rowman & Littlefield Publishers Inc., 2011), 408.
5. Rabindranath Tagore, *The Essential Tagore*, eds. Fakrul Alam and Radha Chakravarty (Cambridge: Belknap of Harvard University Press, 2011), 14.
6. Krishna Dutta and Andrew Robinson, *Rabindranath Tagore: The Myriad-Minded Man* (New York: St. Martin's Press, 1995), 251 (emphasis mine).
7. Benoy K. Sarkar, *The Futurism of Young Asia: and Other Essays on the Relations between the East and the West* (Berlin: J. Springer, 1922), iv; also quoted in Stolte and Fischer-Tiné, "Imagining Asia in India," 65–92.
8. Jawaharlal Nehru, India in the Brussels Congress, *Indian Quarterly Register* 1–2, 1927, 155–156, quoted in Tansen Sen, "The End of Pan-Asianism? India, China, and the Asian Relations Conference in 1947," Talk at King's College London, 10 March 2014.

9. Mohandas K. Gandhi, "On Revolutions," Editorial, *Young India*, 1 March 1928, 67.
10. "Indian Nationalism and Japanese Imperialism", *The Indian Annual Register*, 1938, 49, quoted in Tansen Sen, "The End of Pan-Asianism? India, China, and the Asian Relations Conference in 1947," Talk at King's College London, 10 March 2014.
11. Mohandas K. Gandhi, *Harijan*, 24 December 1938, in *Harijan: Collected Issues of Gandhi's Journal* 1933–1955, 19 vols., ed. Joan V. Bondurant (New York: Garland Publishing, 1973), 394.
12. Madhavi Thampi makes the point that the invasion of Manchuria turned India's attention back to China and away from Japan; see Madhavi Thampi, *Indians in China, 1800-1949* (New Delhi: Manohar, 2005), 200–201.
13. For analyses of this aspect of the Asian Relations Conference, see Angadipuram Appadorai, "The Asian Relations Conference in Perspective," *International Studies* 18, 3 (1979): 275–285; Amitav Acharya, "Will Asia's Past Be Its Future?" *International Security* 28, 3 (2003/04): 149–164. For a fascinating account from an observer present at the conference itself, see J.A. McCallum, "The Asian Relations Conference," *The Australian Quarterly* 19, 2 (1947): 13–17.
14. John Steadman, *The Myth of Asia* (New York: Simon and Schuster, 1969), 35.
15. See Tansen Sen, "The Intricacies of Premodern Asian Connections," *The Journal of Asian Studies* 69, 4 (2010): 991–999.
16. See Mark Mazower, *No Enchanted Palace: The End of Empire and the Ideological Origins of the United Nations* (Princeton: Princeton University Press, 2009), 248.
17. Manu Bhagavan, *The Peacemakers: India and the Quest for One World*, (New York: Harper Collins, 2012), 260.
18. Y.D. Gundevia, "Some Interesting Aspects of Nehru's Policies," Speech given to the Poona Branch of the Indian Council of World Affairs,

Subject File No. 7, Y.D. Gundevia Papers, *Nehru Memorial Museum and Library* (*NMML*), New Delhi, India.

19. Sunil Khilnani, "Making Asia: India, China and the Struggle for an Idea," *Jawaharlal Nehru Memorial Lecture*, November 2012, 3, accessed 26 October 2014, http://www.cambridgetrust.org/assets/documents/Lecture_33.pdf.
20. Kumara P. S. Menon, *Many Worlds: An Autobiography* (London: Oxford University Press, 1965), 260.
21. Gandhi had said, "His nationalism is equal to internationalism"; quoted in Priya Chacko, "The Internationalist Nationalist: Pursuing an Ethical Modernity with Jawaharlal Nehru," in *International Relations and Non-Western Thought: Imperialism, Colonialism and Investigations of Global Modernity*, ed. Robbie Shilliam (London & New York: Routledge, 2011), 179.
22. Manmath N. Das, *The Political Philosophy of Jawaharlal Nehru* (New York: John Day Publishers, 1961), 189.
23. "India's Korean Policy," Statement in Parliament, 3 August 1950, *SWJN*, 2nd ser., vol. 15, 344.
24. "First Information Report on the Work of the UNTCOK," UN Document A/523, 9 February 1948, *United Nations Archives and Records Management Section (UNARMS)*, New York, U.S.A., 2.
25. "Statement of Mr. KPS Menon, Chairman of the United Nations Temporary Commission on Korea, as the Interim Committee," Ministry of External Affairs File No. D8714-CJK/50, 19 February 1948, 21, *National Archives of India (NAI)*, New Delhi, India.
26. "Letter of 20 February 1948," G. Parthasarathi ed. *Jawaharlal Nehru, Letters to Chief Ministers 1947-1964* vol. 1, (Delhi: Oxford University Press, 1985), 69.
27. "From Kondapi to KPS Menon, Note on the working of the United Nations Commission and the General Economic and Political Situation in South Korea," Ministry of External Affairs File No. D3361-CJK/50, 1950, 5, *NAI*.

28. "Message to Thakin Nu," 2 August 1950, *The Selected Works of Jawaharlal Nehru (SWJN),* 2nd ser., vol. 15, Part 1, ed. Sarvepalli Gopal, (New Delhi: Jawaharlal Nehru Memorial Fund), 331–332.
29. See Sergeĭ Nikolaevich Goncharov, *Uncertain Partners: Stalin, Mao, and the Korean War* (Stanford: Stanford University Press, 1993), 393.
30. "India's Korean Policy," Statement in Parliament, 3 August 1950, *SWJN,* 2nd ser., vol. 15, 344.
31. Kavalam M. Panikkar was a diplomat and historian specialized on China; see Kavalam M. Panikkar *In Two Chinas: Memoirs of a Diplomat* (London: G. Allen & Unwin, 1955), 184, for an account of the Korean War.
32. "Memorandum of Conversation, Charles Noyes, New York, 25 June 1950," *Foreign Relations of the United States (FRUS)*, 1950, Volume VII, Korea (Washington: Government Printing Office, 1998) 144–147, accessed 29 October 2014, http://digital.library.wisc.edu/1711.dl/FRUS.FRUS1950v07.
33. Fifth Year No.15, 473rd Meeting, New York, 25 June 1950, *United Nations Security Council Official Records (UNSCOR)*, 1–13.
34. "Letter From Singh and Kondapi to KPS Menon," Ministry of External Affairs File No. D11/86-CJK/50, *NAI.*
35. "Acheson – Henderson, Washington, June 27, 1950," *FRUS*, 1950, Volume VII, Korea, 230–231.
36. "Vijaya Lakshmi Pandit to Jawaharlal Nehru," Subject File no. 59 (Washington), Pandit Papers, 1st Instalment, 29 June 1950, *NMML.*
37. "Secretary General GS Bajpai to Indian Permanent Representative B N Rau, New Delhi," Ministry of External Affairs File No. CJK 67-CJK/50, 29 June 1950, *NAI.*
38. "Report No.2 UNCOK - A brief resume of the work of the UNCOK from March 1st to 21st and other developments in Korea," Ministry of External Affairs File No. D2545/CJK-50, 1950, *NAI.*
39. "Question No. 589 to be answered in Parliament on 1st August 1950," Ministry of External Affairs File No. 67/CJK/50, 1950, *NAI.*

40. "Secretary General GS Bajpai to Indian Permanent Representative B N Rau, New Delhi," Ministry of External Affairs File No. CJK 67-CJK/50, 29 June 1950, *NAI.*
41. "Press Release by President Truman Announcing Military Assistance to Indochina, 27 June 1950,"The Pentagon Papers, Volume 1, Document 8, *The National Archives and Records Administration (NARA)*, Washington, 372–373, accessed 15 September 2014, http://www.archives.gov/research/pentagon-papers/.
42. "Letter from Jawaharlal Nehru," B.N. Rau Papers, 1st Instalment, 1 July 1950, *NMML*, 2–3.
43. Stueck says, "India whose contribution of troops would have been of great political significance, offered *merely* a field ambulance unit", Stueck, *Korean War,* 72, (emphasis mine).
44. "Troops to Korea," 11 December 1951, *The Selected Works of Jawaharlal Nehru (SWJN),* 2nd ser., vol. 17, ed. Sarvepalli Gopal, (New Delhi: Jawaharlal Nehru Memorial Fund), 519–520. For a good description of this policy decision, see Yedezad. D. Gundevia, *Outside the Archives* (Hyderabad: Sangam Books, 1987), 93, 344–345.
45. "Letter from Jawaharlal Nehru, Letter of 27 August 1950" B.N. Rau Papers, 1st Instalment, 27 August 1950, *NMML*, 1. He also goes on to say, "Some of the speeches delivered in the Security Council by Austin or Jebb seem from here to be just pompous and silly nonsense."
46. "India's Stand on Korea," MEA File No D4492/51-AMS – Annual Political Report from the Embassy of India, Washington D.C. for 1951, 31 December 1951, *NAI.*
47. Frank Moraes, *Jawaharlal Nehru: A Biography*, (New Delhi: Jaico Publishing House), 469–470.
48. Second Session, Plenary Meetings, Volume 1, *General Assembly Official Records (GAOR)*, 134, 137–138.
49. "India's Korean Policy," Statement in Parliament, 3 August 1950, *SWJN,* 2nd ser., vol. 15, 343.
50. Ibid. n2.

51. "Reply to Gopal Menon (Indian Delegation to the UN) from KPS Menon (FS)," Ministry of External Affairs File No. D-9632-CJK/50, *NAI*. "Our fears that if the UN troops precipitately cross the 38th Parallel, China might intervene, and the war might spread, seem to be coming true."
52. "Correspondence with Nehru." Pandit Papers, 1st Instalment, 10 August 1950, *NMML*.
53. "Acheson-Austin, Washington, 15 August 1950," *FRUS*, 1950, Volume VII, Korea, 585–586.
54. Peter Russo, "38th Parallel & After? Mediation by Asian Neutrals May Be Solution," *The Argus*, 22 August 1950, accessed 15 September 2014, http://trove.nla.gov.au/ndp/del/article/22899041.
55. Manmath N. Das, *The Political Philosophy of Jawaharlal Nehru*, 237.
56. Quoted in, and see detailed description of the incident in "The VFW Incident," in Stanley Sandler, ed. *The Korean War: An Encyclopaedia* (New York: Taylor & Francis, 1995), 153.
57. Mao had already spoken of "the possibility that the US government may send troops to occupy some of the coastal cities and fight us directly. We should continue to prepare for this now so as to avoid being taken by surprise if it really occurs." "The Present Situation and the Party's Task in 1949," *Mao Zedong Junshi Wenxuan (Selected Military Papers of Mao Zedong)* (Beijing: Soldiers' Press, 1981), 328–329, quoted in Chen Jian, "The Sino-Soviet Alliance and China's Entry into the Korean War" (Working Paper No. 1, Cold War International History Project, Woodrow Wilson International Center for Scholars, Washington, D.C., 1992).
58. Kavalam M. Panikkar, *An Autobiography* (London: Oxford University Press, 1979), 235–236.
59. Zhou Enlai, "We Will Intervene if US Troops Cross the 38th Parallel", *Zhou Enlai Waijao Wenxuan* (Selected Diplomatic Documents of Zhou Enlai), Beijing, 1990, 25–27, Document 64, 3 October 1950.
60. Ibid.

61. Panikkar, *An Autobiography*, 235–236.
62. "Telegram from Loy Henderson to Secretary of State, October 6, 1950, 1 pm from New Delhi," *FRUS*, 1950, Volume VII, Korea,1950, 889–890.
63. "Telegram from Loy Henderson to Secretary of State, October 7, 1950, 1 pm from New Delhi," *FRUS*, 1950, Volume VII, Korea, 901–902.
64. "Telegram from Loy Henderson to Secretary of State, October 10, 1950, 1 pm from New Delhi," *FRUS*, 1950, Volume VII, Korea, 920.
65. UNSC Fifth Year No. 62 520th Meeting, New York, 8 November 1950, 3–10, quoted in Barnes, *U.S., the U.N. and the Korean War*, 300.
66. UNSC Fifth Year Number 72, 530th Meeting, New York, 30 November 1950, quoted in ibid., 22–24.
67. Vijaya Lakshmi Pandit, *The Scope of Happiness: A Personal Memoir* (New York: Crown Publishers, 1979), 257.
68. See "UNCURK in Seoul," *TIME Magazine*, 4 December 1950, accessed 28 October 2014, http://content.time.com/time/magazine/article/0,9171,813950,00.html.
69. "Avoiding Hasty Decisions," 20 January 1951, *SWJN,* 2nd ser., vol. 15, Part 2, 485.
70. Fifth Session, First Committee, 346–350th Meetings, New York, 30 September–3 October 1950, *GAOR*.
71. For a detailed exposition of this process, see Barnes, "Between the Blocs," 263–286.
72. "Cable to V K Krishna Menon," 22 December 1950, *SWJN,* 2nd ser., vol. 15, Part 2, 455.
73. "Telegram from Austin to Acheson, Washington, 28 December 1950," *FRUS*, 1950, Volume VII, Korea, 1620–1624.
74. See, Barnes, "Between the Blocs," 263–286.
75. Pandit says that the ceasefire committee was considered unsuccessful; see Pandit, *The Scope of Happiness*, 258.
76. Both Barnes, "Between the Blocs," and Stueck, *Korean War*, 152, 163–164, make the point that although Nehru was unable to stop the

American resolution from going forward, India amongst other members helped to stall the war cries against China from the US for retaliation.

77. "Message to CR Attlee," 22 December 1950, *SWJN,* 2nd ser., vol. 15, Part 2, 456.
78. "Cable to V K Krishna Menon," 2 July 1952, *SWJN,* 2nd ser., vol.18, 549, Quoting from Chang Han-Fu, Vice-Minister of Foreign Affairs, Central People's Government of the Republic of China.
79. "To B.G. Kher," 15 August 1952, *SWJN,* 2nd ser., vol. 19, 588.
80. "Letter from Jawaharlal Nehru," B.N. Rau Papers, 1st Instalment, 1 July 1950, *NMML*, 2–3.
81. "'Avoiding Hasty Decisions', Interview to the Press, Rome, 20 January 1951. From the *National Herald*, 21 January 1951," *SWJN,* 2nd ser., vol. 15, Part 2, 485.
82. Nehru says. "It is no good our asking China to do this or that." "Letter from Jawaharlal Nehru," B.N. Rau Papers, 1st Instalment, 17 April 1951, *NMML.*
83. "In Pursuit of Peace," 12 February 1951, *SWJN,* 2nd ser., vol. 15, Part 2, 503.
84. Sarvepalli Gopal, *Jawaharlal Nehru: A Biography* (New Delhi: Oxford University Press India, 2004), 134.
85. W.H. Lawrence, "Truman Relieves McArthur of All His Posts; Finds Him Unable to Back US-UN Policies; Ridgway Named to Far Eastern Commands," *New York Times*, 11 April 1951, accessed 15 September 2014, http://www.nytimes.com/learning/general/onthisday/big/0411.html#article.
86. "Ridgway agrees to ceasefire talks," *BBC News*, 3 July 1951, accessed 15 September 2014, http://news.bbc.co.uk/onthisday/hi/dates/stories/july/3/newsid_2785000/2785543.stm.
87. For possible Soviet influence, see "Report, Chinese International Department, Regarding Soviet Suggestion towards Ceasefire Negotiations," 26 June 1951, Foreign Ministry Archives of China, 113-00105-01, 1–8, History and Public Policy Program Digital Archive,

accessed 15 September 2014 http://digitalarchive.wilsoncenter.org/document/117406.

88. "Letter to Chief Ministers," 19 August 1951, *SWJN*, 2nd ser., vol. 16, Part 2, 700–707; Also see [Cover page missing], Ministry of External Affairs File No. 25 (6)/51, PMS, *NAI*; Also see, G. Parthasarathi ed. *Jawaharlal Nehru, Letters to Chief Ministers 1947-1964* vol. 1, 19 August 1951.
89. See [Cover page missing], Ministry of External Affairs File No. 25 (6)/51, PMS, *NAI*.
90. "Fortnightly Report from the Consul-General New York for the Period Ending November 1951," Ministry of External Affairs File No. F-34-4/51/AMS, *NAI*.
91. Ibid.
92. "Summary of the Fortnightly Report for the Period Ending September 15, 1951 from Washington," Ministry of External Affairs File No. F-34-4/51/AMS, *NAI*. The report says, "the small man in Government here is probably not averse to making and administering his own foreign relations."
93. Quote from "The Lost Leader," *New York Times*, 28 August 1951 "... His statesmanship is not inspiring people and nations to do things but only to leave them undone. How the mighty have fallen!"; see Gopal, *Jawaharlal Nehru*, 134, in the chapter titled "The Korean Settlement," in Gopal, *Jawaharlal Nehru*, 137.
94. Quote from "Nehru Idealist or Appeaser?" *The Economist*, 28 April 1951; see ibid., 136.
95. "Annual Political Report from the Embassy of India, Washington D.C. for 1951, Section titled 'India's Stand on Korea'" Ministry of External Affairs File No. D4492/51-AMS, *NAI*.
96. "Fortnightly Report from the Consul-General New York for the Period Ending October 1951," Ministry of External Affairs File No. F-34-4/51/AMS, *NAI*.
97. "UN Admits Bomb Fell on Korea," *Red Eagle*, 23 January 1952, accessed 15 September 2014, http://news.google.com/newspapers?id=OJItAAAAIBAJ&sjid=fp0FAAAAIBAJ&pg=6719%2C104.0730.

98. For accounts of the course of the armistice talks during this period, see Sydney Bailey, *The Korean Armistice* (Basingstoke: Macmillan, 1992), 70–126; Rosemary Foot, "Negotiating with Friends and Enemies: The Politics of Peacemaking in Korea," in *Korea and the Cold War: Division, Destruction, and Disarmament* eds. Kim Chull Baum and James Matray (Claremont: Regina Books, 1993), 193–208; Rosemary Foot, *A Substitute for Victory: The Politics of Peacemaking at the Korean Armistice Talks* (New York: Cornell University Press, 1990), 42–107, 130–52.
99. "Summary of the Fortnightly Report for the Period Ending 31st December 1951 from Washington," Ministry of External Affairs File No. F-34-4/51/AMS, *NAI*.
100. Ibid.
101. Gopal, *Jawaharlal Nehru*, 134.
102. "Memorandum of Conversation (Acheson), 29 October 1952," *Foreign Relations of the United States (FRUS)*, 1952–1954, Volume XV, Part 1, Korea (in two parts), ed. Edward C. Keefer (Washington: Government Printing Office, 1984), Document 293.
103. See Barnes, "Between the Blocs," 263–286.
104. "320/11–1252: Telegram, The Secretary of State to the Department of State, New York, November 12, 1952, 10:26 p. m.," *FRUS*, 1952–1954, Volume XV, Part 1, Korea (in two parts), ed. Keefer, Document 315.
105. "IO files, lot 71 D 440, Minutes of the Thirteenth Meeting of the United States Delegation at the United Nations General Assembly, New York, November 17, 1952," *FRUS*, 1952–1954, Volume XV, Part 1, Korea (in two parts), ed. Keefer, Document 333.
106. Seventh Session, First Committee, 525th Meeting, New York, 19 November 1952, *GAOR*, 111–115.
107. "Nehru-Pandit Correspondence," Pandit Papers, 1st Instalment, Subject File No.47, 18 November 1952, *NMML*.
108. "Telegram from Austin to the Department of State, p.6 Dec 1952," *FRUS*, 1952–1954, Volume XV, Part 1, Korea (in two parts), ed. Keefer, Document 360.

109. "To Thakin Nu," 25 January 1953, *The Selected Works of Jawaharlal Nehru (SWJN),* 2nd ser., vol. 21, ed. Sarvepalli Gopal, (New Delhi: Jawaharlal Nehru Memorial Fund) 446–448n3.
110. Seventh Session, First Committee, 529th Meeting, New York, 24 November 1952, *GAOR*, 135–141.
111. "Memorandum of Conversation, by Maurice M. Bernbaum, Adviser to the United States Delegation at the United Nations General Assembly[1] (#fn2), New York, November 27, 1952," *FRUS*, 1952–1954, Volume XV, Part 1, Korea (in two parts), ed. Keefer, Document 353, https://history.state.gov/historicaldocuments/frus1952-54v15p1/d353.
112. "795.00/11–2652: Telegram, The Ambassador in India (Bowles) to the Department of State, New Delhi, November 26, 1952—7 p. m.," *FRUS*, 1952–1954, Volume XV, Part 1, Korea (in two parts), ed. Keefer, Document 348.
113. "To Thakin Nu," 25 January 1953, *SWJN*, 2nd ser., vol. 21, 446–448.
114. Gopal, *Jawaharlal Nehru*, 134
115. "Cable to N Raghavan," 26 November 1952, *SWJN*, 2nd ser., vol. 20, 435.
116. "Memorandum by Assistant Secretary of State for the UN Affairs (Hickerson) to Under Secretary of State (Bruce), Washington, 2 May 1952," *FRUS*, 1952–1954, Volume XV, Part 1, Korea (in two parts), ed. Keefer, Document, 112.
117. "Cable to N Raghavan," 25 January 1953, *SWJN*, 2nd ser., vol. 21, 449.
118. The Americans also thought this had formed some sort of coalition – "We cannot safely assume this 'coalition' has been dissolved nor that it may not again attempt assume further initiative." "320/12–652: Telegram – The United States Representative at the United Nations (Austin) to the Department of State New York, December 6, 1952—6:27 p. m.," *FRUS*, 1952–1954, Volume XV, Part 1, Korea (in two parts), ed. Keefer, Document 360.
119. "To Girja Shankar Bajpai, December 2, 1952," *SWJN*, 2nd ser., vol. 19, 447.

120. *UNGA*, *Seventh Session*, *First Committee* 535–536th Meetings, New York, 1–2 December 1952, 173–85; *UNGA*, *Seventh Session*, *Plenary* 399th Meeting, New York, 3 December 1952, 295–308.
121. Nehru had misgivings about the process, but it met with some success, see Barnes, "Between the Blocs," 23–24.
122. "Cable to N. Raghavan," 27 November 1952, *SWJN*, 2nd ser., vol. 20, 438.
123. "Nehru to G. L. Mehta," 10 December 1952, *SWJN*, 2nd ser., vol. 20, 458–459; also see "Nehru to KPS Menon," 16 December 1952, *SWJN*, 2nd ser., vol. 19, 464.
124. "Letter of 20 November 1952," in ed. G. Parthasarathi, *Jawaharlal Nehru, Letters to Chief Ministers 1947-1964*, vol. 3, (Delhi: Oxford University Press, 1988), 167.
125. "Memorandum of Conversation, by the Secretary of State, New Delhi, 21 May 1953—11:30 a. m.," *FRUS*, 1952–1954, Volume XV, Part 1, Korea (in two parts), ed. Keefer, Document 537.
126. "Nehru-Pandit Correspondence," Pandit Papers, 1st Instalment, Subject File No.47, 12 October 1952, *NMML*.
127. For an interesting note on the perception of VK Krishna Menon's appointment to the UN, see Vernon M. Hewitt, *The New International Politics of South Asia* (Manchester: Manchester University Press, 1997), 89–90; for a critical view of Menon's dealings with diplomats from Asian states, see Godrey H. Jansen, *Nonalignment and the Afro-Asian State* (New York: Praeger, 1966), 108–113; for reference on how Krishna Menon came to be responsible for the Korean question, see Gopal, *Jawaharlal Nehru*, 134. On Menon's correspondence with regards to the Korean problem, see "Papers relating to Korean issues.", V.K. Krishna Menon Papers, 1st and 2nd Instalment, File No. 852, 1950–1954, *NMML*; "Papers relating to the Korean issues in the UN." V.K. Krishna Menon Papers, 1st and 2nd Instalment, File No. 855, 1952–1953, *NMML*.

128. "Interview with Mr. Lester Pearson, President of the UN General Assembly, New York," Vijaya Lakshmi Pandit Papers, 2nd Instalment, Subject File No. 4, 25 February 1953, *NMML*.
129. See "Statement of Molotov, Minister of Foreign Affairs on the Korean Question," 31 March 1953, History and Public Policy Program Digital Archive, obtained by Andrei Mefodievich Ledovskii, accessed 15 September 2014, http://digitalarchive.wilsoncenter.org/document/117426.
130. "Indian Ambassador to the Soviet Union K.P.S. Menon Interview with Stalin," 18 February 1953, History and Public Policy Program Digital Archive, reprinted from K.P.S. Menon, *The Flying Troika* (London, Oxford University Press) 1963, 330, accessible at http://digitalarchive.wilsoncenter.org/document/134393.
131. The "Peace Offensive" was originally a Stalinist concept, the phrasing was later appropriated by Khrushchev; for the effect it had on Sino-Soviet relations, see Odd Arne Westad, *Brothers in Arms: The Rise and Fall of the Sino-Soviet Alliance, 1945-1963* (Stanford: Stanford University Press, 1998), 22–26.
132. Stueck has an excellent description of this change in attitude, also on the North Korean front. Stueck, *Korean War*, 307–313, 326–7, 341; William Stueck, *Rethinking the Korean War: A New Diplomatic and Strategic History* (Princeton: Princeton University Press, 2002), 173–174.
133. Statement of Zhou Enlai, 30 March 1953, quoted in Gopal, "The Korean Settlement," *Jawaharlal Nehru*, 147n58.
134. Seventh Session, First Committee, 594th Meeting, New York, 9 April 1953, *GAOR*, 582.
135. Seventh Session, First Committee, 602nd–603rd Meetings, New York, 15–16 April 1953, *GAOR*, 637–648. Barnes has a thorough explanation of the various viewpoints and historiography of the signing of the Korean Armistice Agreement; see Barnes, *US, the UN and the Korean War*, 31–32, 31–32nn55–57.

136. "Memorandum of Conversation, by the Secretary of State, New Delhi, 22 May 1953," *FRUS*, 1952–1954, Volume XV, Part 1, Korea (in two parts), ed. Keefer, Document 529.
137. Dwight D. Eisenhower, "Exchange of Messages Between the President and Prime Minister Nehru of India on the Prisoner of War Agreement Reached at Panmunjom," 12 June 1953, online by Gerhard Peters and John T. Woolley, The American Presidency Project, accessed 15 September 2014, http://www.presidency.ucsb.edu/ws/?pid=9604.
138. "Letter of 24 May 1953," in G. Parthasarathi ed. *Jawaharlal Nehru, Letters to Chief Ministers 1947-1964 vol.3*, 310–311, Point 16.
139. Gopal, "The Korean Settlement," *Jawaharlal Nehru*, 148.
140. "Letter of 19 April 1953," in G. Parthasarathi ed. *Jawaharlal Nehru, Letters to Chief Ministers 1947-1964 vol. 3*, 285n61; For accounts of the course of the armistice talks during this period, see Foot: *A Substitute for Victory*, 159–189.
141. "Letter of 2 July 1953," in G. Parthasarathi ed. *Jawaharlal Nehru, Letters to Chief Ministers 1947-1964 vol. 3*, 323.
142. "Memorandum of Conversation, by the Secretary of State, New Delhi, 22 May 1953," *FRUS*, 1952–1954, Volume XV, Part 1, Korea (in two parts), ed. Keefer, Document 539.
143. Ibid.
144. "Cable to Vijaya Lakshmi Pandit," 26 January 1955, *The Selected Works of Jawaharlal Nehru (SWJN)*, 2nd ser., vol. 27, eds. Ravinder Kumar, H.Y. Sharada Prasad, (New Delhi: Jawaharlal Nehru Memorial Fund), 218–219.
145. V. K. Krishna Menon at the UN took a more assertive view on India's membership of the NNRC, which Nehru found presumptuous; see, Jawaharlal Nehru, "Correspondence in 1953 as President of the UN General Assembly, Letter from Nehru," Pandit Papers, 1st Instalment, 26 October 1953, *NMML*, 8; also see "Telegrams from VK Krishna Menon to Nehru relating to international affairs with a special focus

on problems of Korea." V.K. Krishna Menon Papers, 1st and 2nd Instalment, File No. 854, 1952–1953, *NMML*.

146. Nehru's statements, see Frank Moraes, *Jawaharlal Nehru: A Biography*, 2nd ed., (Mumbai: Jaico Publishing House, 2008), 469–470; For India's reply to the UN request, see Reports of the UN Commission for the Unification and Rehabilitation of Korea, General Assembly A/C.1/734, 17 November 1952, Cordier Collection, Box 132, UN Files, Subject Files, Asia – 1. Cablegram dated 29 July 1950 from the Prime Minister and Minister for External Affairs of India to the Secretary General in Reply to the Secretary General's Cablegram of 14 July 1950 (8/1619) concerning the Security Council Resolution of 25 and 27 June and 7 July 1950 (S/1501, S/1511, S/1588).
147. For the official history of the CFI, see Nandan Prasad, *History of the Custodian Force (India) in Korea, 1953-54*, (New Delhi: Historical Section, Ministry of Defence, Government of India, 1976). The Indians named the DMZ camp they stayed in "Hind Nagar (Indian City)" and the other camp, which housed all members from other countries "Shanti Nagar" (City of Peace).
148. "Publicity Arrangements for the NNRC," Ministry of External Affairs File No. 35/48 –XPP/53, *NAI*. — India's functions included: 1) Custody of the prisoners of war and the running of camps (Sole Indian responsibility), 2) Supervision of the explanations and interviews as well as observations of these by the opposite side (Commission's responsibility); and 3) Red Cross Services for the Prisoners of War (Indian responsibility).
149. "Telegram, The Commander in Chief United Nations Command (Clark) to the Joint Chiefs of Staff, Tokyo, 3 April 1953," *FRUS*, 1952–1954, Volume XV, Part 1, Korea (in two parts), ed. Keefer, Document 439.
150. "Telegram, The Commander in Chief, United Nations Command (Clark) to the Joint Chiefs of Staff, Tokyo, 16 May 1953," *FRUS*, 1952–1954, Volume XV, Part 1, Korea (in two parts), ed. Keefer, Document 525.

151. "The Political Adviser for the Armistice Negotiations (Murphy) to the Department of State, Tokyo, 21 May 1953," *FRUS*, 1952–1954, Volume XV, Part 1, Korea (in two parts), ed. Keefer, Document 538.
152. "To U Nu," 11 May 1953, *The Selected Works of Jawaharlal Nehru (SWJN)*, 2nd ser., vol. 22, eds. Sarvepalli Gopal, Ravinder Kumar, H.Y. Sharada Prasad, (New Delhi: Jawaharlal Nehru Memorial Fund), 434–436.
153. Rhee had not allowed Indian troops to land on South Korean soil, so they had had to be airlifted to the DMZ. Jawaharlal Nehru, "Nehru to Pandit," Pandit Papers, 1st Instalment, 28 December 1953, *NMML*, 19–23.
154. "The Ambassador in Korea (Briggs) to the Department of State, Seoul, January 1, 1954—8 p. m.," *Foreign Relations of the United States (FRUS)*, 1952–1954, Volume XV, Part 2, Korea (in two parts), ed. Edward C. Keefer (Washington: Government Printing Office, 1984), Document 829.
155. "The Ambassador in Korea (Briggs) to the Department of State, Seoul, January 5, 1954-1 a. m.," *FRUS*, 1952–1954, Volume XV, Part 2, Korea (in two parts), ed. Keefer, Document 833.
156. "Mark W. Clark Collection, Archives-Museum, The Citadel, The President of the Republic of Korea (Rhee) to the Commander in Chief, United Nations Command (Clark)1 (#fn2), Seoul, June 18, 1953," *FRUS*, 1952–1954, Volume XV, Part 2, Korea (in two parts), ed. Keefer, Document 607.
157. "Cable to MA Rauf," 12 June 1953, *SWJN*, 2nd ser., vol. 22, 453; "Cable to Rajeshwar Dayal," 21 June 1953, *SWJN*, 2nd ser., vol. 22, 463n2.
158. "Towards Armistice and Repatriation," 27 June 1953, *SWJN*, 2nd ser., vol. 22, 472.
159. "Dag Hammarskjold to Pandit," Pandit Papers, 1st Instalment, *NMML*.
160. "Memorandum of Conversation, Arthur Dean, [Washington], October 6, 1953," *FRUS*, 1952–1954, Volume XV, Part 2, Korea (in two parts), ed. Keefer, Document 765.

161. "Memorandum of Conversation, by the Director of the Office of Northeast Asian Affairs (Young) [Seoul], August 5, 1953," *FRUS*, 1952–1954, Volume XV, Part 2, Korea (in two parts), ed. Keefer, Document 734.
162. Report from Reid to Pearson in Escott Reid, *Envoy to Nehru* (New York: Oxford University Press, 1981), 49.
163. Ibid.
164. "Memorandum of Conversation, by the Secretary of State, Denver, 10 August 1953," *FRUS*, 1952–1954, Volume XV, Part 2, Korea (in two parts), ed. Keefer, Document 742.
165. "Memorandum by the Deputy Assistant Secretary of State for United Nations Affairs (Sandifer) to the Secretary of State 1 (#fn2), Washington, 18 August 1953," *FRUS*, 1952–1954, Volume XV, Part 2, Korea (in two parts), ed. Keefer, Document 749.
166. "Move to Exclude India?", *The Sydney Morning Herald*, 24 August 1953, accessed 28 October 2014, http://trove.nla.gov.au/ndp/del/article/18387570.
167. "Telegram, The Ambassador in India (Allen) to the Department of State, New Delhi, 26 August 1953," *FRUS*, 1952–1954, Volume XV, Part 2, Korea (in two parts), ed. Keefer, Document 750.
168. "Nehru Charges US Flouts Asia", *The Spokesman Review*, 18 September 1953, accessed 23 January 2014, http://news.google.com/newspapers?nid=1314&dat=19530918&id=by9WAAAAIBAJ&sjid=JeYDAAAAIBAJ&pg=7186,3307603.
169. Ibid.
170. Krishna Menon, "'World Tension And The Path To Peace,' Statement of 28 September 1953," in *Krishna Menon, Selected Speeches At The United Nations – I. India And The World*, eds. E.S. Reddy & A.K. Damodaran (New Delhi: Sanchar Publishing House, 1994).
171. "Correspondence in 1953 as President of the UN General Assembly, 'Letter of 26 October 1953,'" Pandit Papers, 1st Instalment, 26 October 1953, *NMML*, 8.

172. "South Korean delegation is expected to make vicious speech. Krishna Menon proposes not to take any notice of it." See "Indian Delegation to the UN to Foreign Secretary, India," Ministry of External Affairs File No. D-5832-FEA/54, *NAI.*
173. "An Impartial and Objective Role," 20 January 1954, *The Selected Works of Jawaharlal Nehru (SWJN),* 2nd ser., vol. 24, eds. Ravinder Kumar, H.Y. Sharada Prasad, (New Delhi: Jawaharlal Nehru Memorial Fund), 547–548.
174. "Message to Indian Soldiers in Korea, 6 November 1953," in ibid., 513–514.
175. See Nehru's Cables to Gen. K.S. Thimayya, 5 October 1953–18 January 1954, *SWJN,* 2nd ser., vol. 24, 481–548.
176. "The Korean Question: Reports of the Neutral National Repatriation Commission," UN General Assembly Eight Session/Official Records, P.N. Haksar Papers, 3rd Instalment, File No. 409, September 1953 to 21 February 1954, *NMML.* For a previous report, see "Reports of the UN Commission for the unification and rehabilitation of Korea." V.K. Krishna Menon Papers, 1st and 2nd Instalment, File No. 856, 1952–1953, *NMML.*
177. T.N. Kaul, "Legal Opinion on the Disposal of the Korean Prisoners of War," Ministry of External Affairs File No. 15 (7) –FEA/55, *NAI.*
178. The Maha Vir Chakra is the second highest military decoration in India and is awarded for acts of conspicuous gallantry. [Cover page missing], Ministry of External Affairs File No. C/551(4)/64-KS], *NAI,* (Appendix B).
179. "Letter from Eisenhower to Nehru," File No. 6, Thimayya Papers, 25 February 1954, *NMML,* 2; Also see Dwight D. Eisenhower, "Message to Prime Minister Nehru Commending the Indian Custodial Forces in Korea," 19 February 1954, The American Presidency Project, accessed 15 September 2014, http://www.presidency.ucsb.edu/ws/?pid=101.
180. Krishna Menon, quoted in Michael Brecher, *India and World Politics: Krishna Menon's View of the World* (Toronto: Oxford University Press, 1968), 41–42.

181. This matter was brought up repeatedly later, most notably in the meetings between Premier Zhou Enlai and Prime Minister Nehru in 1954 and subsequent correspondence. See "Talking Points from Premier Zhou Enlai's Third Meeting with Nehru," 21 October 1954, History and Public Policy Program Digital Archive, PRC FMA 204-00007-06, 51–57. Obtained by Chen Jian and translated by 7Brands, accessible at http://digitalarchive.wilsoncenter.org/document/121742; and "Jawaharlal Nehru, 'Note on Visit to China and Indo-China'," 14 November 1954, History and Public Policy Program Digital Archive, National Archives Department of Myanmar, Ascension Number 203, Series 12/3, "Letter from Jawaharlal Nehru to U Nu, relating to Note on Visit to China and Indo-China (16.11.54)." Obtained by You Chenxue, accessible at http://digitalarchive.wilsoncenter.org/document/121651.
182. On how the NNRC dealt with the Prisoners of War situation and minutes of all NNRC meetings, see "Papers relating to Prisoners of War from China and Korea." V.K. Krishna Menon Papers, 1st and 2nd Instalment, File No. 909, 1953–1955, *NMML*.
183. "'Marked Turn for the Better,' Press Conference at London, 8 June 1953," *SWJN*, 2nd ser., vol. 22, 448–450.
184. Jawaharlal Nehru, *India's Foreign Policy: Selected Speeches, September 1946-April 1961* (New Delhi: Publications Division, Ministry of Information and Broadcasting, Government of India, 1961), 79–80.
185. "Letter of 4 November 1959," in G. Parthasarathi ed. *Jawaharlal Nehru, Letters to Chief Ministers 1947-1964 vol. 3*, 329–330.
186. "India's Korean Policy," *SWJN*, 2nd ser., vol. 15, Part 1, 337.
187. Krishna Menon Speech, 492nd Plenary Meeting Wednesday, 6 October 1954, at 3 p.m. New York.
188. Vijaya Lakshmi Pandit, "India's Foreign Policy, *Foreign Affairs* 34, 3 (1956): 435.
189. V.K. Krishna Menon, Statement at the U.N.G.A., 8th Plenary Meeting, 28 September 1953, New York, accessed 15 September 2014, https://www.pminewyork.org/adminpart/uploadpdf/73877lms8.pdf.

190. "'Promotion of Mutual Understanding' (Address to the National Press Club, Washington D.C. 14 October 1949. From The Hindustan Times, 15 October and The Hindu and the National Herald, 16 October 1949," *The Selected Works of Jawaharlal Nehru (SWJN)*, 2nd ser., vol. 13, ed. Sarvepalli Gopal, (New Delhi: Jawaharlal Nehru Memorial Fund), 305–307.
191. "Message to Chou-En Lai," 23 January 1951, *SWJN*, 2nd ser., vol. 15, Part 2, 491–493.
192. "India's Korean Policy", 3 August 1950, *SWJN*, 2nd ser., vol. 15, Part 1, 345.
193. "Efforts to Localize Conflict," 12 February 1953, *SWJN*, 2nd ser., vol. 21, 457n2.
194. Nehru quoted in Angadipuram Appadorai, *National Interest and India's Foreign Policy*, (New Delhi: Kalinga Publications, 1992), 51, 153.
195. "Cable to BN Rau," 12 December 1950, *SWJN*, 2nd ser., vol. 15, Part 2, 453.
196. "Cable to KM Panikkar," 23 January 1951, in ibid., 493.
197. A. Appadorai, *National Interest and India's Foreign Policy*, Kalinga Publications, Delhi, 1992, 12.
198. Ibid., 12.
199. "Political Report for the Month Ending November 15, 1951 from Embassy of India, Washington D.C.," Ministry of External Affairs File No F-34-4/51/AMS, *NAI*.
200. Cable to Vijaya Lakshmi Pandit," 25 November 1952, *SWJN*, 2nd ser., vol. 20, 429–431.
201. "The Ambassador in the Soviet Union (Bohlen) to the Department of State, Moscow, January 9, 1954," *FRUS*, 1952–1954, Volume XV, Part 2, Korea (in two parts), ed. Keefer, Document 843. (Emphasis mine).
202. Chester Bowles, "New India," *Foreign Affairs* 31, 1 (1952): 79–94, 80.
203. See Gundevia, *Outside the Archives*, 93, 344–345.
204. Nehru quoting Dulles's statement of 17 October 1958 in "Letter of 4 November 1959," ed. G. Parthasarathi *Jawaharlal Nehru, Letters to Chief*

Ministers 1947-1964 vol. 5, (Delhi: Oxford University Press, 1990), 329–330.

205. For correspondence between New Delhi and Peking and Chinese reactions to UN resolutions, statements by and correspondence with Zhou Enlai, see "Papers relating to peaceful settlement of Korean question at the UN." V.K. Krishna Menon Papers, 1st and 2nd Instalment, File No. 857, 1952–1954, *NMML*; "Papers relating to resolutions on peace plans for Korea." V.K. Krishna Menon Papers, 1st and 2nd Instalment, File No. 859, 1953, *NMML*. For conversations between Nehru and Zhou Enlai, see "Papers relating to Korea issue in the UN." V.K. Krishna Menon Papers, 1st and 2nd Instalment, File No. 858, 1952–1955, *NMML*. For Zhou Enlai's negotiations with Indian Ambassador to China N. Raghavan, see "Papers relating to Korean question." V.K. Krishna Menon Papers, 1st and 2nd Instalment, File No. 860, 1953–1954, *NMML*.
206. Quoted in Appadorai, *National Interest*, 49–50.
207. See Gundevia, *Outside the Archives*, 93, 344–345.
208. "From Singh and Kondapi to KPS Menon," Ministry of External Affairs File No. D11/86-CJK/50, 1950, *NAI*.
209. "From Anup Singh to KPS Menon," Ministry of External Affairs File No. D12/05-CJK/50, 1950, *NAI*.
210. "Political Report for the month ending October 15, 1951 from Embassy of India, Washington D.C.," Ministry of External Affairs File No. F-34-4/51/AMS, 1951, *NAI*.
211. Benegal N. Rau, Statement at the U.N.G.A, 5th Session, 286th Plenary Meeting, 27 September 1950, Flushing Meadow, New York, 9, accessed 15 September 2014, https://www.pminewyork.org/adminpart/uploadpdf/94699lms05a.pdf.
212. "Germ Warfare in Korea," 27 November 1952, *SWJN*, 2nd ser., vol. 19, 439–440, In response to a question in Parliament regarding possible germ warfare in Korea and the need to send Indian scientists to ascertain the facts, Nehru replied saying, "No Sir. This is a foreign

country and the Government of India does not function in territories outside India."

213. "'Marked Turn for the Better,' Press Conference at London, 8 June 1953," *SWJN*, 2nd ser., vol. 22, 448–450.
214. India continued being involved in various ways, including attending the Geneva Conference of 1954. For records of India's participation at the conference on the Korean question, see "Papers relating to Geneva Conference on Korea." V.K. Krishna Menon Papers, 1st and 2nd Instalment, File No. 861, 1953–1954, *NMML*.
215. See "Statement of Mr. KPS Menon, Chairman of the United Nations Temporary Commission on Korea, as the Interim Committee, On 19 February 1948," Ministry of External Affairs File No. D8714-CJK/50, 1950, *NAI*.

4. The Fog of War

1. Even the Americans noted this affinity; see Chester Bowles, *Ambassador's Report* (New York: Harper & Brothers, 1954), 106.
2. Nehru quoted in Subimal Dutt, *With Nehru in the Foreign Office* (Columbia: South Asia Books, 1977), 188.
3. Ramachandra Guha, introduction to *Nationalism*, by Rabindranath Tagore (New Delhi: Penguin, 2009), xliii.
4. Abdul G. Noorani, "Nehru and The Cold Wars", *Frontline*, 14–27 February 2004.
5. See Paul F. Power, "Indian Foreign Policy: The Age of Nehru", *The Review of Politics* 26, 2 (1964): 268–269.
6. On the shift in Nehru's policy on Hungary, see "Reaffirmation of Neutralism", *The Economic Weekly* IX, 26–27–28 (1957): 787–788.
7. Gopal is in contrast with Gundevia who more accurately refers to the Korean War as the first international test. See Sarvepalli Gopal, *Imperialists, Nationalists, Democrats: The Collected Essays*, ed. Srinath Raghavan (Hyderabad: Orient Blackswan, 2013) 228; Y.D. Gundevia, *Outside the Archives* (Hyderabad: Sangam Books, 1987), 445.

8. Tony Judt, *Postwar: A History of Europe Since 1945* (New York: Penguin, 2006), 294–295. Krishna Menon also makes a similar assessment, see Michael Brecher, *India and World Politics: Krishna Menon's View of the World* (Toronto: Oxford University Press, 1968), 62.
9. Macmillan's phrase in his diary entry of 27 July 1956, see Harold Macmillan, *Riding the Storm, 1956-59* (London: Macmillan, 1971), 101.
10. Guy Mollet denounced Nasser as a "would-be dictator" and "imitator of Adolf Hitler", saying Nasser's pamphlet "The Philosophy of Revolution" should have been entitled "Mein Kampf". See "Cabinet Meeting on the Suez Crisis", 4 August 1956, in *Selected Works of Jawaharlal Nehru (SWJN),* 2nd ser., vol. 34, eds., H.Y. Sharada Prasad, A.K. Damodaran, Mushirul Hasan, (New Delhi: Jawaharlal Nehru Memorial Fund), 332nn2–3.
11. Judt, *Postwar: A History of Europe Since 1945*, 294–295.
12. Jawaharlal Nehru, quoted in Nicolas Blarel, *The Evolution of India's Israel Policy: Continuity, Change, and Compromise Since 1922*, (New Delhi: Oxford University Press India, 2014), 472.
13. Jawaharlal Nehru, "Addressing a Press Conference in Cairo on 16 February", in *SWJN*, 2nd ser., vol. 28, eds., Sarvepalli Gopal, Ravinder Kumar, H.Y. Sharada Prasad (New Delhi: Jawaharlal Nehru Memorial Fund), 216n4.
14. Mohammed M. Rahman, *The Politics of Non-Alignment* (New Delhi: Associated Publishing House, 1969), 128.
15. "Visit of the PM to Cairo on his Way Back to India from the European Tour - Joint Statement Issued on the Occasion by the PMs of India and Egypt", Ministry of External Affairs File No. F 4(75)-AWT/55, *National Archives of India (NAI)*, New Delhi, India.
16. Brecher, *India and World Politics*, 63.
17. The treaty was signed by Mahmoud Fawzi on the Egyptian side and the new Indian Ambassador Nawab Ali Yavar Jung Bahadur. For the full text of the treaty, see Ministry of External Affairs, Government of India, *Treaty of Friendship Between the Union of India and the Republic*

of Egypt, 1955, Commonwealth Legal Information Institute, Ministry of External Affairs, India Databases, 1955.

18. "Conversation with Gamal Abdel Nasser", 14 April 1955, *SWJN*, 2nd ser., vol. 28, eds., Sarvepalli Gopal, Ravinder Kumar, H.Y. Sharada Prasad, (New Delhi: Jawaharlal Nehru Memorial Fund), 216–217n3.
19. Ibid.
20. "Conversation with Gamal Abdel Nasser", 2 May 1955, *SWJN*, 2nd ser., vol. 28, eds., Sarvepalli Gopal, Ravinder Kumar, H.Y. Sharada Prasad, (New Delhi: Jawaharlal Nehru Memorial Fund), 219–222.
21. Ibid., n2.
22. See, for instance, ""Letter of 7 January 1952", in G. Parthasarathi, ed. *Jawaharlal Nehru, Letters to Chief Ministers 1947-1964 vol. 2*, (Delhi: Oxford University Press, 1986), 540.
23. Apa Pant was India's first Commissioner to East and Central Africa and served there from 1948 to 1955. See Apa Pant, *A Moment in Time* (India: Orient Longman, 1974); and Apa Pant, *Undiplomatic Incidents* (Bombay: Orient Longman Limited, 1987).
24. For a detailed description of the historical context of the new political momentum in Egypt, see "General Note on Certain Problems of Africa", Ministry of External Affairs File No. F-39/9/55-AFR II, *National Archives of India (NAI)*, New Delhi, India.
25. "Anti-India Propaganda in West Asia," May 1955, in *SWJN*, 2nd ser., vol. 28, eds., Sarvepalli Gopal, Ravinder Kumar, H.Y. Sharada Prasad, (New Delhi: Jawaharlal Nehru Memorial Fund), 228.
26. For the consequences of the Suez Canal Crisis on India-Israel relations, see Blarel, *Evolution of India's Israel Policy,* 472.
27. "Cable to Ali Yavar Jung" in *SWJN*, 2nd ser., vol. 28, eds., Sarvepalli Gopal, Ravinder Kumar, H.Y. Sharada Prasad, (New Delhi: Jawaharlal Nehru Memorial Fund), 229.
28. "Nehru's Note," Nehru Papers, 19 December 1954, *NMML*, quoted in Gopal, *Imperialists, Nationalists, Democrats*, 228.
29. Rahman also makes the assessment that the move from neutralism to

non-alignment took place during Nasser's time and that he was able to identify Arab nationalism with Arab non-alignment, a possibility that Nehru grasped quite quickly. See Rahman, *Politics of Non-Alignment*, 123–124.

30. For a fascinating account of this meeting, see Nataša Mišković, "Between Idealism and Pragmatism. Tito, Nehru and the Hungarian Crisis 1956," in *The Non-Aligned Movement and the Cold War. Delhi – Bandung – Belgrade*, eds., Nataša Mišković, Harald Fischer-Tine and Nada Bodškovska (Oxon/New York: Routledge, 2014), 250.
31. Judt, *Postwar*, 295.
32. Egypt also withdrew recognition from Nationalist China; Al Gumhouria explicitly said that in undertaking this action, "Gamal Abdul Nasser put Eden's noose around Eden's own neck". See Rahman, *Politics of Non-Alignment*, 127.
33. Jung had this information from the Soviet Ambassador Kiselev; see "Cable to Ali Yavar Jung", 27 July 1956, *SWJN*, 2nd ser., vol. 34, 319–320n2,5.
34. "Background Note for Indian Missions", 31 July 1956, *SWJN*, 2nd ser., vol. 34, 324.
35. Mohammad H. Haykal, *The Cairo Document: The Inside Story of Nasser and His Relationship with World Leaders, Rebels, and Statesmen* (New York: Doubleday, 1973), 67–68, 280. Also quoted in Sarvepalli Gopal, *Jawaharlal Nehru: A Biography*, vol. 3 (New Delhi: Oxford University Press, 2012), 298.
36. "Cable to Ali Yavar Jung", 26 July 1956, *SWJN*, 2nd ser., vol. 34, 319–320.
37. "Nehru's Note," Nehru Papers, 9 September 1958, *Nehru Memorial Museum and Library*, New Delhi, India, 228–229n3.
38. Nasser's Statement of 24 July 1956 quoted in "Cable to Ali Yavar Jung", 26 July 1956, *SWJN, 2nd ser.*, vol. 34, 319–320n4.
39. "Background Note for Indian Missions", 31 July 1956, *SWJN*, 2nd ser., vol. 34, 324.

40. For Jung's correspondence to Delhi, see "Papers and top secret telegrams exchanged with Ali Yavar Jung relating to Suez crisis." V.K. Krishna Menon Papers, 1st and 2nd Instalment, File No. 952, 1956–1957, *NMML*.
41. Ibid., 331.
42. "Message to Gamal Abdel Nasser," 2 August 1956, *SWJN*, 2nd ser., vol. 34, 327–328.
43. Dutt, *With Nehru in the Foreign Office*, 159.
44. Nehru was right to have these fears, as later it came to light that Eden was confused and thought Nehru had supported Nasser's actions. See Iverach McDonald, *A Man of the Times* (London: Hamish Hamilton, 1976), 144, n10.
45. "Cable to Vijaya Lakshmi Pandit", 28 July 1956, in *SWJN*, 2nd ser., vol. 34, 321.
46. Nehru repeats the message to SWRD Bandarnaike and also to Tito sent the same day, see *SWJN*, 2nd ser., vol. 34, 322–323.
47. Ibid., 323n2.
48. "Message to Josip Broz Tito", 5 August 1956, in *SWJN*, 2nd ser., vol. 34, 340n2. Rajeshwar Dayal, who was the Indian Ambassador in Belgrade, had reported that the press had uncritically backed Egypt.
49. "Cable to Ali Yavar Jung, 27 July 1956" in *SWJN*, 2nd ser., vol. 34, 329.
50. "Statement in Parliament", 8 August 1956, *SWJN*, 2nd ser., vol. 34, 348–354, n4.
51. Nasser had also told Nehru that he would honour "all international obligations and both the Convention of 1888 and the assurance given in the Anglo-Egyptian Agreement of 1954." "Cable to Vijaya Lakshmi Pandit," 2 August 1956, in *SWJN*, 2nd ser., vol. 34, 325–326.
52. Sarvepalli Gopal, *Jawaharlal Nehru: A Biography*, vol. 2, (New Delhi: Oxford University Press, 2012), 278.
53. "Cable to Vijaya Lakshmi Pandit," 27 July 1956, *SWJN*, 2nd ser., vol. 34, 318–319n5.
54. "Cabinet Meeting on the Suez Crisis", 4 August 1956, in *SWJN*, 2nd ser., vol. 34, 332n2–3.

55. India had Soviet-style five-year plans; Ibid.
56. All through the crisis, India maintained that Egypt was competent to nationalize the Suez Canal but should have done so in "the normal way of international expropriation." See Lok Sabha Statement, 31 July 1956, in Dutt, *With Nehru in the Foreign Office*, 160. See a copy of Menon's statement at the Conference in U.S. Department of State, FRUS, 1955–1957, Suez Crisis, 26 July–31 December 1956, vol. 16 (Washington: G.P.O., 1956), 159–178.
57. "Message to Gamal Abdel Nasser," in *SWJN*, 2nd ser., vol. 34, 336–337nn3–4.
58. "Vijaya Lakshmi Pandit to Nehru," Nehru Papers, 1 August 1956, *NMML*.
59. "Nehru to Vijaya Lakshmi Pandit", Nehru Papers, 2 August 1956, *NMML*.
60. On India's role at the London Conference, statistical material and background notes, see "Papers Relating to Suez Canal Issue", V.K. Krishna Menon Papers, 1st and 2nd Instalment, File No. 946, 1956, *NMML*; "Papers pertaining to the Suez Canal Conference held in London 16-23 August 1956", V.K. Krishna Menon Papers, 1st and 2nd Instalment, File No. 947, 1956, *NMML*; "Papers Relating to Suez Canal Issue", V.K. Krishna Menon Papers, 1st and 2nd Instalment, File No. 948, 1956, *NMML*.
61. Eisenhower, deeply annoyed is quoted as saying "nothing justifies double-crossing us". See Odd A. Westad, *The Global Cold War: Third World Interventions and the Making of Our Times* (Cambridge: Cambridge University Press, 2007), 125–126n26.
62. For correspondence on participation of Yugoslavia, see "Message to Josip Broz Tito, 5 August 1956," in *SWJN-SS*, vol. 34, 340n3 in which Rajeshwar Dayal conveys the laments of Koca Popovic, the Yugoslav Secretary for Foreign Affairs saying that the conference was "designed to ensure majority decision for Anglo-French position". For correspondence on exclusion of Indonesia, see "Nehru to Ali

Sastroamidjojo, 6 August 1956," in *SWJN-SS*, vol. 34, 341, where Nehru says "in any event there can be no settlement without Egypt."

63. "Message to Nasser," Nehru Papers, 2 August 1956, *NMML*.
64. "Message to Gamal Abdel Nasser," 5 August 1956, *SWJN*, 2nd ser., vol. 34, 337–338.
65. Haykal, *The Cairo Documents*, 282.
66. "Message to Gamal Abdel Nasser," 5 August 1956, *SWJN*, 2nd ser., vol. 34, 337–338.
67. "Cable to Ali Yavar Jung" in *SWJN*, 2nd ser., vol. 34, 354–355.
68. Ibid.
69. Gundevia, *Outside the Archives*, 175–176.
70. "Cable to Ali Yavar Jung," 7 August 1956, *SWJN*, 2nd ser., vol. 34, 342–343n3.
71. "Message to Anthony Eden," 4 August 1956, *SWJN*, 2nd ser., vol. 34, 335–336; "Message to Anthony Eden," 5 August 1956, *SWJN-SS*, vol. 34, 339.
72. "Nehru to Nasser, 5 August 1956, MEA Files" quoted in Gopal, *Imperialists, Nationalists, Democrats*, 234.
73. "Message to Anthony Eden," 5 August 1956, *SWJN-SS*, vol. 34, 339.
74. "Statement in Parliament," 8 August 1956, *SWJN*, 2nd ser., vol. 34, 351n5.
75. "Cable to Ali Yavar Jung," 7 August 1956, *SWJN*, 2nd ser., vol. 34, 342–343n4; Eden had also assured Nehru that participation in the London Conference would not imply acceptance of British demand for an international authority, see "Eden to Nehru - 7 August 1956, MEA Files," quoted in Gopal, Imperialists, Nationalists, Democrats, 234.
76. "Cable to Ali Yavar Jung," 7 August 1956, *SWJN*, 2nd ser., vol. 34, 342–343n4.
77. "Message to U Ba Swe," 7 August 1956, *SWJN*, 2nd ser., vol. 34, 346–347.
78. "Memorandum of a Conversation Between the President and the Secretary of State, White House, Washington, August 8, 1956, 11:30

a.m.1 (#fn1) Washington, August 8, 1956, 11:30 a.m," *FRUS*, 1955–1957, Volume XVI, Suez Crisis, ed., Noring, Document 71.

79. "Cable to RK Nehru," 7 August 1956, *SWJN*, 2nd ser., vol. 34, 348n1. R.K. Nehru had met Zhou Enlai to explain the Indian position on 4 August 1956.
80. From a copy of the Soviet draft reply to the invitation of the London Conference, KPS Menon reported to Nehru that this was a "spirited defence of Egypt's action and vehement denunciation of reaction of Western Powers." See "Message to Dimitri Shepilov," 7 August 1956, *SWJN*, 2nd ser., vol. 34, 345n3.
81. Nehru's note to Vijaya Lakshmi Pandit, quoted in Dutt, *With Nehru in the Foreign Office*, 163.
82. "Statement in Parliament," 8 August 1956, *SWJN*, 2nd ser., vol. 34, 348–354.
83. Ibid.
84. "To Vijaya Lakshmi Pandit," 11 August 1956, *SWJN*, 2nd ser., vol. 34, 365.
85. "Message to Anthony Eden," in *SWJN*, 2nd ser., vol. 34, 363.
86. "Cable to GL Mehta," 10 August 1956, *SWJN*, 2nd ser., vol. 34, 360nn4–7.
87. For details of what these preparations were, see Dutt, *With Nehru in the Foreign Office*, 160–161.
88. Nasser's radio broadcast of 12 August 1956, quoted in "Cable to Ali Yavar Jung," 12 August 1956, *SWJN*, 2nd ser., vol. 34, 367n3.
89. Ibid.
90. Reid, *Envoy to Nehru*, 165.
91. "The Suez Crisis and India's Commonwealth Connection", 9 August 1956, *SWJN*, 2nd ser., vol. 34, 358. Sarvepalli Gopal says "Nehru was not only among the first creators of the new Commonwealth, he was also in its first major crisis, its savior," see Gopal, *Jawaharlal Nehru*, 304. Yet, it is also significant to note that withdrawing from the Commonwealth would have also placed an additional financial strain on India's already

imperiled economy in light of the crisis, see Rahman, *Politics of Non-Alignment*, 145.

92. In this, no doubt, he was encouraged by the correspondence he received from other sections of the British public, who expressed varying degrees of regret at Eden's policies. See, for instance, Gopal, "Philip Noel-Baker to Nehru," *Jawaharlal Nehru*, vol. 2, 285–286.
93. Gopal, "Nehru to Rajagopalachari," *Jawaharlal Nehru*, vol. 2, 280n43.
94. "Letter of 12 August 1956," in G. Parthasarathi, ed. *Jawaharlal Nehru, Letters to Chief Ministers 1947-1964 vol. 4*, (Delhi: Oxford University Press, 1990), 395.
95. Dutt, *With Nehru in the Foreign Office*, 163–164.
96. "Letter of 16 August 1956," in G. Parthasarathi, ed. *Jawaharlal Nehru, Letters to Chief Ministers 1947-1964 vol. 4*, 418–419.
97. Krishna Menon's telegram to Nehru, MEA Files 15 August 1956, quoted in Gopal, *Imperialists, Nationalists, Democrats*, 235.
98. Ibid.
99. "Cable to G L Mehta," 10 August 1956, *SWJN*, 2nd ser., vol. 34, 360nn1–7.
100. For Indian correspondence and background notes, see "Papers pertaining to the Suez Canal Conference held in London 16-23 August 1956." V.K. Krishna Menon Papers, 1st and 2nd Instalment, File No. 947, 1956, *NMML.*
101. "Cable to V K Krishna Menon," 21 August 1956, *SWJN*, 2nd ser., vol. 34, 370n2.
102. "Cable to V K Krishna Menon," 27 August 1956, *SWJN*, 2nd ser., vol. 34, 375n3.
103. Ibid., n5.
104. Ibid.
105. "Nehru to Menon, 21 August 1956, MEA Files," quoted in Gopal, *Imperialists, Nationalists, Democrats*, 235–236.
106. "Nehru to Menon, 22/23 August 1956 MEA Files," quoted in ibid., 236.

107. Ibid., 236.
108. Rahman thinks this was Menon's call, see Rahman, *Politics of Non-Alignment*, 138. But it was actually Nehru who didn't want to appear to be undercutting any efforts not led by India, "Cable to V K Krishna Menon," in *SWJN-SS,* vol. 34, 375n5.
109. Tito agreed with this stand and thought Egypt was in a difficult position, according to reports from Rajeshwar Dayal, the Ambassador in Belgrade; see Gopal, *Imperialists, Nationalists, Democrats*, 236.
110. Nasser had repeatedly sent messages through Ali Yavar Jung to say that Eden must be convinced to take a flexible position before he committed himself in Parliament; see ibid., 235–236.
111. "Message to Gamal Abdel Nasser," 13 September 1956, *SWJN*, 2nd ser., vol. 35, eds., H.Y. Sharada Prasad, A.K. Damodaran, Mushirul Hasan, (New Delhi: Jawaharlal Nehru Memorial Fund), 399.
112. Rahman, *Politics of Non-Alignment*, 139. See also "Papers relating to Suez Crisis. Includes statement by Prime Minister in Lok Sabha on 13 September 1956 on Suez issuc, etc." V.K. Krishna Menon Papers, 1st and 2nd Instalment, File No. 950, 1956–1957, *NMML*.
113. Nehru, "Nehru to Foreign Secretary," Nehru Papers, 17 September 1956, *NMML*.
114. "Cable to V K Krishna Menon," 17 September 1956, *SWJN*, 2nd ser., vol. 35, 413.
115. Gopal, *Jawaharlal Nehru*, 302; "Message to John Foster Dulles, 14 September 1956," *SWJN-SS*, vol. 35, 405n16.
116. Krishna Menon believed that it was difficult therefore to convince Nehru of the urgency of the matter. See Brecher, *India & World Politics*, 65–66.
117. Gopal, *Imperialists, Nationalists, Democrats*, 228–229.
118. "Cable to Ali Yavar Jung," 7 September 1956, *SWJN*, 2nd ser., vol. 35, 392.
119. Nasser had proposed a memorandum while rejecting the Dulles Plan. "Cable to Ali Yavar Jung," 12 August 1956, *SWJN*, 2nd ser., vol. 34, 367.

120. "Message to Dwight D Eisenhower," 11 September 1956, in *SWJN*, 2nd ser., vol. 35, 396n3.
121. "Message to Selwyn Lloyd," 14 September 1956, *SWJN*, 2nd ser., vol. 35, 403–405.
122. Gopal, *Imperialists, Nationalists, Democrats*, 241–242.
123. "Records of conversations of Lloyd and of Eden (telephone) with Menon, 28 September 1956, PREM 11/1102 PRO," in ibid., 242.
124. "Menon's telegram to Nehru from London, 29 September 1956, MEA Files," quoted in ibid., 242–243.
125. "Nehru's note on interview with British High Commissioner, 1 October 1956," quoted in ibid., 242–243.
126. "Nehru to Eden, 4 October 1956, MEA," quoted in ibid., 242–243.
127. The Americans thought they should talk directly with the Egyptians but were glad to have Indian efforts pitched in. See, "Letter From the Acting Secretary of State to the President1 (#fn1) Washington, October 10, 1956, " *FRUS*, 1955–1957, Volume XVI, Suez Crisis, ed. Noring, Document 323.
128. "Papers relating to Suez Canal and situation in Egypt. Includes note on the Egyptian situation arising out of the Anglo-French and Israeli attack by Arthur Lall, etc." V.K. Krishna Menon Papers, 1st and 2nd Instalment, File No. 949, 1956–1957, *NMML*.
129. "Message to Dwight D. Eisenhower," 31 October 1956, *SWJN*, 2nd ser., vol. 35, 421n3. Also see Dutt, *With Nehru in the Foreign Office*, 163.
130. "Message to Gamal Abdel Nasser," 31 October 1956, *SWJN*, 2nd ser., vol. 35, 424.
131. Ibid.
132. "Message to Josip Broz Tito," 31 October 1956, *SWJN*, 2nd ser., vol. 35, 426.
133. "Message to Dag Hammarskjold," 31 October 1956, *SWJN*, 2nd ser., vol. 35, 425.
134. "Message to John Foster Dulles," 31 October 1956, *SWJN*, 2nd ser., vol. 35, 423. For Nehru's statement on behalf of the GOI, see Escott Reid,

Hungary and Suez 1956: A View from Delhi (Oakville: Mosaic Press, 1986), 39.

135. *Interview with Arthur Lall*, United Nations Oral History Project, 27 June 1990, accessed 17 July 2014, http://www.unmultimedia.org/oralhistory/2011/10/lall-arthur-samuel/.
136. National Security Council, *A Documentary on Egypt-Israel Disturbances*, Central Intelligence Agency, ARC646996/LI 263 398, –1957, *National Archives and Records Administration (NARA)*, United States of America.
137. Eden should have tried "to save something from the wreck, by going for the Indian compromise proposals or something like them." William Hayter, "Eden on Suez: The Cost of Force", *The Observer*, London, 28 February 1960, quoted in Reid, *Hungary and Suez 1956*, 24.
138. "Message to Anthony Eden," 1 November 1956, *SWJN*, 2nd ser., vol. 35, 427–428.
139. "British High Commissioner after interview with Nehru, Foreign Officc 371/121785 PRO," quoted in Gopal, *Imperialists, Nationalists, Democrats*, 243.
140. *Interview with Arthur Lall*, United Nations Oral History Project, 27 June 1990. Lall speaks at length about India-Egyptian cooperation on the resolution of the crisis saying Senior Advisor and Cabinet Minister Ali Sabry was "in our meeting room every morning at 8 o'clock"; Lall also says that this idea of taking the issue to the UNGA under the United For Peace Resolution was his and Josua Brilej's (Yugoslavian Representative).
141. The US had urgently undertaken the task of proposing a moderate formula as they thought that most of the nations in Asia and Africa had a dim view of Britain, France or Israel and so a Soviet proposal for severe and immediate punishment would take root unless an alternative plan was made available. See, "Memorandum by the President1 (#fn1) Washington, November 1, 1956," *FRUS*, 1955–1957, Volume XVI, Suez Crisis, ed. Noring, Document 461.

142. "Memorandum of a Conference With the President, White House, Washington, November 2, 1956, 2:32–3:25 p.m.1 (#fn1) Washington, November 2, 1956, 2:32–3:25 p.m.," *FRUS*, 1955–1957, Volume XVI, Suez Crisis, ed. Noring, Document 470.
143. "Memorandum From the Under Secretary of State (Hoover) to the Secretary of State1 (#fn1) Washington, November 2, 1956," *FRUS*, 1955–1957, Volume XVI, Suez Crisis, ed. Noring, Document 469.
144. Lall had earlier suggested that there was no need to create a new organization but that they should use the UN Truce Supervision Organization; Scc, *Interview with Arthur Lall*, 1990.
145. "GL Mehta to S Dutt – About meeting with German Amb Heinz I Krekeler," Ministry of External Affairs File No. X-4564/AMS-56, *National Archives of India (NAI)*, New Delhi, India.
146. "Message to N A Bulganin," 6 November 1956, *SWJN*, 2nd ser., vol. 35, 436–437n2.
147. Ibid.
148. For the President's views on the matter, see Dwight D. Eisenhower, *The White House Years: Mandate for Change 1953-56* (Garden City: Doubleday, 1963), 83.
149. Eisenhower To Nehru, Messages of 5 and 6 November 1956," *SWJN*, 2nd ser., vol. 35, 439–440; "Nehru to Eisenhower, 7 November 1956," ibid.
150. Message to Dwight D. Eisenhower," 7 November 1956, *SWJN*, 2nd ser., vol. 35, 439–440.
151. "Telegram from Indian CDA Rajwade to FS, 6 November 1956," quoted in Gopal, *Jawaharlal Nehru*, vol. 2, 287.
152. Lall also says that the Egyptians were very keen on the force having a low profile and not coming across as an occupation force; says the Indians were the largest contributors by far. See *Interview with Arthur Lall*, 1990.
153. "Lester Pearson, The International Years, 1973," quoted *SWJN*, 2nd ser., vol. 35, 445n3.

154. Gopal, *Jawaharlal Nehru*, 303. Also Gopal, *Jawaharlal Nehru*, vol. 2, 286–287.
155. "Nehru to Krishna Menon, 6 November 1956," *SWJN*, 2nd ser., vol. 35, 438.
156. "Message to Gamal Abdel Nasser," 8 November 1956, *SWJN*, 2nd ser., vol. 35, 441n2.
157. Ibid., n2.
158. S. Gopal, *Imperialists, Nationalists, Democrats*, 245; S. Gopal, *Nehru*, vol. 2, 288.
159. "Indian Contingent for Egypt," 15 November 1956, *SWJN*, 2nd ser., vol. 35, 444. A minor controversy erupted at this time when Md Fawzi insisted that Indian troops would not be welcome in Egypt because "no close friends or foes" would form part of the UNEF but was overruled by Nasser who said the Egyptian public should not think of Indian forces as an occupying force; "Indian Amb telegram from Cairo 12 November 1956," quoted in Gopal, *Imperialists, Nationalists, Democrats*, 245.
160. Rahman, *Politics of Non-Alignment*, 159.
161. UN Doc, A/PV.594, "594th Plenary Meeting", General Assembly, Eleventh Session, 24 November 1956, 305.
162. See Indar J. Rikhye, *The Sinai Blunder* (London/Totowa: Frank Cass & Co., 1980).
163. Pearson's correspondence with Nehru, quoted in Gopal, *Imperialists, Nationalists, Democrats*, 246–247.
164. For Krishna Menon's advice to the Canadians, see Reid, *Envoy to Nehru*, 185.
165. See "Top secret telegrams exchanged with Nehru, Ali Yavar Jung, others, relating to Suez crisis and role of India in resolving the crisis. Includes Nehru's personal message to Gamal Abdel Nasser requesting him to refrain from taking steps to compel a large number of foreign nationals to leave Egypt in penurious circumstances, etc.", V.K. Krishna Menon Papers, 1st and 2nd Instalment, File No. 951, 1956–1957, *NMML*.

166. "Cable to Ali Yavar Jung," 26 December 1956, in *SWJN*, 2nd ser., vol. 36, eds., Sarvepalli Gopal, Ravinder Kumar, H.Y. Sharada Prasad, A.K. Damodaran, Mushirul Hasan, Mridula Mukherjee and Aditya Mukherjee (New Delhi: Jawaharlal Nehru Memorial Fund), 551–552.
167. Jawaharlal Nehru, "Nehru to Tito," Nehru Papers, 2 December 1956, *NMML*, quoted in Gopal, *Imperialists, Nationalists, Democrats*, 247.
168. "Letter of 8 December 1956," in G. Parthasarathi, ed. *Jawaharlal Nehru, Letters to Chief Ministers 1947-1964 vol. 4*, 463.
169. "Nehru to Padmaja Naidu, 10 March 1956," quoted in Gopal, *Jawaharlal Nehru*, vol. 2, 274, n9.
170. Gopal, *Jawaharlal Nehru*, vol. 2, 276n15.
171. Fortnightly report from the Consul-General New York for the Period Ending 15 October 1951," Ministry of External Affairs File No E 34-4/51/AMS, 30 October 1951, *NAI*.
172. "Summary of the political report for the month ending 15 November 1951 from the Embassy of India, Washington," Ministry of External Affairs File No E 34-4/51/AMS, 30 November 1951, *NAI*.
173. "Memorandum of a Conversation Between Secretary of State Dulles and Prime Minister Nehru, Blair House1 (#fn1) Washington, December 16, 1956," *FRUS*, 1955–1957, Volume VIII, South Asia, eds. Robert J. MacMahon and Stanley Shaloff (Washington: Government Printing Office, 1987), Document 163.
174. Brecher, *India and World Politics*, 71.
175. See, for instance, Andreas Hilger, "The Soviet Union and India: The Years of Late Stalinism," in *Indo-Soviet Relations during the Cold War: New Russian and German Evidence* ed. Andreas Hilger et al. (Zurich: Parallel History Project on Cooperative Security, 2009), and for a contemporary perspective from the Indian side, see K.P.S. Menon, *The Flying Troika: Extracts from a Diary* (London: Oxford University Press, 1963).
176. See, "Record of the meeting between S.A. Dange and Soviet leaders in 1947," in *Indo-Russian Relations: 1929-1947, Part 2 of Indo-Russian*

Relations, 1917-1947: Select Documents from the Archives of the Russian Federation, eds., Purabi Roy, Sobhanlal Datta Gupta and Hari S. Vasudevan (Calcutta: Asiatic Society, 2000), 443.

177. Power, "Indian Foreign Policy", 272.
178. This is not the Bandung Declaration of 1955 but one issued by Nehru, Sukarno and Zhou Enlai. Stalin said, "Not a bad declaration. If they had presented it to us, we would have been glad to sign it." See, Stalin, quoted in "India," *Memoirs of Nikita Khrushchev: Statesman, 1953-1964*, vol. 3, ed., Sergei Khrushchev (University Park: Pennsylvania State University Press, 2007), 725.
179. Westad says that to Khrushchev and Bulganin amongst others "the Boss's Third World policy seemed self-defeating", see Westad, *The Global Cold War*, 67.
180. South Asia became a key spot for American-Soviet competition in the 1950s. See David C. Engerman, "South Asia and the Cold War," in *The Cold War in the Third World*, ed. Robert J. McMahon (New York: Oxford University Press, 2013).
181. P.N. Kaul's assessment "the US was "picking off one weak or compliant Asian State after another and hitching it to its wagon", quoted in Vojtech Mastny, "The Soviet Union's Partnership with India", *Journal of Cold War Studies*, 12 (3): 50–90.
182. Mišković says Nehru saw in Tito "a competent consultant", in Mišković, "Between Idealism and Pragmatism", 250.
183. These responses were noted with satisfaction in an Indian Embassy Report from Moscow. "Reactions in the Soviet Press Over the Bandung Conference", Ministry of External Affairs File No. D 886/AAC-55, 31 May 1955, *NAI*.
184. "Pravda, 14, 26 and 30 April 1955," quoted in Zafar Imam, "Soviet View of Non-Alignment", *International Studies*, 20 (1/2): 445–469. This view had changed in less than a decade. "It is abundantly clear that it (the NAM) can no longer persuade the Soviet Union to give its support or to involve itself merely by highlighting the colonial exploitation of

the past or by complaining constantly on the non-conducive nature of world politics". See "Central Committee Reports to the 22nd, 23rd, 24th Congresses of the CPSU 1961-1971," quoted in ibid., 468.

185. Speech in Dynamo stadium in Moscow on 21 June 1955 quoted in Dutt, *With Nehru in the Foreign Office*, 193.
186. Ibid.,197–198.
187. "Military Blocs Condemned", *Ceylon Daily News*, 16 November 1955.
188. Burmese Prime Minister U Nu got into trouble with other Asian-African leaders for inviting the Soviets to the next Asian-African Conference, see "Second Asian-African Conference: Participation of USSR," Ministry of External Affairs File No. F1(63) AAC/55, *NAI* and Ministry of External Affairs File No. D-2192-AAC/55, *NAI*
189. "Summary record of a talk between Prime Minister of India and Mr NA Bulganin and Mr NS Khrushchev at the Prime Minister's House," Subimal Dutt papers, 12 December 1955, Subject File No. 17, *Nehru Memorial Museum and Library*, New Delhi, India; and "Note by the Prime Minister on the Visit of the Soviet Leaders to India," undated, Subimal Dutt papers, Subject File No. 17, *NMML*.
190. Westad, *The Global Cold War*, 67.
191. Escott Reid, *Envoy to Nehru* (New York: Oxford University Press, 1981), 139.
192. Ibid. 134–136.
193. Ibid., 68.
194. Krishnan Srinivasan, *Diplomatic Channels* (New Delhi: Manohar Publishers, 2012), 69.
195. On the background to the speech and its consequences, see https://history.state.gov/milestones/1953-1960/khrushchev-20th-congress
196. "Letter of 14 October 1956," G. Parthasarathi, ed. *Jawaharlal Nehru, Letters to Chief Ministers 1947-1964 vol. 4,* 457–458.
197. Reid, *Envoy to Nehru*, 147.
198. For a full account, see Csaba Békés, "The 1956 Hungarian Revolution and World Politics." Working Paper No.16, Cold War International

History Project, (Woodrow Wilson International Center for Scholars, 1996).

199. On the tense relationship between Hungary and the Soviet Union, and not just that it was affected by the Polish reforms, see Laszlo Borhi, "Hungary in the Soviet Empire, 1945–1956: New Evidence, New Interpretations", *Hungarian Studies* 20, 1 (2005): 21–30.
200. *The Hungarian Revolution 1956 – Documents*, Volume I, Part I, Ministry of External Affairs Archives, New Delhi India, 1–5. For a report on the situation until 1 November 1956, see 12–26.
201. Reid, *Envoy to Nehru*, 148–149.
202. Krishna Menon had made a speech saying this was like the riots in Ahmedabad. Kamath said the implication of Menon's statement was "more or less that Hungary is a province of the Soviet empire"; see Escott Reid, *Hungary and Suez 1956*, 111.
203. For Soviet anxieties about revolutionary spillover into the Soviet Union, see "Working Notes from the Session of the CPSU CC Presidium on 4 November 1956," 4 November 1956, History and Public Policy Program Digital Archive, TsKhSD, F. 3, Op. 12, D. 1006, Ll. 34-36ob, compiled by V. N. Malin. Published in CWIHP Bulletin 8–9, 398–399, accessible at http://digitalarchive.wilsoncenter.org/document/111887.
204. Dutt, *With Nehru in the Foreign Office*, 175.
205. Ibid.,176.
206. "Telegram from MEA to Indian Embassy in DC, 30 October 56," in Gopal, *Jawaharlal Nehru*, vol. 2, 291n1.
207. Dutt, *With Nehru in the Foreign Office*, 175.
208. Reid, *Envoy to Nehru*, 145.
209. Ibid., 153.
210. Indeed, some of the criticism came from within the MEA, with Dutt and Reid sharing their concerns, see ibid.
211. "Conversation between the President and the Secretary of State, Washington, October 29, 1956," *FRUS*, 1955–1957, Volume XXV, Eastern Europe, eds. Edward C. Keefer, Ronald D. Landa and Stanley

Shaloff (Washington: Government Printing Office, 1990), Document 131.

212. Dutt, *With Nehru in the Foreign Office*, 177. See the UN Secretary General's assessment of the order of things: "If you disregard all other aspects and look at the time sequence, I think it is perfectly clear to you that Suez had a time priority on the thinking and on the policy making of the main body in the UN." Dag Hammarskjold, quoted in Henry P. Van Dusen, *Dag Hammarskjöld: The Statesman and His Faith* (New York: Harper & Row, 1964), 141–142.
213. Vincent Sheean, *Nehru: The Years of Power* (New York: Random House, 1960), 161.
214. In a comprehensively analytical note, Rahman lists the following factors as "instrumental in filling the powder keg": a) Economic deterioration, b) The reign of the Stalinists, c) The rehabilitation, d) Soviet troops, e) Titoism. See "Note from Rahman to the Foreign Secretary, MEA India," *The Hungarian Revolution 1956 – Documents,* Volume I, Part I, Ministry of External Affairs Archives, 12.
215. Ibid.
216. Lazslo Borhi, *Hungary in the Cold War 1945-1956: Between the United States and the Soviet Union* (Budapest: Central European University Press, 2004), 298n181. However, Borhi wrongly lists the Indian Ambassador in Moscow as being "Krishna Menon", rather than K.P.S. Menon.
217. Dutt, *With Nehru in the Foreign Office*, 178.
218. Ibid., 178–179; See Reid, *Hungary and Suez 1956*, 37, on how Nehru termed the Hungarian Revolution a "civil war" in his speech on 28 October, and then again on 9 November.
219. Bekes, "1956 Hungarian Revolution and World Politics". Bekes neglects to mention Indian diplomacy at the UN, even in the section titled "The United Nations and the Third World".
220. For a fascinating insight into how the events of the Suez Canal Crisis affected Soviet thinking on the Hungarian Revolution, see "Imre

Horvath's Notes of Khrushchev's Speech at the 3 November Session," 3 November 1956, History and Public Policy Program Digital Archive, Magyar Orszagos Leveltar, XIX J- 1-K Horvath Imre kulugyminiszter iratai, 55, doboz. Published in CWIHP Bulletin 8–9, 398, accessible at http://digitalarchive.wilsoncenter.org/document/111886. This assessment is also included in Editor's Note 4.

221. Csaba Békés, Malcolm Byrne and M. János Rainer, *The 1956 Hungarian Revolution: A History in Documents*, (Budapest: Central European University Press, 2002), 268.
222. Working Notes from the session of the CPSU CC Presidium on 31 October 1956, History and Public Policy Program Digital Archive, accessed 15 September 2014, http://digitalarchive.wilsoncenter.org/document/117064.pdf?v=634f40572566c230c25ec5951095e1d2.
223. Reid, *Envoy to Nehru*, 153.
224. Reid, *Hungary and Suez 1956*, 41.
225. Reid says N.R. Pillai sent Nehru a memo warning him against applying double standards to the cases of Suez and Hungary. See Reid, *Envoy to Nehru*, 154.
226. Rahman reports "All Hungarian borders sealed by Russian troops and Budapest completely encircled." See "Telegram dated November 3, 1956, through Indembassy, Prague," *The Hungarian Revolution 1956 – Documents*, Volume I, Part I, Ministry of External Affairs Archives, 29–30.
227. Record of Conversation Between Zhou En Lai and Agoston Szkladan, 2 November 1956, History and Public Policy Programme Digital Archive, PRC FMA, 109-01038-02, accessed 15 September 2014, http://digitalarchive.wilsoncenter.org/document/117695.
228. "Cable to KPS Menon," 4 November 1956, *SWJN*, 2nd ser., vol. 35, 455.
229. Ibid.
230. Second Emergency Special Session of the UNGA - 1004-E.S.(II) ; also see ibid., n3.3. For a detailed view of India at the session, see "Papers relating to the UNGA emergency special sessions on the situation in

Hungary. Includes speeches, draft resolutions and adopted resolutions on the situation in Hungary at the UN." V.K. Krishna Menon Papers, 1st and 2nd Instalment, File No. 953, November 1956–December 1957, *NMML*.

231. "A cynical and shameful betrayal of the moral unity of the Commonwealth and indeed of all free nations". James Eayrs, quoted in Escott Reid, *Envoy to Nehru*, 162–163.
232. Dutt, *With Nehru in the Foreign Office*, 179–180. However, Krishna Menon's statement at the UNGA clearly states that India "abstained because we agreed with some parts of it but did not agree with others", see "Statement by Krishna Menon at the UNGA on November 8, 1956," *The Hungarian Revolution 1956 – Documents*, Volume I, Part II, Ministry of External Affairs Archives, New Delhi, India, 141–145.
233. "Cable to GL Mehta," 5 November 1956, *SWJN*, 2nd ser., vol. 35, 456.
234. "Cable to Mohan Sinha Mehta," 5 November 1956, *SWJN*, 2nd ser., vol. 35, 457.
235. Stenographic record of 4 November 1956 meeting of Party activists, 4 November 1956, History and Public Policy Program Digital Archive, APRF, Fond 52, Opis 1, Delo 261, List 74–110, Published in "Istochnik", Moscow, No. 6, 2003, 63–75, accessed 15 September 2014, http://digitalarchive.wilsoncenter.org/document/113337.
236. Reid, *Envoy to Nehru*, 157.
237. Rahman, *The Hungarian Revolution 1956 – Documents*, Volume I, Part I, Ministry of External Affairs Archives, 36.
238. Brought on by Lall's comment that he did not know why his country had abstained in the 4 November vote; see "Notes on the 44th Meeting of Special Committee on Soviet and Related Problems, Washington, November 6, 1956," *FRUS*, 1955–1957, Volume XXV, Eastern Europe, eds. Keefer, Landa and Shaloff, Document 171, 103n11.
239. *Paths To Peace: India's Voices in UNESCO, 64 years of UNESCO-India Co-operation* (New Delhi: UNESCO, 2009), 16–17.

240. Reid points out how this statement provided him with some temporary satisfaction, although Nehru continued to insist that there was a "dispute about the facts" in a meeting later that day. See Reid, *Envoy to Nehru*, 158–159.
241. Gopal, *Jawaharlal Nehru*, vol. 2, 292.
242. Ibid.
243. As Reid puts it, "The United States and India were now the only great powers with clean hands. Only Eisenhower and Nehru could speak for the conscience of mankind." Reid, *Envoy to Nehru*, 157.
244. Reid alludes to the closeness of the relationship: "Nehru's willingness to receive advice from Eisenhower had been greatly increased by Eisenhower's forthright opposition to the aggression of Britain, France and Israel against Egypt." Reid, *Hungary and Suez 1956*, 20.
245. "Telegram From the Department of State to the Mission at the United Nations1 (#fn1) Washington, November 6, 1956, 9:24 p.m.," *FRUS*, 1955–1957, Volume XXV, Eastern Europe, eds. Keefer, Landa and Shaloff, Document 172.
246. Ibid., n3; Reid, *Hungary and Suez 1956*, 57.
247. "Memorandum of Telephone Conversations With the President, November 9, 1956," *FRUS*, 1955–1957, Volume XXV, Eastern Europe, eds. Keefer, Landa and Shaloff, Document 178.
248. Reid, *Envoy to Nehru*, 161. Canada had no mission in Budapest and Rahman's own reports were arriving at a week's delay.
249. "Memorandum of Telephone Conversations With the President, November 9, 1956," *FRUS*, 1955–1957, Volume XXV, Eastern Europe, eds. Keefer, Landa and Shaloff, Document 178, [FN 11]; for Reid's position, see Reid, *Hungary and Suez*, 15–17.
250. Reid, *Envoy to Nehru*, 166–167.
251. "Nehru to Eisenhower, 7 November 1956 - sent through Krishna Menon," in *SWJN-SS*, vol. 35, 439–440.
252. "Memorandum of Discussion at the 303rd Meeting of the National Security Council, Washington, November 8, 1956, 9–11:25 a.m.1

(#fn1)," *FRUS*, 1955–1957, Volume XXV, Eastern Europe, eds. Keefer, Landa and Shaloff, Document 175.

253. Ibid.

254. These were UNGA Resolution Nos. 1005-(ES II), 1006-(ES II) and 1007-(ES II).

255. "Cable to V K Krishna Menon, 11 November 1956" in *SWJN,* 2nd ser., vol. 35, 459n2; Brecher is of the view that "On the contrary, when India opposed the proposal to send UN observers and the call for a UN-controlled election in Hungary, it was clear that Delhi wanted to avoid a precedent for Kashmir." He also says that Nehru's instructions to Menon were that he should abstain, but that Menon voted against it, see Michael Brecher, *Nehru: A Political Biography* (New York: Oxford University Press, 1959), 573; Subimal Dutt says no instructions were sent to Menon and that he acted of his own accord, see Dutt, *With Nehru in the Foreign Office*, 181.

256. Escott Reid refers to Vijaya Lakshmi Pandit's account of Nehru's telephone conversation with Menon that says Nehru told Menon he should use his own discretion. Reid also discusses Nehru's Principal Private Secretary Mathai's allegation that Nehru had sent Menon a telegram instructing Krishna Menon to abstain in the vote on the resolution and that Menon claimed that the telegram had arrived too late but that this was a lie. See Reid, *Hungary and Suez 1956*, 106.

257. Berkes/Bedi are of the view that "The total absence of recriminatory clauses in either the preamble or the operative sections of the Austrian resolution was clearly the consideration which won India's support." See Ross N. Berkes and Mohinder S. Bedi, *The Diplomacy of India: Indian Foreign Policy in the United Nations* (Stanford: Stanford University Press, 1958), 53.

258. Nikhil Chakrvarty interview, Rethinking Russia, 80–81, quoted in Sreemati Ganguly, *Indo Russian Relations: Making of a Relationship 1992-2002* (Delhi: Shipra Publications, 2009), 43n112.

259. "Cable to GL Mehta and Vijaya Lakshmi Pandit," 15 November 1956, *SWJN,* 2nd ser., vol. 35, 462.

260. Ibid.
261. Reid, *Hungary and Suez 1956*, 84.
262. "Cable to V K Krishna Menon," 11 November 1956," *SWJN*, 2nd ser., vol. 35, 459.
263. "Cable to V K Krishna Menon," 16 November, *SWJN*, 2nd ser., vol. 35, 464.
264. "Menon's telegram to Nehru, 11 November 1956," in Gopal, *Jawaharlal Nehru*, vol. 2, 294n11. A more elaborate justification can be found in Brecher, *India and World Politics*, 85–96.
265. Ibid., 294n13.
266. Brecher, *India and World Politics*, 53, 85.
267. Ibid., 90, 93–94.
268. Tito's Pula Speech, see Rahman, *The Politics of Non-Alignment*, 167; "Nehru to Menon, Subimal Dutt Papers, 20 November 1956", quoted in *SWJN*, 2nd ser., vol. 35, 469–471.
269. "Nehru Condemns Pacts," *The Hindu*, 13 November 1956.
270. "Nehru's note to FS 18 November 1956," in Gopal, *Jawaharlal Nehru*, vol. 2, 295.
271. "16th November 1956 to FS; from FS," Ministry of External Affairs File No. 15 (38) – UNI/56, *National Archives of India*, New Delhi, India.
272. Dutt, *With Nehru in the Foreign Office*, 181.
273. "India's Stand on UN Resolution on Hungary," 17 November 1956, *SWJN*, 2nd ser., vol. 35, 466.
274. See Dutt, *With Nehru in the Foreign Office*, 184; "India for Speedy Withdrawal of Soviet Forces", 18 November 1956, *SWJN*, 2nd ser., vol. 35, 467n4.
275. Nehru's response was "Rahman should maintain correct attitude and not intervene in any way in internal politics, though he can of course meet people if they wish to see him and report to us." Ibid.
276. "Message to Arthur S. Lall, 18 November 1956," *SWJN*, 2nd ser., vol. 35, 468–469.
277. Western countries followed Nehru's speech with some interest, hoping

that it would help decipher the second Soviet intervention. See Reid, *Hungary and Suez 1956*, 20–21.

278. Dutt, *With Nehru in the Foreign Office*, 182.
279. Rahman, *The Politics of Non-Alignment*, 175.
280. Ibid. Although he didn't bring up Kashmir at all, AK Gopalan, a member of the Communist Party of India did.
281. "Cable to V K Krishna Menon," 20 November 1956," *SWJN*, 2nd ser., vol. 35, 469–471. Also see Reid, *Envoy to Nehru*, 178.
282. Acharya J.B. Kripalani, "For Principled Neutrality: A New Appraisal of Indian Foreign Policy", *Foreign Affairs* 38, 1 (1959): 58.
283. "Gerald Priestland, 20 November 1956, BBC" quoted in Gopal, *Jawaharlal Nehru*, vol. 2, 296.
284. Dutt, *With Nehru in the Foreign Office*, 183; Rahman, *Politics of Non-Alignment*, 172.
285. Reid, *Envoy to Nehru*, 177.
286. "Cable to V K Krishna Menon," 21 November 1956, *SWJN*, 2nd ser., vol. 35, 471.
287. Ibid.
288. The first and second Soviet interventions in Budapest. Mišković, "Between Idealism and Pragmatism", 128.
289. "Cable to V K Krishna Menon," 20 November 1956," *SWJN*, 2nd ser., vol. 35, 469–471.
290. Ibid. 472–473.
291. Rahman, *Politics of Non-Alignment*, 168–170.
292. Menon cautioned Nehru by saying, "I do not think we shall make any progress by our telling the Soviet Government in public what to do." Quoted in S. Gopal, *Jawaharlal Nehru*, vol. 2, 297.
293. "Message to N A Bulganin," 22 November 1956, *SWJN*, 2nd ser., vol. 35, 474–476.
294. "Cable to J N Khosla," 22 November 1956, *SWJN*, 2nd ser., vol. 35, 477–478.
295. Ibid., 484–485.

296. "Letter dated November 30, 1956 from J N Khosla to Foreign Secretary containing an account of his meeting with Hungarian PM Kadar," *The Hungarian Revolution 1956 – Documents*, Volume I, Part I, Ministry of External Affairs Archives, 58–59.
297. "PM Kadar's Letter dated November 29, 1956 to PM Nehru in response to letter from Nehru," *The Hungarian Revolution 1956 – Documents*, Volume I, Part I, Ministry of External Affairs Archives, 60–66.
298. "Message to Josip Broz Tito, 22 November 1956," in *SWJN*, 2nd ser., vol. 35, 478–479n6.
299. For details of Khrushchev's and Malenko's secret meeting with Tito in Brioni, see Mišković, "Between Idealism and Pragmatism", 123–124.
300. "To Josip Broz Tito," 2 December 1956, *SWJN*, 2nd ser., vol. 36, 555–556.
301. Ibid. n6.
302. Gopal, *Jawaharlal Nehru*, vol. 2, 297.
303. Nehru quoted in ibid., 296. For the change in Nehru's attitude see "Letter to CDA Rahman dated November 23, 1956 from New Delhi by the Hungarian Indologist Erwin Baktay," *The Hungarian Revolution 1956 – Documents*, Volume I, Part I, Ministry of External Affairs Archives, 53–56.
304. "Cable to V K Krishna Menon," 2 December 1956, *SWJN*, 2nd ser., vol. 36, 557–558n5. Yugoslavia had indicated that diplomatic channels having failed, they would be "compelled to speak out in the UN".
305. "Cable to V K Krishna Menon", 23 November 1956, *SWJN*, 2nd ser., vol. 35, 481–482.
306. "Cable to V K Krishna Menon," 2 December 1956, *SWJN*, 2nd ser., vol. 36, 557–558.
307. For the correspondence, see *SWJN*, 2nd ser., vol. 36, 562–567, 569–570.
308. Dutt, *With Nehru in the Foreign Office*, 184–185.
309. Rahman, *Politics of Non-Alignment*, 177.
310. "Cable to V K Krishna Menon," 3 December 1956, *SWJN*, 2nd ser., vol. 36, 560.

311. "Cable to V K Krishna Menon," 9 December 1956, *SWJN,* 2nd ser., vol. 36, 565–566.
312. "Cable to V K Krishna Menon," 10 December 1956, *SWJN,* 2nd ser., vol. 36, 569–570n2.
313. Rahman noted that the uprising was staged "by sullen protest rather than violence"; *The Hungarian Revolution 1956 – Documents*, Volume I, Part I, Ministry of External Affairs Archives, 16.
314. "Cable to V K Krishna Menon", 23 November 1956, *SWJN,* 2nd ser., vol. 35, 481–482.
315. "Cable to V K Krishna Menon," 2 December 1956, *SWJN,* 2nd ser., vol. 36, 557–558.
316. "Talks with Zhou-En Lai-I," Record of talks held on 31 December 1956 and 1 January 1957, *SWJN,* 2nd ser., vol. 36, 583–603.
317. Ibid.
318. Ibid.
319. "Cable to V K Krishna Menon," 2 December 1956, *SWJN,* 2nd ser., vol. 36, 557–558. Zhou said he would ask the Chinese representative in Budapest Ho Te-Ching to enquire (presumably with Kadar).
320. "Talks with Chou-En Lai-I," Record of talks held on 31 December 1956 and 1 January 1957, *SWJN,* 2nd ser., vol. 36, 583–603.
321. Brecher, *India and World Politics*, 13.
322. On how exactly the Indian position on the crisis evolved over time, see "Papers relating to Hungary Crisis. Includes letters, telegrams exchanged between Indian delegation to the UN, MEA, through Nehru, Krishna Menon, NR Pillai, MO Mathai, JN Khosla, others, etc." V.K. Krishna Menon Papers, 1st and 2nd Instalment, File No. 954, 1956–1957, *NMML*.
323. Menon said, "I want to point out that the sponsors of the draft resolution have pursued the paths of mediation, of trying to solve a problem, and of moderation." Official Records, Eleventh Session of the General Assembly, (1956–1957), I, 307, quoted in Berkes and Bedi, *Diplomacy of India*, 43–44n16. See also "Papers relating to Suez Canal

question." V.K. Krishna Menon Papers, 1st and 2nd Instalment, File No. 945, 1956, *NMML*.

324. Official Records, General Assembly Emergency Session I, 1–10 November 1956, 31, quoted in ibid., 41n13.
325. Berkes and Bedi, *Diplomacy of India*, 41n14.
326. Ibid., 52n26.
327. Ibid., 55n28.
328. Ibid., 55n27.
329. Menon speaking on the resolution of Hungarian refugees; Ibid, 52–53.
330. Berkes and Bedi, *Diplomacy of India*, 50–54.
331. Official Records, General Assembly, Emergency Session II, 4–10 November 1956, 44, quoted in ibid.
332. Quoting Nehru's speech in Parliament, Menon says this. Official records, Eleventh Session of the General Assembly (1956–1957), I, 524, quoted in ibid., 104–105.
333. Official Records, Eleventh Session of the General Assembly, (1956–1957), III, 1428–1429, quoted in ibid., 55–58n29.
334. Munro of New Zealand quoted in Berkes/Bedi, *Diplomacy of India*, 49–50.
335. Jarring of Sweden quoted in Berkes/Bedi, *Diplomacy of India*, 8–24.
336. T.F. Tsiang, the head of the increasingly isolated Nationalist Chinese delegations, quoted in ibid.
337. Noorani, "Nehru and the cold wars".
338. Nehru, Interview to Sulzberger of *The New York Times*, reprinted the *Times of India*, 27 April 1950, quoted in Noorani, "Nehru and the Cold Wars."
339. 344th Plenary Meeting, Wednesday, 14 November 1951, at 3 p.m. Palais de Chaillot, Paris, Official Records, General Assembly, Sixth Session.
340. "Memorandum of Conversations between Secretary of State Dulles and PM Nehru, PM's Residence," *FRUS*, 1955–1957, Volume VII, South Asia, eds. MacMahon and Shaloff, Document 156.
341. See Power, "Indian Foreign Policy", 257–286.

342. Dragon Protitch, *FRUS*, 1955–1957, Volume XXV, Eastern Europe, eds. Keefer, Landa and Shaloff, Document 206.
343. "Talks with Chou-En Lai-I," Record of talks held on 31 December 1956 and 1 January 1957, *SWJN,* 2nd ser., vol. 36, 587.
344. For a discussion of these, see "Third World Reaction to Hungary and Suez 1956: A Soviet Foreign Ministry Analysis," Top Secret, Copy No. 1, accessed 15 September 2014, http://digitalarchive.wilsoncenter.org/document/111097.
345. Bekes, Byrne and Rainer, *1956 Hungarian Revolution*, 501.
346. Mazower's phrase, Mark Mazower, *Governing the World: The History of an Idea* (Penguin Press HC, 2012), 249.
347. "Text of the hand-bills circulated in Budapest requesting the public to give an affectionate reception to Ambassador KPS Menon," *The Hungarian Revolution 1956 – Documents*, Volume I, Part I, Ministry of External Affairs, 124–25.
348. "14 December 1956 - Letter from Ferenc Farkas (SG of the Petofi/National Peasant Party to KPS Menon, "Embassador [sic] of Bharat)," The Hungarian Revolution 1956 – Documents, Volume II, Part I, Ministry of External Affairs Archives, 58–59.
349. Jawaharlal Nehru, "12 November 1948," in *A Bunch of Old Letters: Written Mostly to Jawaharlal Nehru and Some Written by Him* (New Delhi: Penguin Books India, 2005), 523.
350. *The Hungarian Revolution 1956 – Documents*, Volume I, Part I, Ministry of External Affairs Archives.
351. "Telegram from the Embassy in the UK to the Department of State, London, 26 October, 1956," *FRUS*, 1955–1957, Volume XXV, Eastern Europe, eds. Keefer, Landa and Shaloff, Document 118.
352. "Letter of 8 December 1956," in G. Parthasarathi, ed. *Jawaharlal Nehru, Letters to Chief Ministers 1947-1964 vol. 4,* 466–467.
353. Ibid.
354. Krishna Menon quoted in Berkes and Bedi, *Diplomacy of India*, 59.

355. "Interview between Nehru and The New York Times, 20 December 1956," quoted in ibid., 60–61.
356. "Official Records, Eight Session of the General Assembly (1953)," Krishna Menon quoted in ibid., 97–99.
357. Ibid.; Nehru quoted in Jairam Ramesh, *Text of The 13th Lester Pearson Memorial Lecture, Delhi University*, 23 April 2007, "How India and Canada Manage Diversities," *The Hindu*, 26 April 2007, accessed 26 October 2014, http://www.thehindu.com/todays-paper/tp-opinion/how-india-canada-manage-diversities/article1833713.ece.
358. K.P.S. Menon quoted in Rahman, *Politics of Non-Alignment*, 169.
359. For these criticisms, see Dutt Diaries, entries from 4 to 11 November, quoted in Krishnan Srinivasan, *Diplomatic Channels*, 77; Kripalani, "For Principled Neutrality", 50. "Peaceful coexistence in such cases will be that of the lamb with lion, when the lamb is safe in its belly" and Gopal, *Jawaharlal Nehru*, vol. 2, 295. "A government may follow a broad line of policy, but usually its policy is the resultant of various pulls and urges. Sometimes one pull is greater than the other." Nehru's note to Siquerios, the Mexican mural artist, 14 November 1956.
360. Jagat Mehta's analysis in Srinivasan, *Diplomatic Channels*, 145.
361. Sisir Gupta, *India and the International System* (New Delhi: Vikas Books, 1981), 47.
362. "Third World Reaction to Hungary and Suez 1956," 61–64.
363. Dutt Diaries, 3 June 1957, quoted in Krishnan Srinivasan, *Diplomatic Channels*, 85.
364. Westad, *The Global Cold War*, 125–126n25.
365. "Official records, Eleventh Session of the General Assembly (1956–1957), I," quoted in Berkes and Bedi, *Diplomacy of India*, 608.
366. "Nehru to Menon, 31 December 1956," in Gopal, *Jawaharlal Nehru*, vol. 2, 298.
367. "To Herbert V Evatt," 27 June 1958 and "To KPS Menon," 28 June 1958, *SWJN*, 2nd ser., vol. 42, eds., Mridula Mukherjee and Aditya Mukherjee (New Delhi: Jawaharlal Nehru Memorial Fund), 653–654.

In response to the execution, Nehru refused to raise the status of diplomatic representation to embassy level until December 1959, see Dutt, *With Nehru in the Foreign Office*, 187.

368. "We would only give moral support but no political asylum. Of course, we will not say this openly for that will make matters worse". Dutt, *With Nehru in the Foreign Office*, 186–187.

5. "Bad Ethics and Worse Policy"

1. The officials, whose names appear in the paper in their appropriate context, include Rajeshwar Dayal (Special Representative of the Secretary General in the Congo, 8 September 1960–25 May 1961), Brig. Indar Jit Rikhye (Military Adviser to the Secretary General under Dag Hammarskjöld and then Military Adviser in General under U Thant), D. N. Chatterji (India's first Ambassador to the Congo), Brig. K.A.S. Raja (UN commander in Katanga, March 1961–April 1962) and Maj. Gen. Dewan Prem Chand (UN commander in Katanga, May 1962–April 1963).
2. M.M. Rahman's and one of Rajeshwar Dayal's books had specific chapters devoted to India's role in ending the crisis. Dayal's other book and Chatterji's too are devoted entirely to this episode in India's international relations. See Mohammed M. Rahman, *The Politics of Non-Alignment* (New Delhi: Associated Publishing House, 1969), 181–210; D.N. Chatterji, *Storm Over the Congo* (New Delhi: Vikas, 1980), 251; Rajeshwar Dayal, *A Life of Our Times* (New Delhi: Sangam Books, 1998) 390–416; Rajeshwar Dayal, *Mission for Hammarskjöld: Congo Crisis* (Princeton: Princeton University Press, 1975), 350.
3. Indar Jit Rikhye, *Military Adviser to the Secretary General: U.N. Peacekeeping and the Congo Crisis*, (London: Hurst Publishers Co, 1993), 326.
4. Sarvepalli Gopal, *Jawaharlal Nehru: A Biography*, vol. 3, (New Delhi: Oxford University Press, 2012), 145–161; Sarvepalli Gopal, ed., *Jawaharlal Nehru: A Biography*, 3 vols., (New Delhi: Oxford University

Press, 2012); Robert B. Rakove, *Kennedy, Johnson and the Nonaligned World* (New York: Cambridge University Press, 2013), 291. Rakove discusses the crisis vis-à-vis nonaligned leaders, while Gopal is more specifically focused on Nehru.

5. The OAU was eventually replaced by the African Union in 2002.
6. For the definitive work on the organization of Black African identity around self-determination and decolonization, see Adom Getachew, *Worldmaking After Empire: The Rise and Fall of Self-Determination* (Princeton: Princeton University Press, 2019), 288. For an interesting study of how these connections were forged, see Penny M. Von Eschen, *Race Against Empire: Black Americans and Anticolonialism, 1937-1957* (New York: Cornell University Press, 1997), 259.
7. For how Asian and African nations conducted diplomacy at the UN, see Swapna Kona Nayudu, "We Were Once Colonized: Nehru, India and Afro-Asianism at the UN," in *How Democracy Survives: Global Challenges in the Anthropocene*, eds. Michael Holm & Richard Samuel Deese (Boston: Routledge, 2022), 29–42.
8. See for instance, Christopher J. Lee, *Making a World after Empire: The Bandung Moment and Its Political Afterlives*, (Athens: Ohio University Press, 2010), 400.
9. G.L. Mehta, *Understanding India* (New York: Asia Publishing House, 1959), 31.
10. See David Kimche, *The Afro-Asian Movement: Ideology and Foreign Policy of the Third World* (New York: Halstead Press, 1973).
11. See Vijay Prashad, *The Darker Nations: A People's History of the Third World* (New York: New Press, 2007), 384.
12. See Robert A. Mortimer, *The Third World Coalition in International Politics* (New York: Praeger, 1980), 147.
13. For the most eloquent description of this, see Richard Wright, *The Color Curtain: A Report on the Bandung Conference* (Jackson: University Press of Mississippi, 1956), 245.
14. They were also worried about race in relation to pan-Asianism. See,

Mathew Jones, "A "Segregated" Asia?: Race, the Bandung Conference, and Pan-Asianist Fears in American Thought and Policy, 1954–1955," *Diplomatic History* 29, 5 (2005): 841–868.

15. See Angadipuram Appadorai, *The Bandung Conference* (New Delhi: Indian Council of World Affairs, 1955), 32.
16. Jawaharlal Nehru, "Speech to Bandung Conference Political Committee", 1955, Reprinted in George M. Kahin, *The Asian-African Conference* (New York: Cornell University Press, 1956), 64–72.
17. Michael Brecher, *India and World Politics: Krishna Menon's View of the World* (Toronto: Oxford University Press, 1968), 8.
18. Sukarno, Speech at the Opening of the Bandung Conference, 18 April 1955, *Africa-Asia Speaks from Bandong*, (Djakarta: Indonesian Ministry of Foreign Affairs, 1955), 19–29, accessed 15 September 2014, http://www.fordham.edu/halsall/mod/1955sukarno-bandong.html.
19. Neil Howard, "Freedom and Development in Historical Context: A Comparison of Gandhi and Fanon's Approaches to Liberation," *The Journal of Pan African Studies* 4, 7 (2011): 94–108; Hira Singh, "Confronting Colonialism and Racism: Fanon and Gandhi," *Human Architecture: Journal of the Sociology of Self-Knowledge* 5, 3 (2007): 341–352; Neelam Srivastava, "Towards a critique of colonial violence: Fanon, Gandhi and the restoration of agency," *Journal of Postcolonial Writing* 46, 3–4 (2010): 303–309.
20. For the two phases in which these ideas developed, see Ramachandra Guha, *Gandhi Before India* (New Delhi: Penguin, 2013), 688, and *India After Gandhi: The History of the World's Largest Democracy* (London, Basingstoke and Oxford: Macmillan, 1998), 960.
21. Parker calls for the need for "discerning the precise, subtle, and intricate connections between the Cold War, the global postwar "race revolution," and the course of Third World decolonization", see Jason Parker, Cold War II: The Eisenhower Administration, the Bandung Conference, and the Reperiodization of the Postwar Era, *Diplomatic History*, vol. 30, No. 5 (November 2006), 868.

22. Slate's phrase; for an excellent study of these processes between India and the United States, see Nico Slate, *Colored Cosmopolitanism: The Shared Struggle for Freedom in the United States and India* (Cambridge: Harvard University Press, 2012), 344.
23. For a study of the nationalism/cosmopolitanism divide, see Rahul Rao, *Third World Protest: Between Home and the World* (New York: Oxford University Press, 2010), 288.
24. "'Peace and Empire', Presidential Address at the Conference on Peace and Empire, Organized by the India League and the London Federation of Peace Councils, Friends House, London, July 15 and 16, 1938," in Jawaharlal Nehru, *The Unity of India, Collected Writings 1937-1940* (New York: John Day Company, 1942), 268–277.
25. "'India for Universal Freedom', Message to Africans and Indians in Africa printed in the *Hindustan Times*," 12 June 1947, *The Selected Works of Jawaharlal Nehru (SWJN)*, 2nd ser., vol. 3, ed. Sarvepalli Gopal (New Delhi: Jawaharlal Nehru Memorial Fund), 329.
26. A National Intelligence Estimate says "local Asians" in Africa were "not held in high esteem"; see "National Intelligence Estimate Source, October 20, 1959," *FRUS*, 1958–1960, Volume XIV, Africa, eds. Harriet D. Schwar and Stanley Shaloff, (Washington: Government Printing Office, 1992), Document 18.
27. Acting Governor General Mr Cornells to the American Consul at Leopoldville, "Memorandum by the Consul at Leopoldville (McGregor)1 (#fn2) 511.55A/2–354," *FRUS*, 1952–1954, Volume XI, Part 1, Africa and South Asia (in two parts), eds. Paul Claussen, et. al., (Washington: Government Printing Office, 1988), Document 179.
28. "Bandung Conference - Round up of Belgian Opinion," Ministry of External Affairs File No. D 919/AAC-55, *National Archives of India (NAI)*, New Delhi, India.
29. "Memo of Conversations Between Secretary of State Dulles and Prime Minister Nehru, Prime Minister's Residence, New Delhi, March 9, 1956," *FRUS*, 1955–1957, Volume VIII, South Asia, eds. Robert J.

MacMahon and Stanley Shaloff (Washington: Government Printing Office, 1987), Document 156.

30. "Letter of 30 July 1960," ed., G. Parthasarathi, *Jawaharlal Nehru, Letters to Chief Ministers 1947-1964*, vol. 5, (Delhi: Oxford University Press, 1990), 394–395.
31. For India's troop contribution in numbers in comparison to other countries, see Ernest W. Lefever and Wynfred Joshua, *United Nations Peacekeeping in the Congo: 1960-1964: An Analysis of Political, Executive and Military Control in Four Volumes*, Volume 3: Appendixes, 30 June 1966, Appendix H, Charts B, C, D, E and E contd.
32. For India's views on British policies towards the Congo, see *The Selected Works of Jawaharlal Nehru (SWJN),* 2nd ser., vol. 71, ed. Madhavan Palat (New Delhi: Jawaharlal Nehru Memorial Fund), 704–810; *The Selected Works of Jawaharlal Nehru (SWJN),* 2nd ser., vol. 72, ed. Madhavan Palat (New Delhi: Jawaharlal Nehru Memorial Fund), 682–684; *The Selected Works of Jawaharlal Nehru (SWJN),* 2nd ser., vol. 73, ed. Madhavan Palat (New Delhi: Jawaharlal Nehru Memorial Fund), 604–605, 612–616.
33. "Annual Report on the Belgian Congo and Ruanda-Urundi for 1954," Ministry of External Affairs File No. D-3877/55-AFR II, *NAI*, 3.
34. "NA and India-Africa," Sr. No. 42, Apa B. Pant (Ist Installment), Writings by him, Apa Pant Papers, *Nehru Memorial Museum and Library (NMML)*, New Delhi, India, 1; Also see "'General Note on Certain Problems of Africa' by Apa B. Pant," Ministry of External Affairs File No F-39/9/55-AFR II, *NAI*, 8–9. On Apa Pant and Indian diplomacy in Africa, see Bérénice Guyot-Rechard (2022) "Stirring Africa towards India: Apa Pant and the Making of Post-Colonial Diplomacy, 1948–54", *The International History Review*, 44 (4) 892–913.
35. An oft-quoted concept in the context of Indian nation-building, "unity in diversity" became part of government propaganda, popular culture and socio-cultural messaging.
36. India's non-aligned policy towards the crisis in the Congo is often conflated with its membership in the Non-Aligned Movement and

mischaracterised as neutralist. See Alanna O'Malley (2015), "Ghana, India, and the Transnational Dynamics of the Congo Crisis at the United Nations, 1960–1", *The International History Review*, 37(5), 971–972.

37. In fact, Nico Slate is of the opinion that the larger forces of the civil rights movement in America and the Third World movement in Asia and Africa did not bring together the connections between Indian and African freedom struggles. See, Slate, *Colored Cosmopolitanism*, 163.
38. Chatterji, *Storm over the Congo*, 22.
39. W.E.B. Du Bois had warned against substituting "the exploitation of the coloured races by white races, an exploitation of coloured races by coloured men," quoted in Slate, *Colored Cosmopolitanism*, 245.
40. Dayal, *Life of Our Times*, 394.
41. For snapshots of the unfolding of the crisis in New York at UN headquarters, and in Léopoldville, see Rikhye, *Military Adviser to the Secretary General*, 22, 190, 280, 324.
42. "Letter of 30 July 1960," ed., G. Parthasarathi, *Jawaharlal Nehru, Letters to Chief Ministers 1947-1964*, vol. 5, (Delhi: Oxford University Press, 1990), 394–395.
43. Rahman, *Politics of Non-Alignment,* 181.
44. Dayal, *Life of Our Times*, 394.
45. Rahman, *Politics of Non-Alignment,* 182.
46. This was Indar Jit Rikhye, who became a very important part of Hammarskjöld's basic structure of the top command of ONUC. In his words, "In the Congo, he would have a Special Representative, who would be the top man with political responsibility. This was Ralph J. Bunche. Maj. Gen. Carl von Horn was Supreme Commander of the UN Force, and Dr. Sture Linner was Chief of Civilian Operations. At UN headquarters in New York, the chain of responsibility started with the Secretary General and he was assisted by a small group of trusted political advisers which included Andrew Cordier, Heinz Wieschoff and Ralph Bunche. This group also included myself as Military Adviser

to the Secretary General and Sir Alexander MacFarquhar as Adviser on Civilian Operations. It was known as the 'Congo Club'". See, Rikhye, *Military Adviser to the Secretary General*, 16.

47. Ibid.
48. Rahman, *Politics of Non-Alignment*, 188.
49. Rikhye, *Military Adviser to the Secretary*, 22.
50. Letter of 19 August 1960, in Kwame Nkrumah, *The Challenge of the Congo* (London: Thomas Nelson, 1967), 33–35.
51. *The Hindu*, 12 August 1960, quoted in Rahman, *Politics of Non-Alignment*, 196.
52. "Cablegram from C.V. Narasimhan to Secretary General," Cordier Collection, Box 165, UN Files, Subject Files, Africa – Congo – Countries G-J, AWC Congo – India, *CUL: MS*.
53. Rahman, *Politics of Non-Alignment*, 190–193.
54. Nehru quoted in Rahman, *Politics of Non-Alignment*, 197.
55. Rikhye was placed temporarily at the disposal of the Supreme Commander of the UN Force, Major General Carl von Horn, and of the Secretary General's Personal Representative in the Congo; See, Note No. 2226, 27 August 1960, Office of Public Information, U.N., N.Y., Cordier Collection, Box 140, U.N. Files, Subject Files, Africa - Congo - Press Releases Note to Correspondents, *CUL: MS*. For Rikhye's assessment of the operation in the Congo, see Indar Jit Rikhye, *Military Adviser to the Secretary General: U.N. Peacekeeping and the Congo Crisis*, Hurst Publishers Co, 1993, 288.

    Dayal's appointment had been announced on 20 August 1960. See "Statement by the Secretary-General," Press Release SG/949, 20 August 1960, Office of Public Information, U.N., N.Y., Cordier Collection, Box 140, U.N. Files, Subject Files, Africa - Congo - Press Releases, *CUL: MS*.
56. Indar Jit Rikhye, *Military Adviser to the Secretary General: U.N. Peacekeeping and the Congo Crisis*, Hurst Publishers Co, 1993, 288.

57. For Cordier's views of himself, see Emmanuel Gerard, Bruce Kuclick, *Death in the Congo*, 151, 172, 219–220.
58. Spooner, *Canada, the Congo Crisis, and UN Peacekeeping*, 94–95; also see Hoskyns, *The Congo Since Independence*, 204, for an account of the re-opening of airports.
59. Chatterji, *Storm Over the Congo*, 17; see also Spooner, *Canada, the Congo Crisis, and UN Peacekeeping*, 94–95 for very good descriptions of the origins of the coup. For a description of the destruction of documents, see Lise Namikas, *Battleground Africa: Cold War in the Congo, 1960-1965*, (Palo Alto, Stanford University Press, 2013), 106–107.
60. Gopal is of the view that Nehru was less than critical because both Rikhye and Dayal who were at the helm of affairs on the Congo were Indian officers. See "Crusade in the Congo," in Gopal, *Jawaharlal Nehru*, vol. 3, 147.
61. Dayal, *Mission for Hammarskjöld*, 76–77.
62. For Nkrumah's version of non-aligned diplomacy in this period, see Frank Gerits (2015) "'When the Bull Elephants Fight': Kwame Nkrumah, Non- Alignment, and Pan-Africanism as an Interventionist Ideology in the Global Cold War (1957–66)," *The International History Review*, 37:5, 951–969.
63 "Telegram to Krishna Menon at New York, 18 September 1960," in "Crusade in the Congo," in Gopal, *Jawaharlal Nehru*, vol. 3, 147n11.
64. "Exchange of Telegrams Between Frederick H. Boland (New York) and Con Cremin (Dublin), (Nos. 232, 315 and 316), New York and Dublin, 12 and 13 September 1961", in Michael Kennedy, Eunan O'Halpin, Kate O'Malley, Bernadette Whelan, Dermot Keogh (2018), *Documents on Irish Foreign Policy: v. 11: 1957-1961*, Royal Irish Academy, Dublin, 688, 700.
65. Krishna Menon, General Assembly, Fifteenth Session, 906th Plenary Meeting, Monday, 17 October 1960, at 10.30 am, New York, "Papers relating to the situation in Congo." V. K. Krishna Menon Papers, 1st and 2nd Instalment, File No. 873, November 1960–December 1960,

NMML; "Papers relating to the fifteenth session of the UNGA on Congo crisis" V.K. Krishna Menon Papers, 1st and 2nd Instalment, File No. 875, 1960 –1961, *NMML*; "Papers relating to Congo crisis." V.K. Krishna Menon Papers, 1st and 2nd Instalment, File No. 876, 1960 –1961, *NMML.*

66. Ibid.
67. He also disagreed with Tito's proposal that under certain circumstances, the national troops would follow national, not UN command as impractical and dangerous. See, Gopal, *Jawaharlal Nehru*, vol. 3, 153. See also Nehru, "To M J Desai: Assessing the Situation", 17 October 1960, *SWJN*, 2nd ser., vol. 63, 561–562. Also available in Ministry of External Affairs File No. 59/60-AFR-II, Vol-I, 75–77/corr., *NAI.*
68. Gopal, *Jawaharlal Nehru*, vol. 3, 150–151.
69. Namikas, *Battleground Africa*, 107.
70. Kalb, *Congo Cables*, 252. For a discussion of Nehru's views on the Troika plan, see Kalb, *Congo Cables*, 120–121, although the reading of the Nehru-Hammarskjöld relationship is somewhat confused here.
71. "Note on the Conversation Between H.E. Mr. Kosygin and the Prime Minister", 20 February 1961, Ministry of External Affairs File No. 13 (23)-Europe East, 1960, *NAI.*
72. Mazov, *A Distant Front in the Cold War*, 124.
73. Stephen R. Weissman, *American Foreign Policy in the Congo, 1960-1964*, (Ithaca and London: Cornell University Press, 1974), 146.
74. Dayal's approach was in line with the Indian view of the situation, both based on prioritizing the question of the legality of the government in the Congo. See Nehru, "To M J Desai: Good Offices Committee for Congo", 2 November 1960, *SWJN,* 2nd ser., vol. 64, 416–417. See also Nehru, "To M J Desai: Mobutu's Misbehaviour", 17 November 1960, Ministry of External Affairs File No. REP 59/60-AFR-II (Notes), 27/notes, *NAI*, reprinted in *SWJN,* 2nd ser., vol. 64, 419.
75. Kevin A. Spooner, *Canada, the Congo Crisis, and UN Peacekeeping, 1960-64*, (Vancouver: University of British Columbia Press, 2009), 95. For how

American policy, which often came in contradiction with Indian policy, or rather, with Dayal, see John Kent, *America, the UN and Decolonisation: Cold War Conflict in the Congo* (London: Routledge, 2011), 256.

76. Hoskyns, *The Congo Since Independence*, 248.
77. Kent, *America, the UN and Decolonisation*, 32, 38.; for the Belgian reaction to Dayal's report, see Gerard, Kuclick, *Death in the Congo*, 175. For a general discussion of how the Belgians had meddled in the affairs of the Congo, see Emmanuel Gerard, Bruce Kuclick, *Death in the Congo*, especially chapter titled "The Return of the Belgians". For India's view of the Dayal Report, see Nehru, "To M J Desai: Good Offices Committee for Congo", 2 November 1960, *SWJN*, 2nd ser., vol. 64, 416–417.
78. Gerard, Kuclick, *Death in the Congo*, 115.
79. See Hoskyns, *The Congo Since Independence*, 251, 143, 139.
80. Ibid., 179.
81. Ibid., 179–180.
82. Indar Jit Rikhye, *Military Adviser to the Secretary General: U.N. Peacekeeping and the Congo Crisis*, Hurst Publishers Co, 1993, 92, 107, 114, 124, 233–234.
83. Gerard, Kuclick, *Death in the Congo*, 191.
84. Ibid., 93.
85. For an excellent discussion of Soviet policy towards Africa in general, and the Congo specifically, see Namikas, *Battleground Africa*, 27–30, 109–132, although Namikas engages inaccurately with the non-aligned position, mischaracterizing it as either economic policy or neutralism only; also see Mazov, *A Distant Front in the Cold War*, 256. The book deals with Soviet policy, but also tells us an enormous amount about American policy, and indeed, paranoia about Soviet/communist motives in Africa, and the eventual waning of Soviet counterinfluence.
86. Kalb, *Congo Cables*,120.
87. Hoskyns, *The Congo Since Independence*, 471.
88. Nehru speaking in the UNGA, 21 December 1960, Rahman, *Politics of Non-Alignment*, 204.

89. Sarvepalli Gopal, *Jawaharlal Nehru: A Biography*, vol. 1, (New Delhi: Oxford University Press, 2012, 518–519; see also Weissman, *American Foreign Policy in the Congo*, 115; see also Catherine Hosykyns, 310.
90. There was talk of a secret agreement reached between Lumumba and Nehru for the immigration of two million Indians into the Congo as a price for India's support of the Congolese nationalist leaders. Declared by Lokiki, Kasavubu's representative in the Security Council, Rajeshwar Dayal, *Mission for Hammarskjöld*, 221 and Rajeshwar Dayal, *A Life of Our Times*, 452; "Letter from Secretary General to Dragan Protitch," 29 January 1961, Cordier Collection, Box 157, U.N. Files, Subject Files, Africa – Congo – Advisory Committee Conciliation Commission, *CUL: MS*. Also, see Indar Jit Rikhye, *Military Adviser to the Secretary General: U.N. Peacekeeping and the Congo Crisis* (London: Hurst Publishers Co, 1993), 245, 276. See Nehru, "To C S Jha: Army Officers Attacked in Congo", *SWJN,* 2nd ser., vol. 64, 420; see also Nehru, "To M A Rahman: Army Officers Attacked in Congo", *SWJN,* 2nd ser., vol. 64, 420.
91. See Nehru, "In the Lok Sabha: Statement on Congo Incidents", 30 November 1960, *SWJN,* 2nd ser., vol. 64, 435–442; see also Nehru, "In the Rajya Sabha: Statement on Congo Incidents", 30 November 1960, *SWJN,* 2nd ser., vol. 64, 442–448. India had 770–780 troops in the Congo at that point, most engaged in supplies, signaling and hospital work. See Nehru, "In the Lok Sabha: Attack on Indian Officers in Congo", 28 November 1960, in *SWJN,* 2nd ser., vol. 64, 432–433.
92. Report of the CWIHP Conference on the Congo Crisis, *History through Documents and Memory: A CWIHP Critical Oral History Conference of the Congo Crisis, 1960–1961*, accessed 15 September 2014, http://www.wilsoncenter.org/article/history-through-documents-and-memory-report-cwihp-critical-oral-history-conference-the-congo.
93. Nehru, "To Presspersons" (Via National Herald, City Edition, 1), 14 February 1961, *SWJN,* 2nd ser., vol. 66, 507–508.
94. Nehru Telegram to Dag Hammarskjöld, "Message received by UN SG

DH from JN, PM of India," Press Release SG/1007, 15 February 1961, Statement by the Secretary-General, Office of Public Information, U.N., N.Y., Cordier Collection, Box 140, UN Files, Subject Files, Africa – Congo – Press Releases, *CUL: MS.*

95. Nehru, "For Hammarskjöld: Lumumba's Murder", 13 February 1961, *SWJN,* 2nd ser., vol. 66, 506. Corroborated by Rahman, *Politics of Non-Alignment*, 208, as Nehru had also copied this note to him, Nehru, "To M.A. Rahman", 13 February 1961, *SWJN,* 2nd ser., vol. 66, 507.
96. Nehru, "For Dag Hammarskjöld", 25 January 1961, (sent through C.S. Jha, Permanent Representative to the UN, Ministry of External Affairs File No. REP-13/61-AFR-II, Vol I, 84–85/c, *NAI*, reprinted in *SWJN,* 2nd ser., vol. 66, 495–496.
97. Ibid.
98. Ibid.
99. Nehru was under immense pressure from both houses of parliament as is evident from his speech and the subsequent questions he fielded. Nehru, "In the Rajya Sabha: Statement on Congo", 15 February 1961, *SWJN,* 2nd ser., vol. 67, 318–327.
100. Nehru, "For Harold Macmillan", 1 February 1961, (sent through T.N. Kaul, Deputy High Commissioner to the UK), *SWJN,* 2nd ser., vol. 66, 498–499.
101. For India's views on British policy towards the Congo, see *SWJN,* 2nd ser., vol. 71, 704–710; vol. 72, 682–684; vol. 73, 604–605, 612–616.
102. Nehru, "For Harold Macmillan", 12 February 1961, *SWJN,* 2nd ser., vol.66, 504–505.
103. Nehru, "To KPS Menon, Telegram to the Ambassador to the USSR", 17 February 1961, *SWJN,* 2nd ser., vol. 67, 343–344.
104. Nehru, "To NS Khrushchev", 26 February 1961, *SWJN,* 2nd ser., vol. 67, 350–356.
105. Nehru, "For Dean Rusk, Telegram sent through M C Chagla, Indian Ambassador to the US", 5 February 1961, (repeated to C.S. Jha at New York), *SWJN,* 2nd ser., vol. 66, 499–500.

106. Nehru, "To John F Kennedy: Resolution on Congo", 20 February 1961, *SWJN,* 2nd ser., vol. 67, 346–347.
107. Kennedy quoted in *The Hindu*, 17 February 1961, reprinted in Nehru, "In the Rajya Sabha: Statement on Congo", 15 February 1961, *SWJN,* 2nd ser., vol. 67, 318–327, fn8.
108. For continuities between the Eisenhower and Kennedy administrations on US policy towards the Congo, see Kalb, *Congo Cables*, 466, specifically pages 203–206.
109. Nehru, "To Gamal Abdel Nasser: Congo", 1 April 1961, *SWJN,* 2nd ser., vol. 68, 699–700.
110. Nehru, "To CS Jha and MC Chagla: Western Double-Dealing", 3 April 1961, *SWJN,* 2nd ser., vol. 68, 701–702.
111. Nehru, "In the Rajya Sabha: Belgian Ambassador's Provocation", 17 April 1961, *SWJN,* 2nd ser., vol. 68, 703–704.
112. See Kalb, *Congo Cables*, 236–247.
113. Nehru had also agreed to Hammarskjöld's request that Dayal's assignment be prolonged. Nehru, "To CS Jha: Rajeshwar Dayal in Congo", 3 March 1961, *SWJN,* 2nd ser., vol. 67, 362–363.
114. Namikas, *Battleground Africa*, 145.
115. See Kalb, *Congo Cables*, 247; also see Namikas, *Battleground Africa*, 145.
116. Kalb, *Congo Cables*, 262.
117. Hoskyns, *The Congo Since Independence*, 365.
118. Kalb, *Congo Cables*, 262.
119. Nehru, "To CS Jha: Rajeshwar Dayal's Term in Congo", 9 March 1961, *SWJN,* 2nd ser., vol. 67, 371.
120. Nehru, "For Dag Hammarskjöld: Rajeshwar Dayal in Congo" (Telegram to CS Jha for forwarding to the Secretary General), 22 May 1961, *SWJN,* 2nd ser., vol. 69, 530–531.
121. Nehru, "In the Rajya Sabha: Rajeshwar Dayal's Service at the UN", 4 May 1961, *SWJN,* 2nd ser., vol. 68, 704–707; see also Nehru, "In the Lok Sabha: Rajeshwar Dayal's Resignation", 4 May 1961, *SWJN,* 2nd

ser., vol. 69, 612–615; see also Nehru, "In the Rajya Sabha: Rajeshwar Dayal and Congo", 4 May 1961, *SWJN,* 2nd ser., vol. 69, 615–619.

122. Nehru, "To CS Jha: Troop Transport, Dayal's Absence and Belgian Intervention", 10 March 1961, *SWJN,* 2nd ser., vol. 67, 372; see also Nehru, "To Harold Macmillan: British Propaganda against India in Congo", 11 March 1961, *SWJN,* 2nd ser., vol. 67, 373–374.
123. Michael J. Kennedy and Art Magennis (2014), *Ireland, the United Nations and the Congo: A Military and Diplomatic History, 1960-1*, Four Courts Press, Dublin, 42.
124. Gopal, *Jawaharlal Nehru*, vol. 3, 154.
125. Nehru, "For U Nu", 14 February 1961, *SWJN,* 2nd ser., vol. 66, 502–503; see also, Nehru, "For A Sukarno" (sent through J.N. Khosla, Ambassador to Indonesia), 14 February 1961, *SWJN,* 2nd ser., vol. 66, 508–509; see also Nehru, "For Gamal Abdul Nasser", 14 January 1961, *SWJN,* 2nd ser., vol. 66, 509–510 [This date is a printing error, and should be 14 February 1961]; see also Nehru, "For Josip Broz Tito", 14 February 1961, *SWJN,* 2nd ser., vol. 66, 511–512.
126. Dayal, *Mission for Hammarskjöld*, 237.
127. "Cablegram from Dag Hammarskjöld to Nehru", R.J. Bunche/ld. 3053, 2932, 21 January 1961, Cordier Collection, Box 165, U.N. Files, Subject Files, Africa – Congo – Countries G-J, AWC Congo – India, *CUL: MS.*
128. Ibid.
129. "Telegram from the Mission to the United Nations to the Department of State, New York, January 31, 1961, 9 p.m.," *FRUS*, 1961–1963, Volume XX, Congo Crisis, ed. Harriet D. Schwar, (Washington: Government Printing Office, 1994), Document 15.
130. See [Cover page Missing], Ministry of External Affairs File No. D-2442/61-AFR II, *NAI.*
131. See "Prime Minister's Statement in Lok Sabha on the Situation in the Congo," Ministry of External Affairs File No. PQ-16/61-AFR II, 15 February 1961, *NAI.* Catherine Hosykyns calls this "a rally for the UN" – see Hoskyns, *The Congo Since Independence*, 324.

132. Nehru, "In the Lok Sabha: Statement on Congo", 15 February 1961, *SWJN,* 2nd ser., vol. 67, 328–333; for difficulties in sending Indian troops to the Congo, see Nehru, "To CS Jha: Publishing Correspondence with Khrushchev", 1 March 1961, SWJN, 2nd ser., vol. 67, 360–361; for a detailed list of caveats on deciding to send troops, see Nehru, "To CS Jha: Indian Troops for Congo", 3 March 1961, *SWJN,* 2nd ser., vol. 67, 362–363; also see Nehru, "In the Cabinet: Indian Troops for Congo", 4 March 1961, *SWJN,* 2nd ser., vol. 67, 363–364; to explain to parliament India's initial reticence to send troops, and eventual change in policy, see Nehru, "In the Lok Sabha: Indian Troops for Congo", 6 March 1961, *SWJN,* 2nd ser., vol. 67, 368–371; also see Nehru, "To CS Jha: Conditions for Troops Despatch", 23 March 1961, *SWJN,* 2nd ser., vol. 67, 375; and finally, Nehru, "'In the Lok Sabha", 23 March 1961, *SWJN,* 2nd ser., vol. 67, 376–380.
133. "Telegram from C.V. Narasimhan to Dag Hammarskjöld", (Narasimhan was in Delhi to see Nehru), Cordier Collection, Box 165, UN Files, Subject Files, Africa – Congo – Countries G-J, AWC Congo-India, *CUL: MS.*
134. "India Offers Brigade for UN Force in Congo," Statement by the Secretary-General, Press Release SG/1015 + CO/135, 3 March 1961, Office of Public Information, U.N., N.Y., Cordier Collection, Box 140, UN Files, Subject Files, Africa – Congo – Press Releases, *CUL: MS.*
135. "Note for Supplementaries – Lok Sabha Starred Question No. 269 (Final List) for 23 February 1961", Ministry of External Affairs File No. D-1833/61-AFR, 23 February 1961, *NAI.*
136. "Letter from Secretary General Dag Hammarskjöld to Permanent Representative of India", Statement by the Secretary-General, Press Release SG/1016, 4 March 1961, Office of Public Information, U.N., N.Y., Cordier Collection, Box 140, U.N. Files, Subject Files, Africa – Congo – Press Releases, *CUL: MS.*
137. "Cablegram from C.V. Narasimhan to Secretary General," Cordier Collection, Box 165, UN Files, Subject Files, Africa – Congo – Countries G-J, AWC Congo – India, *CUL: MS.*

138. Gopal, *Jawaharlal Nehru*, vol. 3, 156. Nehru seemed to think that anything less than a brigade would only "add to the drift", see Nehru - SWJN/SS - Volume 66 (Congo), 495–496, For Dag Hammarksjöld, 25 January 1961, (sent through CS Jha, Permanent Representative to the UN), MEA File No. REP-13/61-AFR-II, vol. I, 84–85/c.
139. Kennedy and Magennis, *Ireland, the United Nations and the Congo*, 53.
140. Ibid., 156–157.
141. Kennedy and Magennis, *Ireland, the United Nations and the Congo*, 52.
142. Ibid., 156; As a result, Indian troops suffered numerous casualties in Katanga; see [Cover page missing], Ministry of External Affairs File No. D12176/61-AFR, 1961, *NAI*.
143. "Extracts from a letter from Eamonn Kennedy to Con Cremin (Dublin) 'Presentation of Credentials'", Lagos, 9 October 1961 in Kennedy, O'Halpin, O'Malley, Whelan, Keogh, *Documents on Irish Foreign Policy: v. 11: 1957-1961*, 764. On how Indians were "looked upon as the Jews are looked on in Central Europe", see Kennedy and Magennis, *Ireland, the United Nations and the Congo*, 54.
144. For a description of these along with political allegiances, see Dayal, *Life of Our Times*, 439.
145. Ibid., 441–442.
146. "Note to Correspondents," Note No. 2348, 12 June 1961, Office of Public Information, U.N., N.Y., Cordier Collection, Box 140, UN Files, Subject Files, Africa – Congo – Press Releases, *CUL: MS*.
147. "C.S. Jha from the Permanent Mission of India to the UN (on behalf of and transmitting message from Nehru) to DH", File No. S-0844-01-08, 23 May 1961, *UNARMS*.
148. For correspondence on troop deployment, see [Cover Page Missing], Ministry of External Affairs File No. PQA-112/61-AFR II, 1961, *NAI*; [Cover Page Missing], Ministry of External Affairs File No. PQA-99/61-AFR II, 1961, *NAI*; and [Cover Page Missing], Ministry of External Affairs File No. 3875-JSS/61, 1961, *NAI*.
149. Indian 99th Independent Brigade Group in the Congo, 1961–63,

"The Congo Operation 1960-63", Historical Section, Ministry of Defence, Government of India, 1976, Published by the Controller of Publications, accessed 15 September 2014, http://orbat.com/site/cimh/india/99bdecongo.html.

150. For troops deployments, see ibid. For details of Operation Rumpunch, see Hoskyns, *The Congo Since Independence*, 404 onwards, and for troop deployments, 384–467.

151. The original plan was to send the Hunter aircraft, but this was then changed to the Canberras, see "Canberras in the Congo" in Pushpinder Singh Chopra, William Green and Gordon Swanborough, eds. *The Indian Air Force and its Aircraft, IAF Golden Jubilee, 1932-82* (London: Ducimus Books, 1982), 80.

152. Walter Dorn, "The UN's First 'Air Force': Peacekeepers in Combat, Congo, 1960-1964", *The Journal of Military History* 77 (October 2013): 1399–1425.

153. "Canberras in the Congo," in Chopra, Green and Swanborough, *Indian Air Force*. For the strain in Commonwealth relations after an allegation that Britain and France had sabotaged an earlier operation, and subsequent fitting of the Indian Canberras with 1000-pound bombs by the British, see Kalb, *Congo Cables*, 315. For the role of anti-Indian propaganda during the Katangan operations and for India's anger at Britain's role in it, see Hoskyns, *The Congo Since Independence*, 427–441. For Indian Canberras being fitted with British 1000-pound bombs, see Hoskyns, *The Congo Since Independence*, 453. Also see, Namikas, *Battleground Africa*, 172. For a British story about Indian "atrocities" in the Congo that was later soft-pedalled, see Kennedy and Magennis, *Ireland, the United Nations and the Congo*, 128.

154. Cordier Collection, Box 165, UN Files, Subject Files, Africa - Congo - Countries G-J, AWC Congo – India, *CUL: MS*.

155 "Letter from Permanent Mission in New York to MEA," Ministry of External Affairs File No. PQA115/61-AFR II, 1961, *NAI*.

156. Ibid., 159.

157. "Records of the UNGA and Security Council on the question of South West Africa and Congo crisis." V.K. Krishna Menon Papers, 1st and 2nd Instalment, File No. 877, April 1961–October 1961, *NMML.*
158. "Confidential report from Frederick H. Boland to Con Cremin (Dublin) (PR 4 UN (61)) (M/13/6/4) (Confidential) (Copy), New York, 18 September 1961", Kennedy, O'Halpin, O'Malley, Whelan, Keogh, *Documents on Irish Foreign Policy: v. 11: 1957-1961*, 708.
159. "Appeal to General K S Raja of the United Nations Forces in Katanga", "Note to Correspondents," Note No. 2457, 22 December 1961, Office of Public Information, U.N., N.Y., Cordier Collection, Box 140, UN Files, Subject Files, Africa - Congo - Press Releases, *CUL: MS.* The appeal said, "We think that we are all allowed to live. We thank your soldiers in the Elisabeth district of Elisabethville, where it is now possible to walk peacefully."
160. Jawaharlal Nehru, quoted in Gopal, *Jawaharlal Nehru*, vol. 3, 161.
161. "Note to Correspondents," Press Release SG/1124 + CO/186, 23 January 1962, Office of Public Information, U.N., N.Y., Cordier Collection, Box 140, UN Files, Subject Files, Africa - Congo - Press Releases, *CUL: MS.*
162. Kennedy and Magennis, *Ireland, the United Nations and the Congo*, 188.
163. Ibid., 2–3.
164. Gopal, *Jawaharlal Nehru*, vol.3, 160.
165. Chatterji, *Storm over the Congo*, 64.
166. Ibid., 75–79 for discussion on composition of Indian contingent.
167. Ibid., 80.
168. Kent, *America, the UN and Decolonisation*, 115.
169. Kalb, *Congo Cables*, 255.
170. For the movement by 4th Madras and Rajputana Rifles, the Gurka regiment, see ibid., 81–91.
171. Author's interview with Major General Ashok Mehta, who fought with the 2/5th Gurkha Rifles as part of the 99th Infantry Brigade, who fought in the Congo as part of the Indian troops with the ONUC.

172. For an excellent retelling of the end of the secession from Elizabethville but right up to Kolwezi across the Lufira river, see Namikas, *Battleground Africa*, 174.
173. Author's interview with Major General Ashok Mehta, who fought with the 2/5th Gurkha Rifles as part of the 99th Infantry Brigade, who fought in the Congo as part of the Indian troops with the ONUC.
174. V.K. Krishna Menon, UNGA 16th Session Official Records, 1025th Plenary Meeting, 4 October 1961, 249, accessible at https://documents-dds-ny.un.org/doc/UNDOC/GEN/NL6/205/08/PDF/NL620508.pdf?OpenElement
175. Namikas, *Battleground Africa*, 172 onwards. Also see Kalb, *Congo Cables*, 198.
176. Chatterji, *Storm over the Congo*, 87.
177. "The Indian public 'simply would not stand for it'". For Kennedy's understanding of Nehru's dilemma in keeping Indian troops in the Congo even though they were unable to retaliate due to use of force restrictions, see Kalb, *Congo Cables*, 358.
178. See Ministry of External Affairs File No. PQA-194/61-AFR II, *1961, NAI.*
179. Kalb, *Congo Cables*, 466. Kalb lays out ways in which Raja's personality was disliked in the Congo.
180. For criticism of Rikhye, see Kalb, *Congo Cables*, 107–109.
181. For the ill-conduct of UN troops, and Brigadier Raja's efforts at reigning them in, see Hoskyns, *The Congo Since Independence*, 457.
182. For a discussion, See Kalb, *Congo Cables*, 107–109, 121, 125–127, 145, 158, 160.
183. Chatterji, *Storm over the Congo*, 62.
184. T. Ramachandran, "India death toll highest in UN peacekeeping operations", *The Hindu*, 30 October 2014, accessible at http://www.thehindu.com/opinion/blogs/blog-datadelve/article6547767.ece
185. Darya Pushkina (2006) "A recipe for success? Ingredients of a successful peacekeeping mission", *International Peacekeeping*, 13:2, 133–149.

186. For an account of the fighting in Katanga involving Capt. Salaria, see Kennedy and Magennis, *Ireland, the United Nations and the Congo*, 194.
187. Author's interview with Major General Ashok Mehta, who fought with the 2/5th Gurkha Rifles as part of the 99th Infantry Brigade, who fought in the Congo as part of the Indian troops with the ONUC.
188. By courtesy of Michael Kennedy in personal correspondence to the author: "this on the Gurkhas from Lt Jim Condon (B Coy 35th Irish Inf Bn) who wrote in his Congo diary (MA PC 0346) for 12/10/61 'Bn of Gurkhas on Airport – they are real soldiers – we are learning the hard way'"; "Confidential report from Frederick H. Boland to Con Cremin (Dublin), (M/13/6) (Confidential) New York, 12 September 1961", in Kennedy, O'Halpin, O'Malley, Whelan, Keogh, *Documents on Irish Foreign Policy*, vol. 11: 1957–1961, 692.
189. For the special position of the neutrals and the non-aligned in peacekeeping operations, see Hoskyns, *The Congo Since Independence*, 478; see also Spooner, *Canada, the Congo Crisis, and UN Peacekeeping*, 4.
190. Brecher, *India and World Politics*, 97–99.
191. Dayal, *Life of Our Times*, 454–455.
192. Chatterji, *Storm over the Congo*, 185.
193. "Nehru at a Press Conference in London, 7 July 1962," File No. S-0845-10-13, 12 July 1962, *UNARMS*.
194. Spooner, *Canada, the Congo Crisis, and UN Peacekeeping*, 7.
195. Kalb is of the view that force was favoured by Afro-Asians, without specifying the various cleavages in thought amongst this large grouping. Kalb, *Congo Cables*, 290.
196. Nehru, "Inaugural Address to Seminar on Problems of Emergent Africa", 17 February 1961, New Delhi, (the seminar was organized by the Indian Council for Africa and was held between 17 and 19 February 1961), *SWJN*, 2nd ser., vol. 67, 335–342.
197. Harold Macmillan quoted in Kalb, *Congo Cables*, 290.
198. Hoskyns, *The Congo Since Independence*, 256–258.
199. Ibid., 310.

200. Nehru, "For Kwame Nkrumah: No need for Accra Meeting on Congo", 11 May 1961, *SWJN,* 2nd ser., vol. 68, 708–709.
201. Nehru, "Inaugural Address to Seminar on Problems of Emergent Africa", 17 February 1961, New Delhi, (the seminar was organized by the Indian Council for Africa and was held between 17 and 19 February 1961), *SWJN,* 2nd ser., vol. 67, 335–342.
202. Subimal Dutt, *With Nehru in the Foreign Office* (Columbia: South Asia Books, 1977), 272–273.
203. M.C. Chagla, Selected Writings by him, S. No. 29, 19 September 1961, *NMML*, 1–2, "Broadcast on the death of Mr. Hammarskjöld.
204. "Cablegram from C.V. Narasimhan to Secretary General," Cordier Collection, Box 165, UN Files, Subject Files, Africa - Congo - Countries G-J, AWC Congo – India, *CUL: MS.*
205. Rakove, *Kennedy, Johnson and the Nonaligned World*, 99.
206. For an analysis of these moves, see ibid., 99–100.
207. For an excellent discussion, see Dietmar Rothermund, *The Era of Non-Alignment*, in Nataša Mišković, Harald Fischer-Tiné and Nada Boškovska Leimgruber, eds. *The Non-Aligned Movement and the Cold War: Delhi, Bandung, Belgrade* (Oxon; New York: Routledge, 2014), 25–26.
208. Chatterji, *Storm over the Congo*, 150–151.
209. Rakove, *Kennedy, Johnson and the Nonaligned World*, 97. Rakove makes the point that non-aligned leaders had "raised expectations" of American policy, but ignores Nehru, who relied less and less on American support and much more in the Congo Crisis than anywhere else, on Indian initiative.
210. Dayal, *Mission for Hammarskjold,* 121.
211. Chatterji, *Storm over the Congo*, 22.
212. This extended into their communication with the ONUC. See, "Items in Peace-keeping operations – United Nations Operations in the Congo - US Congressional Record – Senator Dodd re: Congo crisis," File No. S-0875-0007-07-00001, 14 July 1961, *UNARMS.*

213. "Communism and Africa," Ministry of External Affairs File No. C/104/15/CH/63, 1963, *NAI*.
214. "Letter from Secretary of State Rusk to the Ambassador to India, Source, Washington, July 31, 1961," *FRUS*, 1961–1963, Volume XIX, South Asia, ed. Smith, Document 33.
215. "Journal Entry of September 30, 1961" in Galbraith, *Ambassador's Journal*, 218.
216. Chatterji, *Storm over the Congo*, 224.
217. Ibid.
218. Ibid., 100.
219. Nehru, "A Foreign Policy for India", 13 September 1927, *SWJN*, 1st ser., vol. 2, 348.
220. This included domestic questions; for instance, when an Indian soldier was killed by a shot fired from the Belgian Consulate Building in Elisabethville, a question was raised in the Indian parliament demanding that a protest be made to the Belgian Government. The matter had to be closed by reminding the house that the Indian troops were working there under the UN command, and therefore not in a national capacity. See Ministry of External Affairs File No. PQA-194/61-AFR II, *1961, NAI*.
221. V.K. Krishna Menon, UNGA 16th Session Official Records, 1025th Plenary Meeting, 4 October 1961, 249, accessible at https://documents-dds-ny.un.org/doc/UNDOC/GEN/NL6/205/08/PDF/NL620508.pdf?OpenElement
222. Ibid.
223. Ibid., 106.
224. Michael Brecher, *India and World Politics: Krishna Menon's View of the World*. (Toronto: Oxford University Press, 1968), 105.
225. Letter of 17 April 1961, Galbraith to J.F.K., in Galbraith, *Ambassador's Journal*, 76.
226. Gopal, *Jawaharlal Nehru*, vol. 3, 145–146.
227. Ibid., 161.

228. Jawaharlal Nehru, "Changing India," *Foreign Affairs* 41, 3 (1963): 453–465.
229. Brecher, *India and World Politics*, 97–99.
230. Gundevia quoted "Cablegram from C.V. Narasimhan to Secretary General," Cordier Collection, Box 165, UN Files, Subject Files, Africa - Congo - Countries G-J, AWC Congo – India, *CUL: MS*.
231. Brecher, *India and World Politics*, 100.
232. Partha Chatterjee, *The Partha Chatterjee Omnibus* (New Delhi: Oxford University Press, 2007), 25.
233. Nehru, Speech in Rajya Sabha, 12 February 1960, quoted in Gopal, *Jawaharlal Nehru*, vol.3, 161.
234. Brecher, *India and World Politics*, 99.
235. "Telegram from the Mission at the United Nations to the Department of State, New York, December 2, 1960. 1592. Congo," *FRUS*, 1958–1960, Volume XIV, Africa, eds. Schwar and Shaloff, Document 2274.
236. Dayal in "The Congo: Exit Raj," *TIME Magazine*, 2 June 1961, accessed 31 October 2014, http://content.time.com/time/magazine/article/0,9171,826993,00.html.
237. Mark Mazower, *Governing the World: The History of an Idea* (New York: Penguin Press, 2012), 267–268.
238. Dayal, *Life of Our Times*, 454–455.
239. Chatterji, *Storm over the Congo*, 185.
240. Nehru, 882nd Plenary Meeting, Monday, 3 October 1960, at 10.30 a.m, 324.
241. Ibid., 325.
242. "Telegram from the Mission at the United Nations to the Department of State, New York, October 15, 1960, 8 p.m.," *FRUS*, 1958–1960, Volume XIV, Africa, eds. Schwar and Shaloff, Document 243.
243. "Nehru at a Press Conference in London, 7 July 1962," File No. S-0845-10-13, 12 July 1962, *UNARMS*.
244. "Press Release BIO/165," File No. S-0875-2-8, 13 August 1962, *UNARMS*.

245. Dayal, *Life of Our Times*, 427–428.
246. Subimal Dutt, *With Nehru in the Foreign Office* (Columbia: South Asia Books, 1977), 272–273.
247. "'General Note on Certain Problems of Africa' by Apa B. Pant," Ministry of External Affairs File No. F-39/9/55-AFR II, 1955, *NAI*, 8–9.
248. Ibid.
249. Ibid.

Epilogue

1. Westad, Odd Arne. *The Global Cold War: Third World Interventions and the Making of Our Times* (New York: Cambridge University Press, 2005), 1.
2. Walker, R.B.J. *Inside/Outside: International Relations as Political Theory* (New York: Cambridge University Press, 1992), 5.
3. Nehru's reply to a question by Andre Malraux, quoted in Sunil Khilnani, "Nehru's Faith", *Outlook*, 9 December 2002.
4. Kamola, I. "IR, the Critic, and the World: From Reifying the Discipline to Decolonising the University", *Millennium: Journal of International Studies*, 2020, vol. 48, no. 3, 245–270.
5. Menon, Dilip M. "Bandung Is Back: Afro-Asian Affinities", *Radical History Review*, vol. 2014, no. 119, 241, https://doi.org/10.1215/01636545-2402153.

Bibliography

Primary Sources

Unpublished Sources

Ministry of External Affairs (MEA) Archives, New Delhi, India

The Hungarian Revolution 1956 – Documents, Volume I, Part I, MEA Archives.

The Hungarian Revolution 1956 – Documents, Volume I, Part II, MEA Archives.

The Hungarian Revolution 1956 – Documents, Volume II, Part I, MEA Archives.

Treaty of Friendship Between the Union of India and the Republic of Egypt, 1955, Commonwealth Legal Information Institute, Ministry of External Affairs, India Databases, 1955.

Ministry of External Affairs Files, 1947–1964, *National Archives of India*, India.

Nehru Memorial Museum and Library (NMML), New Delhi, India

All India Congress Committee (AICC) Files.

M.C. Chagla Papers.

Subimal Dutt Papers.

Y.D. Gundevia Papers.

P.N. Haksar Papers.

Jawaharlal Nehru Papers.

Vijaya Lakshmi Pandit Papers.
Apa Pant Papers.
B.N. Rau Papers.
Thimmayya Papers.
V.K. Krishan Menon Papers

Foreign Relations of the United States (FRUS)

Department of State USA. *Foreign Relations of the United States (FRUS) 1950, Volume VII, Korea.* Washington: Government Printing Office, 1998. http://digital.library.wisc.edu/1711.dl/FRUS.FRUS1950v07.

Claussen, Paul, Joan M. Lee, David W. Mabon, Nina J. Noring, Carl N. Raether, William F. Sanford, Stanley Shaloff, William Z. Slany, and Louis J. Smith, eds. "Foreign Relations of the United States (FRUS), 1952–1954, Volume XI, Part 1, Africa and South Asia (in two parts)." *Department of State USA.* Washington: Government Printing Office, 1988.

Keefer, Edward C., ed. *Foreign Relations of the United States (FRUS), 1952–1954, Volume XV, Part 1, Korea (in two parts).* Washington: Government Printing Office, 1984.

Keefer, Edward C., ed. *Foreign Relations of the United States (FRUS), 1952–1954, Volume XV, Part 2, Korea (in two parts).* Washington: Government Printing Office, 1984.

McMahon, Robert J., and Stanley Shaloof, eds. *Foreign Relations of the United States (FRUS), 1955–1957, Volume VIII, South Asia.* Washington: Government Printing Office, 1987.

Noring, Nina J., ed. *Foreign Relations of the United States (FRUS), 1955–1957, Volume XVI, Suez Crisis, July 26–December 31, 1956.* Washington: Government Printing Office, 1990.

Keefer, Edward C., Ronald D. Landa, and Stanley Shaloff, eds. *Foreign Relations of the United States (FRUS), 1955–1957, Volume XXV, Eastern Europe.* Washington: Government Printing Office, 1990.

Schwar, Harriet D., and Stanley Shaloff, eds. *Foreign Relations of the United*

States (FRUS), 1958–1960, Volume XIV, Africa. Washington: Government Printing Office, 1992.

Smith, Louis J. *Foreign Relations of the United States (FRUS)*, 1961–1963, *Volume XIX, South Asia*. Washington: Government Printing Office, 1996.

Schwar, Harriet D., ed. *Foreign Relations of the United States (FRUS), 1961–1963, Volume XX, Congo Crisis*. Washington: Government Printing Office, 1994.

Howland, Nina D., ed. *Foreign Relations of the United States (FRUS), 1961–1963, Volume XXI, Africa*. Washington: Government Printing Office, 1995.

United Nations Records and Archives Management (UNARMS), New York, U.S.A.

UNARMS. *First Information Report on the work of the UNTCOK*. UN Document A/523, 9 February 1948.

UNARMS. *Krishna Menon's statements during the United Nations Advisory Committee on the Congo Meetings*. File No. S-0849-0001-02-00001, 9–15 November 1960.

UNARMS. *Dag Hammarskjold to Adlai Stevenson*. File No. S-0844-01-08, 27 March 1961.

UNARMS. *Dag Hammarskjold to Nehru letter*. File No. S-0844-01-08, 27 March 1961.

UNARMS. *C.S. Jha from the Permanent Mission of India to the UN (on behalf of and transmitting message from Nehru) to DH*. File No. S-0844-01-08, 23 May 1961.

UNARMS. *Items in Peace-keeping operations - United Nations Operations in the Congo - US Congressional Record - Senator Dodd re: Congo crisis*. File No. S-0875-000 07-00001, 14 July 1961.

UNARMS. *Nehru at a Press Conference in London, 7 July 1962*. File No. S-0845-10-13, 12 July 1962.

UNARMS. *Press Release BIO/165*. File No. S-0875-2-8, 13 August 1962.

UN Official Records

United Nations Library. "Second Session, Plenary Meetings, Volume 1." *General Assembly Official Records (GAOR)*, 134, 137–138. New York, 1947.

United Nations Library. "Fifth Session, First Committee, 346–350th Meetings, 30 September-3 October 1950." *General Assembly Official Records (GAOR)*. New York, 1950.

United Nations Library. "Fifth Year No.15, 473rd Meeting, 25 June 1950." *United Nations Security Council Official Records (UNSCOR)*, 1–13. New York, 1950.

United Nations Library. "344th Plenary Meeting, Wednesday, 14 November at 3p.m. Palais de Chaillot, Paris, Sixth Session." *General Assembly Official Records (GAOR)*. New York, 1951.

United Nations Library. "Seventh Session, First Committee, 525th Meeting, 19 November 1952." *General Assembly Official Records (GAOR)*, 111–115. New York, 1952.

United Nations Library. "Seventh Session, First Committee, 529th Meeting, 24 November 1952. *General Assembly Official Records (GAOR)*, 135–141. New York, 1952.

United Nations Library. "Seventh Session, First Committee, 594th Meeting, 9 April 1953." *General Assembly Official Records (GAOR)*, 582. New York, 1953.

United Nations Library. "Seventh Session, First Committee, 602nd-603rd Meetings, 15–16 April 1953." *General Assembly Official Records (GAOR)*, 637–648. New York, 1953.

United Nations Library. "Second Emergency Special Session of the UNGA - 1004-E.S.(II)." *General Assembly Official Records (GAOR)*. New York, 1956.

Menon, Vengalil Krishnan Krishna. *Statement at the U.N.G.A., 8th Plenary Meeting, 28 September*. New York: United Nations Organisation, 1953. https://www.pminewyork.org/adminpart/uploadpdf/73877lms8.pdf.

Nehru, Jawaharlal. *General Assembly, Fifteenth Session, 882nd Plenary Meeting, Monday, 3 October at 10.30 a.m.* New York: United Nations Organisation,

1960. https://www.pminewyork.org/adminpart/uploadpdf/25273lms15.pdf

Menon, Vengalil Krishnan Krishna. "Speech at the 492nd Plenary Meeting, Wednesday, 6 October at 3 p.m." *General Assembly Official Records (GAOR)*. New York: United Nations Organisation, 1954.

Menon, Vengalil Krishnan Krishna. "Statement at the General Assembly, Fifteenth Session, 906th Plenary Meeting, Monday, 17 October at 10.30 am." *General Assembly Official Records (GAOR)*. New York: United Nations Organisation, 1960.

Rau, Benegal Narsing. "Statement at the U.N.G.A, 5th Session, 286th Plenary Meeting, 27 September, Flushing Meadow." New York, 1950. https://www.pminewyork.org/adminpart/uploadpdf/94699lms05a.pdf.

Columbia University Library, Manuscript Collections (CUL: MS)

"Note to Correspondents." Note No. 2227, Office of Public Information, United Nations (U.N.), New York (N.Y.), Cordier Collection, Box 78, UN Files, Cordier: Official Trips 1956–1962, *CUL: MS*. 27 August 1960.

"Reports of the UN Commission for the Unification and Rehabilitation of Korea." General Assembly A/C.1/734, Cordier Collection, Box 132, U.N. Files, Subject Files, Asia, *CUL: MS*. 17 November 1952.

"Statement by the Secretary-General." Press Release SG/949, Office of Public Information, U.N., N.Y., Cordier Collection, Box 140, U.N. Files, Subject Files, Africa - Congo - Press Releases, *CUL: MS*. 20 August 1960.

Note No.2226, Office of Public Information, U.N., N.Y., Cordier Collection, Box 140, U.N. Files, Subject Files, Africa - Congo - Press Releases Note to Correspondents, *CUL: MS*. 27 August 1960.

"Statement by the Secretary-General." Press Release SG/1003, Office of Public Information, U.N., N.Y., Cordier Collection, Box 140, U.N. Files, Subject Files, Africa - Congo - Press Releases, *CUL: MS*. 6 February 1961.

"Message Received by UN Secretary General Dag Hammarskjold from Jawaharlal Nehru, Prime Minister of India." Press Release SG/1007,

Statement by the Secretary-General, Office of Public Information, U.N., N.Y., Cordier Collection, Box 140, UN Files, Subject Files, Africa - Congo - Press Releases, *CUL: MS*. 15 February 1961.

"Kwame Nkrumah to Secretary General Dag Hammarskjold." Press Release PM/3965, Office of Public Information, U.N., N.Y., Cordier Collection, Box 140, UN Files, Subject Files, Africa - Congo - Press Releases, *CUL: MS*. 18 February 1961.

"India Offers Brigade for UN Force in Congo." Statement by the Secretary General Dag Hammarskjold, Press Release SG/1015 + CO/135, Office of Public Information, U.N., N.Y., Cordier Collection, Box 140, UN Files, Subject Files, Africa - Congo - Press Releases, *CUL: MS*. 3 March 1961.

"Letter from Secretary General Dag Hammarskjold to Permanent Representative of India." Statement by the Secretary-General, Press Release SG/1016, Office of Public Information, U.N., N.Y., Cordier Collection, Box 140, U.N. Files, Subject Files, Africa - Congo - Press Releases, *CUL: MS*. 4 March 1961.

"Statement by Dag Hammarskjold to the General Assembly, 5 April 1961." Statement by the Secretary General, Press Release SG/1020, Office of Public Information, U.N., N.Y., Cordier Collection, Box 140, U.N. Files, Subject Files, Africa - Congo - Press Releases, *CUL: MS*. 5 April 1961.

"Statement by the Secretary General." Press Release SG/1034, Office of Public Information, U.N., N.Y., Cordier Collection, Box 140, UN Files, Subject Files, Africa - Congo - Press Releases, *CUL: MS*. 25 May 1961.

"Note to Correspondents." Note No.2348, Office of Public Information, U.N., N.Y., Cordier Collection, Box 140, UN Files, Subject Files, Africa - Congo - Press Releases, *CUL: MS*. 12 June 1961.

"Note to Correspondents." Note No. 2457, Office of Public Information, U.N., N.Y., Cordier Collection, Box 140, UN Files, Subject Files, Africa - Congo - Press Releases, *CUL: MS*. 22 December 1961.

"Note to Correspondents." Press Release SG/1124 + CO/186, Office of Public Information, U.N., N.Y., Cordier Collection, Box 140, UN Files,

Subject Files, Africa - Congo - Press Releases, *CUL: MS.* 23 January 1962.

Cordier Collection, Box 157, UN Files, Subject Files, Africa - Congo - Advisory Committee Conciliation Commission, *CUL: MS.* 20 January 1961.

"Letter from Dragon Protitch to Secretary-General." Cordier Collection, Box 157, UN Files, Subject Files, Africa - Congo - Advisory Committee Conciliation Commissions, *CUL: MS.* 24 January 1961.

"Letter from Secretary General to Dragan Protitch." Cordier Collection, Box 157, U.N. Files, Subject Files, Africa - Congo - Advisory Committee Conciliation Commission, *CUL: MS.*

Cordier Collection, Box 157, UN Files, Subject Files, Africa - Congo - Advisory Committee Conciliation Commission, *CUL: MS.* 13 February 1961.

"Cablegram from C.V. Narasimhan to Secretary General." Cordier Collection, Box 165, UN Files, Subject Files, Africa - Congo - Countries G-J, AWC Congo – India, *CUL: MS.*

"Cablegram from Dag Hammarskjold to Nehru." R.J. Bunche/ ld 3053, 2932, Cordier Collection, Box 165, U.N. Files, Subject Files, Africa - Congo - Countries G-J, AWC Congo – India, *CUL: MS.* 21 January 1961.

Cordier Collection, Box 165, UN Files, Subject Files, Africa - Congo - Countries G-J, AWC Congo – India, *CUL: MS.*

Constituent Assembly Debates

Constituent Assembly of India, Debates, vol. 1, 13 December 1946. http://parliamentofindia.nic.in/ls/debates/debates.htm.

Indian Constituent Assembly (Legislative), 8 March 1948. India Information, vol. 22, 15 April 1948. http://parliamentofindia.nic.in/ls/debates/debates.htm.

Cold War International History Project

"Report, Chinese International Department, Regarding Soviet Suggestion towards Ceasefire Negotiations, June 26, 1951." 113-00105-01, Ministry Archives of China, History and Public Policy Program Digital Archive, Wilson Center, 1951. http://digitalarchive.wilsoncenter.org/document/117406.

"Statement of Molotov, Minister of Foreign Affairs on the Korean Question, March 31, 1953." History and Public Policy Program Digital Archive, Obtained by Andrei Mefodievich Ledovskii, 1953. http://digitalarchive.wilsoncenter.org/document/117426.

"Working Notes from the Session of the CPSU CC Presidium." History and Public Policy Program Digital Archive, 31 October 1956. http://digitalarchive.wilsoncenter.org/document/117064.pdf?v=634f40572566c230c25ec5951095e1d2.

"Record of Conversation Between Zhou En Lai and Agoston Szkladan." History and Public Policy Programme Digital Archive. PRC FMA, 109-01038-02, 2 November 1956. http://digitalarchive.wilsoncenter.org/document/117695.

"Stenographic Record of 4 November 1956 Meeting of Party Activists." History and Public Policy Program Digital Archive, APRF, Fond 52, Opis 1, Delo 261, List 74–110, Published in "Istochnik", Moscow, No. 6, 2003. http://digitalarchive.wilsoncenter.org/document/113337.

"Third World Reaction to Hungary and Suez 1956: A Soviet Foreign Ministry Analysis." Top Secret, Copy No. 1, 1956. http://digitalarchive.wilsoncenter.org/document/111097.

"Report of the CWIHP Conference on the Congo Crisis." *History through Documents and Memory: A CWIHP Critical Oral History Conference of the Congo Crisis, 1960-1961*. http://www.wilsoncenter.org/article/history-through-documents-and-memory-report-cwihp-critical-oral-history-conference-the-congo.

National Archives and Records Administration (NARA), Washington, U.S.A.

"Press Release by President Truman Announcing Military Assistance to Indochina, 27 June 1950." The Pentagon Papers, Volume 1, Document 8, 372–3. 1950. http://www.archives.gov/research/pentagon-papers/.

National Security Council. *A Documentary on Egypt-Israel Disturbances.* Central Intelligence Agency, ARC646996/LI 263 398, 1957.

Other Unpublished Sources

Eisenhower, Dwight. "Exchange of Messages Between the President and Prime Minister Nehru of India on the Prisoner of War Agreement Reached at Panmunjom." Online by Gerhard Peters and John T. Woolley, *The American Presidency Project*, June 12, 1953. http://www.presidency.ucsb.edu/ws/?pid=9604.

Furey, J.B. "Voting Alignments in the General Assembly." *Columbia University, Doctoral Dissertation Series,* 6620, 1954.

Interview with Arthur Lall, United Nations Oral History Project, 27 June 1990. http://www.unmultimedia.org/oralhistory/2011/10/lall-arthur-samuel/.

"Jawaharlal Nehru Speech Criticising UN Secretary General Dag Hammarskjöld." YouTube video, 1:37, posted 19 April 2014. https://www.youtube.com/watch?v=9RG7LqpSqQY.

Kona, Swapna Nayudu. "The Nehru Years: Indian Non-Alignment as the Critique, Discourse and Practice of Security (1947-1964)." PhD dissertation, King's College London, 2015.

Sukarno. "Speech at the Opening of the Bandung Conference, April 18." *Africa-Asia Speaks from Bandong*. Indonesian Ministry of Foreign Affairs, Djakarta, 1955. http://www.fordham.edu/halsall/mod/1955sukarno-bandong.html.

Published Sources

Gopal, Sarvepalli. ed. *The Selected Works of Jawaharlal Nehru (SWJN), 2nd ser., vol. 3.* New Delhi: Jawaharlal Nehru Memorial Fund, 1997.

Gopal, Sarvepalli. ed. *The Selected Works of Jawaharlal Nehru (SWJN), 2nd ser., vol. 13*. New Delhi: Jawaharlal Nehru Memorial Fund, 1997.

Gopal, Sarvepalli. ed. *The Selected Works of Jawaharlal Nehru (SWJN), 2nd ser., vol. 15. Part 1*. New Delhi: Jawaharlal Nehru Memorial Fund, 1997.

Gopal, Sarvepalli. ed. *The Selected Works of Jawaharlal Nehru (SWJN), 2nd ser., vol. 17*. New Delhi: Jawaharlal Nehru Memorial Fund, 1997.

Gopal, Sarvepalli. ed. *The Selected Works of Jawaharlal Nehru (SWJN), 2nd ser., vol. 21*. New Delhi: Jawaharlal Nehru Memorial Fund, 1997.

Gopal, Sarvepalli, Ravinder Kumar, and H.Y. Sharada Prasad, eds. *The Selected Works of Jawaharlal Nehru (SWJN), 2nd ser., vol. 22*. New Delhi: Jawaharlal Nehru Memorial Fund.

Gopal, Sarvepalli, Ravinder Kumar, and H.Y. Sharada Prasad, eds. *The Selected Works of Jawaharlal Nehru (SWJN), 2nd ser., vol. 28*. New Delhi: Jawaharlal Nehru Memorial Fund.

Kumar, Ravinder, and H.Y. Sharada Prasad, eds. *The Selected Works of Jawaharlal Nehru (SWJN), 2nd ser., vol. 24*. New Delhi: Jawaharlal Nehru Memorial Fund.

Kumar, Ravinder, and H.Y. Sharada Prasad, eds. *The Selected Works of Jawaharlal Nehru (SWJN), 2nd ser., vol. 27*. New Delhi: Jawaharlal Nehru Memorial Fund.

Nehru, Jawaharlal. *India and the World: Essays*. London: G. Allen & Unwin, 1936.

Nehru, Jawaharlal. *The Unity of India, Collected Writings 1937-1940*. New York: John Day Company, 1942.

Nehru, Jawaharlal. *An Autobiography*. New Delhi: Penguin Books India, 2004.

Nehru, Jawaharlal. *Glimpses of World History*. New Delhi: Penguin Books India, 2004.

Nehru, Jawaharlal. *A Bunch of Old Letters: Written Mostly to Jawaharlal Nehru and Some Written by Him*. New Delhi: Penguin Books India, 2005.

Nehru, Jawaharlal. *The Discovery of India*. New Delhi: Penguin Books India, 2008.

Parthasarathi, G., ed. *Jawaharlal Nehru, Letters to Chief Ministers 1947-1964 Volume 1: 1947-1949.* Delhi: Oxford University Press, 1985.

Parthasarathi, G., ed. *Jawaharlal Nehru, Letters to Chief Ministers 1947-1964 Volume 2: 1950-1952,* Delhi, Oxford University Press.

Parthasarathi, G., ed. *Jawaharlal Nehru, Letters to Chief Ministers 1947-1964 Volume 3: 1952-1954.* Delhi: Oxford University Press, 1988.

Parthasarathi, G., ed. *Jawaharlal Nehru, Letters to Chief Ministers 1947-1964 Volume 4: 1954-1957.* Delhi: Oxford University Press, 1990.

Parthasarathi, G., ed. *Jawaharlal Nehru, Letters to Chief Ministers 1947-1964 Volume 5: 1958-1964.* Delhi: Oxford University Press, 1990.

Prasad, H.Y. Sharada, A.K. Damodaran, and Mushirul Hasan, eds. *The Selected Works of Jawaharlal Nehru (SWJN), 2nd ser., vol. 34.* New Delhi: Jawaharlal Nehru Memorial Fund.

Roy, Purabi, S.D. Gupta, and H.S. Vasudevan, eds. *Indo-Russian Relations: 1929-1947, Part 2 of Indo-Russian Relations, 1917-1947: Select Documents from the Archives of the Russian Federation.* Calcutta: Asiatic Society, 2000.

Official Publications

"Asian-African Conference: Live and Let Live in Unity in Diversity." Information Service, Embassy of the Republic of Indonesia, New Delhi, 1955.

"The Asian Relations Being Report of the Proceedings and Documents of the First Asian Relations Conference, March-April 1947." Asian Relations Organization, New Delhi, 1948.

"The Conference of Heads of State or Government of Non-Aligned Countries." Publicistico, Izdavacki Zavod, Belgrade, 1–6 September 1961.

"Commitment to Non-Alignment Has Served India Well." External Affairs Minister Annual Report, *Indian and Foreign Review* 16, no. 12 (1 April 1979): 6.

"The Congo Operation 1960-63," *Indian 99th Independent Brigade Group in the Congo, 1961-63,* Historical Section, Ministry of Defence, Government of India, 1976. http://orbat.com/site/cimh/india/99bdecongo.html

Foreign Policy of India: Texts of Documents 1947-1959, 2nd edition. New Delhi: Lok Sabha Secretariat, 1959.

Nehru, Jawaharlal. *Jawaharlal Nehru's Speeches, March 1953–August 1958, vol. 3*. New Delhi: Ministry of Information and Broadcasting, Government of India, 1958.

Nehru, Jawaharlal. *India's Foreign Policy: Selected Speeches, September 1946–April 1961*. New Delhi: Publications Division, Ministry of Information and Broadcasting, Govt. of India, 1961.

Paths To Peace: India's Voices in UNESCO, 64 Years of UNESCO-India Co-operation. New Delhi: UNESCO, 2009.

Secondary Sources

Books

Acharya, Amitav. *The End of American World Order*. Cambridge: Polity, 2014.

Acharya, Amitav, and Barry Buzan. *Non-Western International Relations Theory: Perspectives On and Beyond Asia*. Oxon: Routledge, 2010.

Alden, Chris, Sally Morphet, and Marco Antonio Vieira. "The Non-Aligned Movement and Group of 77 During the Cold War, 1965–89." In *The South in World Politics*, 57–90. London: Palgrave Macmillan, 2010.

Alker Jr., Hayward R., and Bruce M. Russett. *World Politics in the General Assembly*. New Haven: Yale University Press, 1965.

Allot, Philip. *The Health of Nations*. Cambridge: Cambridge University Press, 2002.

Anderson, Benedict. *Imagined Communities: Reflections on the Origin and Spread of Nationalism*. London: Verso, 1991.

Anthony, Mely Caballero, Ralf Emmers, and Amitav Acharya, eds. *Non-Traditional Security in Asia: Dilemmas in Securitisation*. Aldershot: Ashgate, 2006.

Appadorai, Angadipuram. *The Bandung Conference*. New Delhi: Indian Council of World Affairs, 1955.

Appadorai, Angadipuram. *Dilemma in Foreign Policy in the Modern World*. Delhi: Asia Publishing House, 1963.

Appadorai, Angadipuram. *Select Documents on India's Foreign Policy and Relations 1947–1972, vol. 1*. Oxford: Oxford University Press, 1982.

Appadorai, Angadipuram. *National Interest and India's Foreign Policy*. New Delhi: Kalinga Publications, 1992.

Appiah, Kwame Anthony. *Color Conscious*, Princeton: Princeton University Press, 2000.

Aradau, Claudia. *Rethinking Trafficking in Women: Politics out of Security*. London: Palgrave Macmillan, 2008.

Armitage, David. *Foundations of Modern International Thought*. Cambridge: Cambridge University Press, 2013.

Arnold, Guy. *Third World Handbook*. London: Cassell, 1994.

Arnold, Guy. *The A to Z of the Non-Aligned Movement and Third World, Illustrated edition*. Lanham: Scarecrow Press, 2010.

de Araújo, Caio Simões. ""A Crisis of Confidence": The Postcolonial Moment and the Diplomacy of Decolonization at the United Nations, ca. 1961." In *The United Nations and Decolonization*, edited by Nicole Eggers, Jessica Lynn Pearson, and Aurora Almada e Santos, 125–126. London: Routledge, 2020.

Aydin, Cemil. *The Politics of Anti-Westernism in Asia: Visions of World Order in Pan-Islamic and Pan-Asian Thought*. New York: Columbia University Press, 2007.

Ayoob, Mohammad. *The Third World Security Predicament: State Making, Regional Conflict and the International System*. Boulder: Lynne Rienner Publishers, 1995.

Ayoob, Mohammad. "Defining Security: A Subaltern Realist Perspective." In *Critical Security Studies*, edited by Keith Krause and Michael C. Williams, 121–146. Minnesota: University of Minnesota Press, 1997.

Bailey, Sydney. *The General Assembly of the United Nations*. London: Stevens & Sons Ltd, 1960.

Bailey, Sydney. *The Korean Armistice*. Basingstoke: Macmillan, 1992.

Balzacq, Thierry. "Constructivism and Securitization Studies." In *The Routledge Handbook of Security Studies,* edited by Myriam Dunn Cavelty and Victor Mauer, 56–72. Abingdon and New York: Routledge, 2010.

Balzacq, Thierry, ed. *Securitization Theory: How Security Problems Emerge and Dissolve*. Abingdon and New York: Routledge, 2011.

Balzacq, Thierry. "Enquiries into Methods: A New Framework for Securitization Analysis." In *Securitization Theory: How Security Problems Emerge and Dissolve*, edited by Thierry Balzacq, 31–54. Abingdon and New York: Routledge, 2011.

Bajpai, Girija S. "India and the Balance of Power." In *The Indian Year Book of International Affairs, vol. 1*, edited by Charles H. Alexandrowicz. Madras: The Indian Study Group of International Affairs, University of Madras, 1952.

Bajpai, Kanti. "India." In *Asian Security Practice: Material and Ideational Influences*, edited by Muthiah Alagappa. Stanford: Stanford University Press, 1998.

Bajpai, Kanti, and Siddharth Mallavarapu. *Theorising International Relations: The Region and the Nation*. New Delhi: Orient Longman, 2006.

Bajpai, Kanti, and Siddharth Mallavarapu. "Introduction." In *International Relations in India: Theorising the Region and the Nation*, 1–12. New Delhi: Orient Blackswan, 2009.

Bajpai, Kanti. "Indian Strategic Culture." In *India's Foreign Policy: A Reader*, edited by Kanti Bajpai and Harsh Pant. Oxford University Press India, New Delhi. 2013.

Bajpai, Kanti. "Indian conceptions of order and justice: Nehruvian, Gandhian, Hindutva, and Neo-liberal." In *Order and Justice in International Relations*, edited by Rosemary Foot, John Gaddis, and Andrew Hurrell, 236–61. Oxford: Oxford University Press, 2003.

Bajpai, Uma S. *Non-Alignment: Perspectives and Prospects*. New Delhi: Lancer, 1983.

Barkawi, Tarak. *Soldiers of Empire: Indian and British Armies in World War II*. Cambridge: Cambridge University Press, 2017.

Barnes, Robert. *The US, the UN and the Korean War: Communism in the Far East and the American Struggle for Hegemony in the Cold War*. New York: I.B. Tauris, 2014.

Barros, James. *Trygve Lie and the Cold War: The UN Secretary-General Pursues Peace, 1946–1953*. DeKalb: Northern Illinois University Press, 1989.

Bayly, Christopher. *Recovering Liberties: Indian Thought in the Age of Liberalism and Empire*. Cambridge: Cambridge University Press, 2011.

Békés, Csaba, Malcolm Byrne, and MJ nos Rainer, eds. *The 1956 Hungarian Revolution: A History in Documents*. Budapest: Central European University Press, 2002.

Bell, Duncan. "International Relations and Intellectual History." In *The Oxford Handbook of History and International Relations*, edited by Bukovansky, Keene, Reus-Smit, and Spanu. Oxford: Oxford University Press, 2022 (forthcoming).

Bender, Thomas. *A Nation among Nations: America's Place in World History. 1st ed.* New York: Hill and Wang, 2006.

Berkes, Ross N., and Mohinder S. Bedi. *The Diplomacy of India: Indian Foreign Policy in the United Nations*. Stanford: Stanford University Press, 1958.

Bhagavan, Manu. *The Peacemakers: India and the Quest for One World*. Delhi: Harper Collins India, 2012.

Bigo, Didier. "Security: A Field Left Fallow." In *Foucault on Politics, Security and War*, edited by Michael Dillon and Andrew W. Neal, 93–114. New York: Palgrave Macmillan, 2008.

Blarel, Nicolas. *The Evolution of India's Israel Policy: Continuity, Change, and Compromise Since 1922*. New Delhi: Oxford University Press India, 2014.

Booth, Ken. *Theory of World Security*. Cambridge: Cambridge University Press, 2007.

Borhi, László. *Hungary in the Cold War 1945–1956: Between the United States and the Soviet Union*. Budapest: Central European University Press, 2004.

Bose, Sugata, and Ayesha Jalal, eds. *Nationalism, Democracy, and Development: State and Politics in India*. New Delhi: Oxford University Press India, 1997.

Bose, Sugata, and Kris Manjapra, eds. *Cosmopolitan Thought Zones: South Asia and the Global Circulation of Ideas*. Basingstoke: Palgrave, 2010.

Bose, Sugata. *In Search of Young Asia*. Stanford: Centre for South Asia Lecture Series, Stanford University, 2021.

Bott, Sandra, Jussi M. Hanhimäki, Janick Schaufelbuehl, and Marco Wyss. *Neutrality and Neutralism in the Global Cold War: Between or Within the Blocs?*. London: Routledge, 2016.

Bowles, Chester. *Ambassador's Report*. New York: Harper & Brothers, 1954.

Bradley, Mark Philip. "Decolonization, the Global South, and the Cold War, 1919–1962." In *The Cambridge History of the Cold War. vol. 1*, edited by Melvyn P. Leffler and Odd Arne Westad, 464–485. Cambridge: Cambridge University Press, 2010.

Brecher, Michael. *Nehru: A Political Biography*. New York: Oxford University Press, 1959.

Brecher, Michael. *The New States of Asia: A Political Analysis*. London: Oxford University Press, 1963.

Brecher, Michael. *India and World Politics: Krishna Menon's View of the World*. Toronto: Oxford University Press, 1968.

Burton, Antoinette M. "The Sodalities of Bandung: Toward a Critical 21st Century History." In *Making a World after Empire: The Bandung Moment and Its Political Afterlives*, edited by Christopher J. Lee, 351–361. London: Routledge, 2010.

Buzan, Barry, Ole Wæver, and Jaap De Wilde. *Security: A New Framework for Analysis*. Boulder: Lynne Rienner Publishers, 1998.

Cavelty, Myriam Dunn, and Victor Mauer, eds. *The Routledge Handbook of Security Studies*. Abingdon and New York: Routledge, 2010.

Cavoški, Jovan. "Saving Non-Alignment: Diplomatic Efforts of Major Non-Aligned Countries and the Sino-Indian Border Conflict." In *The Sino-Indian War of 1962: New Perspectives*, edited by Amit R. Dasgupta and Lorenz M. Lüthi, 160–178. Delhi: Routledge India, 2017.

Chacko, Priya. "The Internationalist Nationalist: Pursuing an Ethical Modernity with Jawaharlal Nehru." In *International Relations and Non-*

Western Thought: Imperialism, Colonialism and Investigations of Global Modernity, edited by Robbie Shilliam, 178–196. London & New York: Routledge, 2011.

Chakrabarty, Dipesh. *Provincializing Europe: Postcolonial Thought and Historical Difference*. Princeton: Princeton University Press, 2000.

Chand, Attar. *Nonaligned World Order: Ideology, Strategy, Prospects*. Delhi: UDH Publishers, 1983.

Chatterjee, Partha. *Nationalist Thought and the Colonial World: A Derivative Discourse?* Minneapolis: University of Minnesota Press, 1986.

Chatterjee, Partha. *The Nation and its Fragments: Colonial and Postcolonial Histories*, Princeton: Princeton University Press, 1993.

Chatterjee, Partha. *The Partha Chatterjee Omnibus*. New Delhi: Oxford University Press, 2007.

Chatterjee, Partha. *'Tagore's Non-nation', Lineages of Political Society: Studies in Postcolonial Democracy*. New York: Columbia University Press, 2011.

Chatterjee, Partha. *The Black Hole of Empire: History of a Global Practice of Power*. Princeton: Princeton University Press, 2012.

Chatterji, D.N. *Storm over the Congo*. New Delhi: Vikas, 1980.

Chaudhuri, Rudra. *Forged in Crisis: India and the United States Since 1947*. London: Hurst & Co., 2013.

Chopra, Pushpindar Singh, William Green, and Gordon Swanborough, eds. *The Indian Air Force and its Aircraft, IAF Golden Jubilee, 1932-82*. London: Ducimus Books, 1982.

Coates, Ken. *The Most Dangerous Decade: World Militarism and the New Non-Aligned Peace Movement*. Nottingham: Spokesman, 1984.

Cohen, Stephen. "The World View of India's Strategic Elite." In *India's Foreign Policy: A Reader*, edited by Kanti Bajpai and Harsh Pant, 51–81. New Delhi: Oxford University Press India, 2013.

Collins, Michael. *Empire, Nationalism and the Postcolonial World: Rabindranath Tagore's Writings on History, Politics and Society*. Oxon: Routledge, 2012.

Crabb, Cecil V. *The Elephants and the Grass: A Study of Non-Alignment*. New York: Praegar, 1965.

Curley, Melissa, and Siu-lun Wong, eds. *Security and Migration in Asia: The Dynamics of Securitisation*. London and New York: Routledge, 2008.

Das, Manmath Nath. *The Political Philosophy of Jawaharlal Nehru*. New York: John Day Publishers, 1961.

Davis, Alexander, Vineet Thakur, and Peter Vale. *The Imperial Discipline: Race and the Founding of International Relations*. London: Pluto Press, 2021.

Dayal, Rajeshwar. *Mission for Hammarskjold: Congo Crisis*. Princeton: Princeton University Press, 1975.

Dayal, Rajeshwar. *A Life of Our Times*. New Delhi: Sangam Books, 1998.

Deora, Man Singh, ed. *Documents on India's Role in Afro-Asian Liberation Movements*. New Delhi: Discovery Publishing House, 1994.

Devetak, Richard. *Critical International Theory: An Intellectual History*. Oxford: Oxford University Press, 2018.

Devji, Faisal, ed. *The Impossible Indian: Gandhi and the Temptations of Violence*. London: Hurst Publishers, 2012.

Dinkel, Jürgen. *The Non-Aligned Movement: Genesis, Organization and Politics*. Leiden and Boston: BRILL, 2018.

Dinkel, Jürgen. "'Third World Begins to Flex Its Muscles': The Non-Aligned Movement and the North–South Conflict during the 1970s." In *Neutrality and Neutralism in the Global Cold War*, edited by Jussi M. Hanhimäki, Janick Schaufelbuehl, and Marco Wyss, 108–123. London: Routledge, 2015.

Duara, Prasenjit. *Decolonisation: Perspectives from Now and Then*. London: Routledge, 2003.

Dulffer, Jost, and Marc Frey, eds. *Elites and Decolonization in the Twentieth Century*. Basingstoke: Palgrave Macmillan, 2011.

Dunn, John. *Political Obligation in its Historical Context: Essays in Political Theory*. Cambridge: Cambridge University Press, 2002.

Dunn, John. "Unimagined Community: The Deceptions of Socialist Internationalism." In *Rethinking Modern Political Theory: Essays, 1979–1983*, 103–118. Cambridge: Cambridge University Press, 1985.

Dutt, Subimal. *With Nehru in the Foreign Office*. Calcutta: Minerva Associates, 1977.

Dutta, Krishna, and Andrew Robinson. *Rabindranath Tagore: The Myriad-Minded Man*. New York: St. Martin's Press, 1995.

Eisenhower, Dwight. *The White House Years: Mandate for Change 1953-56*. Garden City: Doubleday, 1963.

Engerman, David. "South Asia and the Cold War." In *The Cold War in the Third World*, edited by Robert J. McMahon, 67–84. New York: Oxford University Press, 2013.

Fierke, Karin. *Critical Approaches to International Security*. Cambridge: Polity Press, 2007.

Fanon, Frantz. *Black Skin, White Masks*. New York: Grove Press, 2008.

Finnane, Antonia. "Bandung as History." In *Bandung 1955: Little Histories*, edited by Antonia Finnane and Derek McDougall, 1–8. Caulfield: Monash University Press, 2010.

Foot, Rosemary. *A Substitute for Victory: The Politics of Peacemaking at the Korean Armistice Talks*. Ithaca: Cornell University Press, 1990.

Foot, Rosemary. "Negotiating with Friends and Enemies: The Politics of Peacemaking in Korea." In *Korea and the Cold War: Division, Destruction, and Disarmament*, edited by Kim, Ch'ŏl-bŏm, and James Irving Matray, 193–208. Claremont: Regina Books, 1993.

Foucault, Michel. *The Archaeology of Knowledge*, Translated by Alan M. Sheridian-Smith. New York: Pantheon, 1972.

Foucault, Michel. *Power/Knowledge: Selected Interviews and Other Writings, 1972–1977*. New York: Random House, 1988.

Foucault, Michel. *Society Must Be Defended: Lectures at the Collège de France, 1975–1976*, Translated by David Macey. New York: Picador, 2003.

Foucault, Michel. "What is Critique?" In *The Politics of Truth,* translated by L. Hochroth and C. Porter, edited by S. Lotringer, 41–82. Los Angeles: Semiotext(e), 1978.

Foucault, Michel. *Security, Territory, Population: Lectures at the College de France 1977–1978,* translated by G. Burchell. New York: Picador, 2009.

Galbraith, John Kenneth. *Ambassador's Journal*. Boston: Houghton Mifflin Co., 1969.

Gandhi, Mohandas K. *Harijan: Collected Issues of Gandhi's Journal 1933–1955, 19 vols.*, edited by Joan V. Bondurant. New York: Garland Publishing, 1973.

Gandhi, Rajmohan. *The Good Boatman*. New Delhi: Penguin Books India, 1997.

Ganguli, Sreemati. *Indo Russian Relations: Making of a Relationship 1992-2002*. Delhi: Shipra Publications, 2009.

Ganguly, Sumit, ed. *India's Foreign Policy: Retrospect and Prospect*. New Delhi: Oxford University Press, 2010.

Gellner, Ernest. *Nations and Nationalism.* Oxford: Blackwell, 1983.

Getachew, Adom. *Worldmaking after Empire: The Rise and Fall of Self-determination*. Princeton: Princeton University Press, 2020.

Goedde, Petra. *The Politics of Peace: A Global Cold War History*. Oxford: Oxford University Press, 2019.

Goldmann, Kjell, Ulf Hannerz, and Charles Westin, eds. *Nationalism and Internationalism in the Post–Cold War Era.* London: Psychology Press, 2000.

Goncharov, Sergei, John W. Lewis, and Litai Xue. *Uncertain Partners: Stalin, Mao, and the Korean War*. Stanford: Stanford University Press, 1993.

Gopal, Sarvepalli. *Jawaharlal Nehru: A Biography*. New Delhi: Oxford University Press India, 2004.

Gopal, Sarvepalli. *Jawaharlal Nehru: A Biography, vol. 1*. New Delhi: Oxford University Press, 2012.

Gopal, Sarvepalli. *Jawaharlal Nehru: A Biography, vol. 2*. New Delhi: Oxford University Press, 2012.

Gopal, Sarvepalli. *Jawaharlal Nehru: A Biography, vol. 3*. New Delhi: Oxford University Press, 2012.

Gopal, Sarvepalli and Srinath Raghavan, eds. *Imperialists, Nationalists, Democrats: The Collected Essays*. New Delhi: Orient Blackswan, 2013.

Grewal, David S. *Network Power: The Social Dynamics of Globalization*. New Haven and London: Yale University Press, 2009.

Grover, Verinder, ed., *International Relations and Foreign Policy of India.* New Delhi: Deep & Deep, 1992.

Guha, Ramachandra. *The Last Liberal and Other Essays*. New Delhi: Permanent Black, 2004.

Guha, Ramachandra. *India After Gandhi: The History of the World's Largest Democracy*. Basingstoke and Oxford: Macmillan, 2007.

Guha, Ramachandra. "Travelling with Tagore." Introduction to *Rabindranath Tagore, Nationalism*. New Delhi: Penguin Classics, 2009.

Guha, Ramachandra, ed. *Makers of Modern India*. Cambridge: Belknap of Harvard University Press, 2011.

Guha, Ramachandra. *Patriots and Partisans: From Nehru to Hindutva and Beyond*. New Delhi: Penguin, 2012.

Guha, Ramachandra. *Gandhi Before India*. New Delhi: Penguin, 2013.

Guha, Ramachandra. *Gopal Krishna Gokhale: The Liberal Reformer*. New Delhi: Penguin Petit Series, 2018.

Guha, Ranajit, ed. *A Subaltern Studies Reader 1986-1995*. Minneapolis: University of Minnesota Press, 1997.

Guha, Ranajit, and Gayatri Spivak, eds. *Selected Subaltern Studies*. New York: Oxford University Press, 1988.

Gundevia, Yezdezard Dinshaw. *Outside the Archives*. Hyderabad: Sangam Books, 1987.

Gupta, Sisir. *India and the International System*. New Delhi: Vikas Books, 1981.

Hall, Stuart. "Old and New Identities, Old and New Ethnicities." In *Culture, Globalization and the World System: Contemporary Conditions for the Representation of Identity*, edited by Anthony D King, 41–68. Minnesota: University of Minnesota Press, 1991.

Hansen, Lene. *Security as Practice: Discourse Analysis and the Bosnian War*. London and New York: Routledge, 2006.

Hardt, Michael, and Antonio Negri. *Empire*. Cambridge: Harvard University Press, 2000.

Heikal, Mohammad H. *The Cairo Document: The Inside Story of Nasser and His Relationship with World Leaders, Rebels, and Statesmen*. New York: Doubleday, 1973.

Hilger, Andreas. "The Soviet Union and India: The Years of Late Stalinism." In *Indo-Soviet Relations during the Cold War: New Russian and German Evidence*, edited by Andreas Hilger, Anna Locher, Roland Popp, Matthias Pintsch, and Shana Goldberg. Zurich: Parallel History Project on Cooperative Security, 2009.

Herz, John. *Political Realism and Political Idealism*. Chicago: University of Chicago Press, 1959.

Hewitt, Vernon. *The New International Politics of South Asia*. Manchester: Manchester University Press, 1997.

Hobson, John A. *Imperialism: A Study*. New York: Cosimo, 2005.

Hovet, Thomas. *Bloc Politics in the United Nations*. Cambridge: Harvard University Press, 1960.

Hovet, Thomas. *Africa in the United Nations*. Evanston: Northwestern University Press, 1963.

Hoskyns, Catherine. *The Congo Since Independence January 1960-December 1961*. London: Oxford University Press, 1965.

Huysmans, Jef. *The Politics of Insecurity: Fear, Migration and Asylum in the EU*. London and New York: Routledge, 2006.

Ishay, Micheline. *Internationalism and Its Betrayal*. Minnesota: University of Minnesota Press, 1995.

Jabri, Vivienne. *War and the Transformation of Global Politics*. New York: Palgrave Macmillan, 2010.

Jackson, Richard. *The Non-Aligned, the UN, and the Superpowers*. New York: Praeger, 1983.

Jahn, Beate. *Liberal Internationalism: Theory, History, Practice.* London: Palgrave Macmillan, 2013.

James, Leslie, and Elisabeth Leake. "Introduction." In *Decolonization and the Cold War: Negotiating Independence,* edited by Leslie James and Elisabeth Leake, 1–18. London: Bloomsbury, 2015.

Jankowitsch, Odette, and Karl Sauvant. *The Third World Without Superpowers: The Collected Documents of the Non-Aligned Countries. 4 vols.* Dobbs Ferry: Oceana, 1978.

Jansen, Godfrey. *Nonalignment and the Afro-Asian State*. New York: Praeger, 1966.

Judt, Tony. *Postwar: A History of Europe Since 1945*. New York: Penguin, 2006.

Kahin, George M. *The Asian-African Conference*. Ithaca: Cornell University Press, 1956.

Kapila, Shruti. *Violent Fraternity: Indian Political Thought in the Global Age*. Princeton: Princeton University Press, 2021.

Kaul, Triloki Nath. *Diplomacy in Peace and War: Recollections and Reflections*. Delhi: Vikas Publishing House, 1979.

Kavic, Lorne. *India's Quest for Security*. Berkeley: University of California Press, 1967.

Kaviraj, Sudipta, ed. *Politics in India*. New Delhi: Oxford University Press, 1997.

Kaviraj, Sudipta. *The Imaginary Institution of India: Politics and Idea.* New York: Columbia University Press, 2010.

Kennedy, Andrew. *The International Ambitions of Mao and Nehru: National Efficacy Beliefs and the Making of Foreign Policy*. New York: Cambridge University Press, 2011.

Kennedy, Michael, and Art Magennis. *Ireland, the United Nations and the Congo: A*

Military and Diplomatic History, 1960–1. Dublin: Four Courts Press, 2014.

Kennedy, Michael, Eunan O'Halpin, Kate O'Malley, Bernadette Whelan, and Dermot Keogh. *Documents on Irish Foreign Policy: v. 11: 1957-1961*. Dublin: Royal Irish Academy, 2018.

Khilnani, Sunil. *The Idea of India*, Farrar. New York: Straus & Giroux, 1999.

Khilnani, Sunil. "Nehru's Judgement." In *Political Judgement: Essays for John Dunn*, edited by Richard Bourke and Raymond Geuss, 257–276. Cambridge: Cambridge University Press, 2009.

Khilnani, Sunil. "Politics and National Identity." In *The Oxford Companion to Politics in India*, edited by Niraja Gopal Jayal and Pratap Bhanu Mehta, 192–204. New Delhi: Oxford University Press, 2010.

Khilnani, Sunil, Rajiv Kumar, Pratap Bhanu Mehta, Prakash Menon,

Nandan Nilekani, Srinath Raghavan, Shyam Saran, and Siddharth Varadarajan. *NonAlignment 2.0: A Foreign and Strategic Policy for India in the 21st Century*. New Delhi: Viking Press, 2013.

Khrushchev, Sergei, ed. *Memoirs of Nikita Khrushchev: Statesman, 1953-1964, vol. 3*, University Park: Pennsylvania State University Press, 2004.

Kimche, David. *The Afro-Asian Movement: Ideology and Foreign Policy of the Third World*. New York: Halstead Press, 1973.

Kothari, Rajni. "The Crisis of the Modern State and the Decline of Democracy." In *Transfer and Transformations: Political Institutions in the Commonwealth*, edited by Peter Lyon and James Manor. Leicester: Leicester University Press, 1983.

Krause, Keith, and Michael C. Williams. "From Strategy to Security: Foundations of Critical Security Studies." In *Critical Security Studies*, edited by Keith Krause and Michael C. Williams, 33–59. Minneapolis: University of Minnesota Press, Minneapolis, 1997.

Kuruppu, Nihal H. *Nonalignment and Peace versus Military Alignment and War*. New Delhi: Academic Foundation, 2004.

Kux, Dennis. *India and the U.S.: Estranged Democracies, 1941-1991*. Washington DC: National Defense University Press, 1992.

Lawrence, Mark A. "The Rise and Fall of Non-Alignment." In *The Cold War in the Third World*, edited by Robert J. McMahon, 139–155. New York: Oxford University Press, 2013.

Lee, Christopher J., ed. *Making a World after Empire: The Bandung Moment and Its Political Afterlives*. Athens: Ohio University Press, 2010.

Lefever, Ernest. *Crisis in the Congo: A United Nations Force in Action*. Washington DC: The Brookings Institution, 1965.

Lefever, Ernest, and Wynfred Joshua. *United Nations Peacekeeping in the Congo: 1960-1964: An Analysis of Political, Executive and Military Control in Four Volumes, Volume 3: Appendices*. Washington DC: The Brookings Institution, 1966.

Lie, Trygve. *In the Cause of Peace. Seven Years with the United Nations*. New York: Macmillan, 1954.

Liska, George. "The 'Third Party': the Rationale of Nonalignment." In *Neutralism and Nonalignment: The New States in World Affairs*, edited by Laurence W. Martin, 88–89. New York: Praeger, 1962.

Long, David, and Brian C. Schmidt, eds. *Imperialism and Internationalism in the Discipline of International Relations,* Albany: SUNY Press, 2006.

Loschke, Angela. "The United Nations Between 'Old Boys' Club' and a Changing World Order: The South African-Indian Dispute at the United Nations, 1945–1955." In *The United Nations and Decolonization*, edited by Nicole Eggers, Jessica Lynn Pearson, and Aurora Almada e Santos, 87–108. London: Routledge, 2020.

Louro, Michele L. "The Making of the League against Imperialism, 1927," in *Comrades against Imperialism: Nehru, India, and Interwar Internationalism (Global and International History*, Cambridge University Press, Cambridge, 2018.

Louro, Michele L. *The League Against Imperialism: Lives and Afterlives*. Leiden: Leiden University Press, 2020.

Lyon, Peter. *Neutralism*. Leicester: University of Leicester Press, 1964.

Mackie, Jamie. *Bandung 1955: Non-Alignment and Afro-Asian Solidarity*. Singapore: Editions Didier Millet, 2005.

Maclean, Kama. *A Revolutionary History of Interwar India: Violence, Image, Voice and Text*. New York: Oxford University Press, 2015.

Macmillan, Harold. *Riding the Storm, 1956-59*. London: Macmillan, 1971.

Malone, David. *Does the Elephant Dance?: Contemporary Indian Foreign Policy*. Oxford: Oxford University Press, 2011.

Manela, Erez. *The Wilsonian Moment: Self-Determination and the International Origins of Anticolonial Nationalism*. New York: Oxford University Press, 2007.

Mates, Leo. *Non-Alignment: Theory and Current Policy*. Belgrade: Institute of International Politics and Economics, 1972.

Mates, Leo. "The Concept of Non-Alignment." In *Issues Before Non-Alignment: Past and Present*, edited by Uma Vasudev, 59–79. New Delhi: Indian Council of World Affairs, 1983.

Mazower, Mark. *No Enchanted Palace: The End of Empire and the Ideological Origins of the United Nations*. Princeton: Princeton University Press, 2009.

Mazower, Mark. *Governing the World: The History of an Idea*. London: Allen Lane, 2012.

Mayer, Arno J. *Wilson vs. Lenin: Political Origins of the New Diplomacy, 1917-1918*. Cleveland: Meridian Books, 1964.

McDonald, Iverach. *A Man of the Times*. London: Hamish Hamilton, 1976.

McGarr, Paul. *The Cold War in South Asia: Britain, the United States and the Indian Subcontinent, 1945-1965*. New York: Cambridge University Press, 2013.

McMahon, Robert J., ed. *The Cold War in the Third World*. New York: Oxford University Press, 2013.

McSweeney, Bill. *Security, Identity and Interests: A Sociology of International Relation.* Cambridge: Cambridge University Press, 2004.

Mehrotra, Raja, ed. *Nehru: Man Among Men*. New Delhi: Mittal Publications, 1990.

Mehta, Gaganvihari L. *Understanding India*. New York: Asia Publishing House, 1959.

Mehta, Pratap B. *The Burden of Democracy*. New Delhi: Penguin Books, 2003.

Mehta, Pratap B. "After Colonialism: The Impossibility of Self-Determination," In *Colonialism and its Legacies*, edited by Jacob Levy, 147–170. New York: Lexington Books, 2011.

Mehta, Uday S. *Liberalism and Empire: A Study in Nineteenth-Century British Liberal Thought*. Chicago: University of Chicago Press, 1999.

Mende, Tibor. *Conversations with Mr. Nehru*. London: Secker & Warburg, 1956.

Mende, Tibor. *Nehru: Conversations on India and World Affairs*. New York: G. Braziller, 1956.

Menon, Kumara P.S. *The Flying Troika: Extracts from a Diary*. London: Oxford University Press, 1963.

Menon, Kumara P.S. *Many Worlds: An Autobiography*. London: Oxford University Press, 1965.

Menon, Venganil K.K. *Krishna Menon, Selected Speeches at The United Nations – I. India and the World, edited by E. S. Reddy and A. K. Damodaran*. New Delhi: Sanchar Publishing House, 1994.

Miller, Manjari. *Wronged by Empire: Post-Imperial Ideology and Foreign Policy in India and China*. Stanford: Stanford University Press, 2013.

Mišković, Natasa. "Between Idealism and Pragmatism. Tito, Nehru and the Hungarian Crisis 1956." In *The Non-Aligned Movement and the Cold War. Delhi – Bandung – Belgrade*, edited by Natasa Mišković, H. Fischer-Tine, and N. Bodškovska, 114–142. Oxon/New York: Routledge, 2014.

Misra, Kashi Prasad. *Studies in Indian Foreign Policy*. New Delhi: Vikas Publications, 1969.

Moraes, Frank. *Jawaharlal Nehru: A Biography, 2nd ed*. Mumbai: Jaico Publishing House, 2008.

Morgan, Patrick. "Security in International Politics: Traditional Approaches." In *Contemporary Security Studies*, edited by Alan Collins, 13–33. Oxford: Oxford University Press, Oxford, 2007.

Morgenthau, Hans J. *Dilemmas of Politics*. Chicago: University of Chicago Press, 1958.

Morphet, Sally. "Three Non-Aligned Summits — Harare 1986; Belgrade 1989 and Jakarta 1992." In *Diplomacy at the Highest Level: The Evolution of International Summitry*, edited by David H. Dunn, 147–162. London: Palgrave Macmillan UK, 1996.

Mortimer, Robert. *The Third World Coalition in International Politics*. New York: Praeger, 1980.

Mukherjee, Radhakamal. *Democracy of the East*. London: P.S. King, 1923.

Muppidi, Himadeep. *The Politics of the Global*. Minneapolis: University of Minnesota Press, 2004.

Mutimer, David. "Critical Security Studies: A Schismatic History." In *Contemporary Security Studies*, edited by Alan Collins, 67–86. Oxford: Oxford University Press, 2007.

Nairn, Tom. "Internationalism: A Critique." In *Faces of Nationalism: Janus Revisited*, edited by Tom Nairn, 25–46. London: Verso, 1998.

Nanda, Balram. *Indian Foreign Policy: The Nehru Years*. New Delhi: Vikas Publishing House, 1976.

Naoroji, Dadabhai. *Poverty and Un-British Rule in India*. London: S. Sonnenschein, 1901.

Nehru, Braj Kumar. *Speaking of India*. Washington: Information Service of India, 1963.

Nehru, Jawaharlal. "Press Statement made in Brussels." In *Selected Works of Jawaharlal Nehru, First Series, vol. 2*, 270–271. New Delhi: Jawaharlal Nehru Memorial Fund, 1927.

Nehru, Jawaharlal. "Indian National Congress Presidential Address in Lahore, 1936." *India and the World: Essays by Jawaharlal Nehru*. London: George Allen and Unwin Ltd., 1936.

Nehru, Jawaharlal. "The Psychology of Indian Nationalism." *Selected Works of Jawaharlal Nehru, First Series, vol. 2*, New Delhi: Orient Longman, 1972.

Nehru, Jawaharlal. "A Foreign Policy for India." In *Selected Works of Jawaharlal Nehru First Series, vol. 2*, 248–264. New Delhi: Orient Longman, 1972.

Nehru, Jawaharlal. *An Autobiography – Towards Freedom*. New Delhi: Penguin Books India, 2004.

Nehru, Jawaharlal. *Glimpses of World History*. New Delhi: Penguin Books India, 2004.

Nehru, Jawaharlal. *The Discovery of India*. New Delhi: Penguin Books India, 2008.

Neocleous, Mark. *Critique of Security*. Edinburgh: Edinburgh University Press, 2008.

Nicholas, Herbert G. *The United Nations as a Political Institution, 2nd ed.* London: Oxford University Press, 1962.

Nkrumah, Kwame. *The Challenge of the Congo*. London: Thomas Nelson, 1967.

Osterhammel, Jürgen. *Unfabling the East – The Enlightenment's Encounter with Asia*. Princeton: Princeton University Press, 2019.

Parekh, Bhikhu C. *Rethinking Multiculturalism: Cultural Diversity and Political Theory*. Basingstoke: Macmillan, 2000.

Pande, Dinesh Chandra. *India's Foreign Policy as an Exercise in Non-Alignment: Nehru-Indira Period, 1946-1977.* Nainital: Gyanodaya Prakashan, 1988.

Pandit, Vijayalakshmi. *The Scope of Happiness: A Personal Memoir*. New Delhi: Crown Publishers, 1979.

Panikkar, Kavalam M. *In Two Chinas: Memoirs of a Diplomat*. London: G. Allen & Unwin, 1955.

Panikkar, Kavalam M. *An Autobiography*. London: Oxford University Press, 1979.

Pant, Apa. *A Moment in Time*. Bombay: Orient Longman, 1974.

Pant, Apa. *Undiplomatic Incidents.* Bombay: Orient Longman Limited, 1987.

Patel, Dinyar P. *Naoroji: Pioneer of Indian Nationalism*. Cambridge: Harvard University Press, 2020.

Patil, Vrushali. *Negotiating Decolonization in the United Nations: Politics of Space, Identity and International Community.* London and New York: Routledge, 2008.

Pedersen, Susan. *The Guardians: The League of Nations and the Crisis of Empire.* Oxford: Oxford University Press, 2015.

Peoples, Columba, and Nick Vaughan-Williams. *Critical Security Studies: An Introduction.* Abingdon and New York: Routledge, 2020.

Peterson, M.J. *The UN General Assembly*. London: Routledge, 2006.

Prasad, B. *The General Experience of Non-Alignment and its Effects for the Future*, New Delhi: s.n, 1968.

Prasad, Sri Nandan. *History of the Custodian Force (India) in Korea, 1953-54.* New Delhi: Historical Section, Ministry of Defence, Government of India, 1976.

Prashad, Vijay. *The Darker Nations: A People's History of the Third World.* New York: New Press, 2007.

Slate, Nico. *Colored Cosmopolitanism: The Shared Struggle for Freedom in the United States and India.* Cambridge: Harvard University Press, 2012.

Steadman, John. *The Myth of Asia.* New York: Simon and Schuster, 1960.

Raghavan, Srinath. *War and Peace in Modern India.* London: Palgrave Macmillan, 2010.

Rajan, Mannaraswamighala S. *Non-Alignment and the Future*. Mysore: University of Mysore, 1970.

Rajan, Mannaraswamighala S., ed. *India's Foreign Relations During the Nehru Era*. Bombay: Asia Publishing House, 1976.

Rajan, Mannaraswamighala S. "The Concept of Non-Alignment and the Basis of the Membership of the Movement." In *Non-Alignment in Contemporary International Relations*. New Delhi: Vikas, 1981.

Mohan, C. Raja. "Beyond Nonalignment." In *India's Foreign Policy: A Reader*, edited by Kanti Bajpai and Harsh Pant, 27–50. New Delhi: Oxford University Press India, 2013.

Rakove, Robert B. *Kennedy, Johnson and the Non-Aligned World*. New York: Cambridge University Press, 2012.

Rana, A.P. *The Imperatives of Nonalignment: A Conceptual study of India's Foreign Policy Strategy in the Nehru Period*. Delhi: Macmillan, 1976.

Rana, A.P. "Detente and Non-Alignment: A Conceptual Study." In *Foreign Policy of India: A Book of Readings*, edited by Kashi Prasad Misra. New Delhi: Thomson Press, 1977.

Rao, Rahul. *Third World Protest: Between Home and the World*. New York: Oxford University Press, 2010.

Rao, Rahul. "Postcolonialism." In *The Oxford Handbook of Political Ideologies*, edited by Michael Freeden, Lyman T. Sargent, and Marc Stears, 271–292. Oxford: Oxford University Press, 2013.

Rao, Rahul. "The Elusiveness of 'Non-Western Cosmopolitanism," In *Politics and Cosmopolitanism in a Global Age*, edited by Sonika Gupta and Sudarsan Padmanabhan, 205–227. Delhi: Routledge India, 2015.

Rasgotra, Maharajakrishna. *A Life in Diplomacy*. London: Penguin UK, 2016.

Rathore, Khushi Singh. "Excavating hidden histories Indian women in the early history of the United Nations." In *Women and the UN*, edited by Rebecca Adami and Dan Plesch, 39–54. London: Routledge, 2021.

Raza, Ali, Francisca Roy, and Benjamin Zachariah, eds. *The Internationalist Moment: South Asia, Worlds and Worldviews, 1917–1939*. London: Sage, 2014.

Reid, Escott. *Hungary and Suez 1956: A View from Delhi*. Oakville: Mosaic Press, 1986.

Rey, Matthieu. "'Fighting Colonialism' Versus 'Non-alignment': Two Arab Points of View on the Bandung Conference." In *The Non-Aligned Movement and the Cold War: Delhi – Bandung – Belgrade*, edited by Natasa Miskovic, Harald Fischer-Tiné, and Nada Boskovska, 163–183. London: Routledge, 2014.

Riggs, Robert E. *Politics in the United Nations.* Urbana: University of Illinois Press, 1958.

Rikhye, Indar Jit. *The Sinai Blunder.* London/Ottawa: Frank Cass & Co., 1988.

Rodman, Peter W. *More Precious than Peace: The Cold War and the Struggle for the Third World.* New York: Scribner's, 1994.

Rothermund, Dietmar, ed. *Memories of Post-Imperial Nations: The Aftermath of Decolonization, 1945–2013*. New Delhi: Cambridge University Press, 2015.

Roy, Allison. *The Soviet Union and the Strategy of Non-Alignment in the Third World*. Cambridge and New York: Cambridge University Press, 1988.

Russell, Bertrand. *Unarmed Victory*. Middlesex: Penguin, 1963.

Russett, Bruce M. *International Regions and the International System: A Study in Political Ecology.* Chicago: Rand McNally, 1967.

Saaler, Sven, and Christopher Szpilman, eds. *Pan-Asianism: A Documentary History, 1920–Present.* Plymouth: Rowman & Littlefield Publishers Inc., 2011.

Saaler, Sven, and J. Victor Koschmann, eds. *Pan-Asianism in Modern Japanese History: Colonialism, Regionalism, and Borders*. London: Routledge, 2007.

Sarkar, Benoy Kumar. *The Futurism of Young Asia: and Other Essays on the Relations between the East and the West*. Berlin: J. Springer, 1922.

Sandler, Stanley, ed. *The Korean War: An Encyclopedia*. New York: Taylor & Francis, 1995.

Schmidt, Brian C., ed. *International Relations and the First Great Debate.* London: Routledge, 2012.

Schmidt, Brian C. "On the History and Historiography of International Relations." In *Handbook of International Relations, 2nd edition*, edited by Walter Carlsnaes, Beth Simmons, and Thomas Risse, 3–23. London: Sage, 2012.

Schmidt, Brian C. *The Political Discourse of Anarchy: A Disciplinary History of International Relations.* Albany: SUNY Press, 2016.

Sen, Amartya. "On Interpreting India's Past." In *Nationalism, Democracy, and Development: State and Politics in India*, edited by Sugata Bose and Ayesha Jalal. New Delhi: Oxford University Press, 1997.

Singham, Arch W., ed. *The Non-Aligned Movement in World Politics.* Westport: Lawrence Hill, 1978.

Singham, Arch W., and Shirley Hune. *Non-Alignment in an Age of Alignments.* London: Lawrence Hill, 1986.

Sheean, Vincent. *Nehru: The Years of Power.* New York: Random House, 1960.

Shukul, Harish C. *India's Foreign Policy: The Strategy of Nonalignment.* Delhi: Chanakya Publications, 1994.

Sluga, Glenda. *Internationalism in the Age of Nationalism.* Philadelphia: University of Pennsylvania Press, 2013.

Smith, Steve. "The Contested Concept of Security." In *Critical Security Studies and World Politics*, edited by Ken Booth, 27–62. Boulder: Lynne Rienner, 2005.

Srinivasan, Krishnan. *Diplomatic Channels.* New Delhi: Manohar, 2012.

Srivastava, Govind N. *India, Non-Alignment and World Peace.* New Delhi: New Delhi Publications, 1984.

Srivastava, Govind N., ed. *India's Foreign Policy: Peace, Security and Co-operation in South Asia,* New Delhi: Indian Institute for Non-Aligned Studies, 1994.

Srivastava, Renu. *India and the Nonaligned Summits: Belgrade to Jakarta.* New Delhi: Northern Book Centre, 1995.

Stölte, Carolien. "'The Asiatic Hour': New Perspectives on the Asian Relations Conference, Delhi, 1947." In *The Non-Aligned Movement and the Cold War: Delhi – Bandung – Belgrade*, edited by Natasa Miskovic, Harald Fischer-Tiné, Nada Boskovska, 57–75. London: Routledge, 2014.

Stokes, Eric. *The English Utilitarians and India.* Oxford: Oxford University Press, 1959.

Stueck, William. *The Korean War: An International History*. Princeton: Princeton University Press, 1995.

Stueck, William. *Rethinking the Korean War: A New Diplomatic and Strategic History*. Princeton: Princeton University Press, 2002.

Tagore, Rabindranath. *Greater India*. Translated by S. Tagore, S. Ganesan. Madras: Triplicane, 1921.

Tagore, Rabindranath. *Nationalism*. New Delhi: Penguin Books, 2009.

Tagore, Rabindranath. *The Essential Tagore*. Edited by F. Alam and R. Chakravarty. Cambridge: Belknap of Harvard University Press, 2011.

Tan, See Seng, and Amitav Acharya, eds. *Bandung Revisited: The Legacy of the 1955 Asian-African Conference for International Order*. Singapore: National University of Singapore Press, 2008.

Taylor, Charles. *Modern Social Imaginaries*. Durham: Duke University Press, 2004.

Thakur, Vineet. *India's First Diplomat: VS Srinivas Sastri and the Rise of Liberal Nationalism*. Bristol: Bristol University Press, 2021.

Thampi, Madhavi. *Indians in China, 1800–1949*. New Delhi: Manohar, 2005.

Thomas, Martin, Bob Moore, and Larry Butler. *Crises of Empire: Decolonization and Europe's Imperial States, 1918–1975*. London: Bloomsbury Academic, 2010.

Tonnies, Ferdinand. "Community and Society." In *The Urban Sociology Reader*, edited by Jan Lin and Christopher Mele, 30–36. London: Routledge, 2005.

Upadhyaya, Priyankar. *Nonaligned States and India's International Conflicts*. New Delhi: South Asian Publishers, 1990.

Vajpeyi, Ananya. *Righteous Republic: The Political Foundations of Modern India*. Cambridge: Harvard University Press, 2012.

Valentine, Chirol. *Indian Unrest*. London: MacMillan, 1910.

Van Dusen, Henry P. *Dag Hammarskjöld: The Statesman and His Faith*. New York: Harper & Row, 1964.

Van Reybrouck, David. *Congo: The Epic History of a People*. New York: HarperCollins, 2014.

Varkey, K.T. *V. K. Krishna Menon and India's Foreign Policy*. New Delhi: Indian Publishers Distributors, 2002.

Von Eschen, Penny M. *Race Against Empire: Black Americans and Anticolonialism, 1937-1957*. New York: Cornell University Press, 1997.

Wæver, Ole, Barry Buzan, Morten Kelstrup, and Pierre Lemaitre. *Identity, Migration and the New Security Agenda in Europe*. London: Pinter, 1993.

Wæver, Ole. "Securitization and Desecuritization." In *On Security*. edited by Ronnie Lipschutz, 44–86. New York: Columbia University Press, 1995.

Wæver, Ole. "The EU as a Security Actor: Reflections from a Pessimistic Constructivist on Post Sovereign Security Order." In *International Relations Theory and the Politics of European Integration*, edited by Morten Kelstrup and Michael C. Williams, 250–294. London: Routledge, 2000.

Wagner, Florian. *Colonial Internationalism and the Governmentality of Empire, 1893–1982*. Cambridge: Cambridge University Press, Cambridge, 2022.

Walker, R.B.J. *Inside/Outside: International Relations as Political Theory*. New York: Cambridge University Press, 1992.

Wendt, Alexander. *Social Theory of International Politics*. Cambridge: Cambridge University Press, 1999.

Wertheim, Stephen. *Tomorrow, the World: The Birth of U.S. Global Supremacy*. Cambridge: Harvard University Press, 2020.

Westad, Odd Arne. *Brothers in Arms: The Rise and Fall of the Sino-Soviet Alliance, 1945-1963*. Stanford: Stanford University Press, 1998.

Westad, Odd Arne. *The Global Cold War: Third World Interventions and the Making of Our Times*. New York: Cambridge University Press, 2005.

Westad, Odd Arne. "Epilogue." In *The Cold War in the Third World*, edited by Robert J. McMahon, 208–220. New York: Oxford University Press, 2013.

Willetts, Peter. *The Non-Aligned Movement: The Origins of a Third World Alliance*. London: Pinter, 1978.

Williams, Gwyneth. "The Non-Aligned Movement." In *Third-World Political Organizations: A Review of Developments*, edited by Gwyneth Williams, 50–71. London: Palgrave Macmillan, 1987.

Wright, Richard. *The Color Curtain: A Report on the Bandung Conference*. Jackson: University Press of Mississipi, 1956.

Wrigley, Charles. *Toward an Orderly System for International Decision-Making: The Experience of the United Nations General Assembly*. Philadelphia: Peace Research Society (International), Third Conference, University of Pennsylvania, 1965.

Wyn Jones, Richard. *Security, Strategy, and Critical Theory*. Boulder: Lynne Rienner Publishers, 1999.

Wyn Jones, Richard. "On Emancipation: Necessity, Capacity and Concrete Utopias." In *Critical Security Studies and World Politics*, edited by Ken Booth, 215–235. Boulder: Lynne Rienner Publishers, 2005.

Journals and Periodicals:

Abraham, Itty. "Science and Secrecy in Making of Postcolonial State." *Economic and Political Weekly* 32, no. 33/34 (1997): 2136–2146.

Abraham, Itty. "From Bandung to NAM: Non-Alignment and Indian Foreign Policy, 1947–65." *Commonwealth & Comparative Politics* 46, no. 2 (2008): 195–219.

Acharya, Amitav. "Ideas, Identity, and Institution-Building: From the 'ASEAN way' to the 'Asia-Pacific way'?" *The Pacific Review* 10, no. 3 (1997): 319–346.

Acharya, Amitav. "Will Asia's Past Be Its Future?" *International Security* 28, no. 3 (2003): 149–164.

Acharya, Amitav. "Global International Relations (IR) and Regional Worlds." *International Studies Quarterly* 58, no. 4 (2014): 647–659.

Acharya, Amitav, and Barry Buzan. "Why is There No Non-Western IR theory: Reflections on and from Asia." *International Relations of Asia Pacific* 7, no. 3 (2007): 287–312.

Acharya, Amitav, and Barry Buzan, "Conclusion: On the possibility of a non-Western IR theory in Asia." *International Relations of the Asia Pacific* 7, no. 3 (2007): 427–438.

Alagappa, Muthiah. "International Relations Studies in Asia: Distinctive Trajectories." *International Relations of the Asia-Pacific* 11, no. 2 (2011): 193–230.

Alam, Muhammad Badiul. "The Concept of Non-alignment: A Critical Analysis." *World Affairs*, 140, no. 2 (1977): 166–185.

Alker, Hayward R. "On Securitization Politics as Contexted Texts and Talk." *Journal for International Relations and Development* 9, no. 1 (2006): 70–80.

Alker, Hayward R. "Supranationalism in the United Nations." *Peace Research Society International) Papers, vol. 3* (1965): 197–212.

Alker, Hayward R. "Dimensions of Conflict in the General Assembly." *American Political Science Review* 58, no. 3 (1964): 642–657.

Amrith, Sunil, and Glenda Sluga. "New Histories of the United Nations." *Journal of World History* 19, no. 3 (2008): 251–274.

Anabtawi, Samir N. "The Afro-Asian States and the Hungarian Question." *International Organization* 17, no. 4 (1963): 872–900.

Anabtawi, Samir N. "Neutralists and Neutralism." *The Journal of Politics* 27, no. 2 (1965): 351–361.

Anderson, Perry. "Internationalism: A Breviary." *New Left Review* 14, (2002): 5–25.

Andersen, Walter. "The Domestic Roots of Indian Foreign Policy." *Asian Affairs* 10, no. 3 (1983): 45–46.

Anon. "The Non-aligned: How Relevant?" *Economic and Political Weekly* 11, no. 22 (1976): 794.

Appadorai, Angadipuram. "Non-Alignment: Some Important Issues." *International Studies*, 20, no. 1–2 (1981): 3–11.

Appadorai, Angadipuram. "The Bandung Conference." *India Quarterly* 11, no. 3 (1955): 207–235.

Appadorai, Angadipuram. "The Asian Relations Conference in Perspective." *International Studies* 18, no. 3 (1979): 275–285.

Aradau, Claudia. "Security and the Democratic Scene: Desecuritization and Emancipation." *Journal for International Relations and Development* 7, no. 4 (2004): 388–413.

Aradau, Claudia. "Limits of Security, Limits of Politics? A response." *Journal for International Relations and Development* 9, no. 1 (2006): 81–90.

Aradau, Claudia and Rens Van Munster. "Exceptionalism and the 'War on Terror': Criminology Meets International Relations." *British Journal of Criminology* 49, no. 5 (2009): 686–701.

Armstrong, Hamilton F. "Neutrality: Varying Tunes." *Foreign Affairs* 35, no. 1 (1956): 57–83.

Babaa, Khalid. "The "Third Force" and the United Nations." *The Annals of the American Academy of Political and Social Science* 362, no. 1 (1965): 81–91. https://doi.org/10.1177/000271626536200110.

Babaa, Khalid, and Cecil Crabb. "Nonalignment as a Diplomatic and Ideological Credo." *The Annals of the American Academy of Political and Social Science* 362, no. 1 (1965): 6–17.

Baldwin, David A. "The Concept of Security." *Review of International Studies* 23, no. 1 (1997): 5–26.

Ball, Margaret. "Bloc Voting in the General Assembly." *International Organisation* 5, no. 1 (1951): 3–31.

Balzacq, Thierry. "The Three Faces of Securitization: Political Agency, Audience and Context." *European Journal of International Relations* 11, no. 2 (2005): 171–201.

Bandarnaike, Sirimavo. "The Non-Aligned Movement and the United Nations." *The Black Scholar: The Non-Aligned Movement* 8, no. 3 (1976): 27–38.

Bandyopadhyaya, Jayantanuja. "The Non-Aligned Movement and International Relations." *India Quarterly* 33, no. 2 (1977): 137–64. https://doi.org/10.1177/097492847703300201.

Banerji, Malabika. "Institutionalization of the Non-Aligned Movement." *International Studies* 20, no. 3–4 (1981): 549–563. https://doi.org/10.1177/002088178102000304.

Barkawi, Tarak, and Mark Laffey. "The Postcolonial Moment in Security Studies." *Review of International Studies* 32, no. 2 (2006): 329–352.

Barkawi, Tarak, and Shane Brighton. "Powers of War: Fighting, Knowledge, and Critique." *International Political Sociology* 5, no. 2 (2011): 126–143.

Barnes, Robert. "On the Limits of New Foundations: A Commentary on R. Harrison Wagner, War and the State." *International Theory* 2, no. 2 (2010): 317–332.

Barnes, Robert. "Between the Blocs: India, the United Nations, and Ending the Korean War." *Journal of Korean Studies* 18, no. 2 (2013): 263–286.

Basu, BK. "The Bandung Conference in Retrospect." *Indian and Foreign Review* 22, no. 14 (1985): 11–13.

Bharucha, Rustom. "Under the Sign of 'Asia': Rethinking Creative Unity Beyond the Rebirth of Traditional Arts." *Inter-Asia Cultural Studies* 2, no. 1 (2001): 151–156.

Bhugaloo, Heeralall. "The Relevance of Non-Alignment." *India International Centre Quarterly: Role of Non-alignment in a Changing World* 3, no. 3 (1976): 16–24.

Bilgrami, Akeel. "Gandhi, the Philosopher." *Economic and Political Weekly* 38–39, (2003): 4159–4165.

Board, Editorial. "Reaffirmation of Neutralism [Editorial]." *The Economic Weekly* 9, no. 26–27–28 (1957): 787–788.

Booth, Ken. "Security and Emancipation." *Review of International Studies* 17, no. 4 (1991): 313–326.

Borhi, László. "Hungary in the Soviet Empire, 1945–1956: New Evidence, New Interpretations." *Hungarian Studies* 20, no. 1 (2005): 21–30.

Bose, Sugata. "Post-Colonial Histories of South Asia: Some Reflections." *Journal of Contemporary History* 38, no. 1 (2003): 133–146.

Bowles, Chester. "New India." *Foreign Affairs* 31, no. 1 (1952): 79–94.

Brecher, Michael. "Neutralism: An Analysis." *International Journal* 117, no. 3 (1962): 224–236.

Brown, Irene. "Studies on Non-Alignment." *The Journal of Modern African Studies* 4, no. 4 (1966): 517–527.

Bubandt, Nils. "Vernacular Security: The Politics of Feeling Safe in Global, National and Local Worlds." *Security Dialogue* 36, no. 3 (2005): 275–296.

Burke, Roland. "'The Compelling Dialogue of Freedom': Human Rights at the Bandung Conference." *Human Rights Quarterly* 28, no. 4 (2004): 947–965.

Buzan, Barry, and Ole Wæver. "Slippery? Contradictory? Sociologically Untenable? The Copenhagen School Replies." *Review of International Studies* 23, no. 2 (1997): 241–250.

Collective, CASE. "Critical Approaches to Security in Europe: A Networked Manifesto." *Security Dialogue* 37, no. 4 (2006): 443–487.

Chakravarthy, I.N. "Towards a Nonaligned News Pool." *Indian and Foreign Review* 13, no. 18 (1976): 15–16.

Chari, P.R. "Non-alignment and International Security." *India International Centre Quarterly: Role of Non-alignment in a Changing World* 3, no. 3 (1976): 68–81.

Chari, P.R. "Nonalignment – Contemporary Justification and Challenges." *Indian and Foreign Review* 13, no. 16 (1976): 13–15.

Chatterjee, Partha. "Empire and Nation Revisited: 50 Years after Bandung." *Inter-Asia Cultural Studies* 6, no. 4 (2005): 487–496.

Chatterji, N.C. "Non-Alignment: A Scriptural Interpretation." *Indian and Foreign Review* 20, no. 11 (1983): 19–20.

Chaudhuri, Rudra. "The Limits of Executive Power: Domestic Politics and Alliance Behaviour in Nehru's India." *India Review* 11, no. 2 (2012): 95–115.

Chavan, Yashwantrao. "United Nations and the Third World." *Indian and Foreign Review* 13, no. 15 (1976): 13–14.

Chavan, Yashwantrao. "Ideals of Nonalignment – World Peace and Prosperity." *Indian and Foreign Review* 13, no. 17 (1976): 13–15.

Chavan, Yashwantrao. "The Methodology of Non-Alignment." *Indian and Foreign Review* 20, no. 10 (1983): 24–26, 45.

Chen, Ching-Chang. "The Absence of Non-western IR theory in Asia Reconsidered." *International Relations of the Asia-Pacific* 11, no. 1 (2011): 1–23.

Cho, Hee-Yeon, and Kuan-Hsing Chen. "Editorial Introduction: Bandung/Third Worldism." *Inter-Asia Cultural Studies* 6, no. 4 (2005): 473–475.

Choucri, Nazli. "The Nonalignment of Afro-Asian States: Policy, Perception, and Behaviour." *Canadian Journal of Political Science/Revue Canadienne de Science Politique* 2, no. 1 (1969): 1–17. https://doi.org/10.1017/S0008423900024574.

Clark, Claire. "Soviet and Afro-Asian Voting in the UN General Assembly, 1946–65." *Australian Outlook* 24, no. 3 (1970): 296–308.

Cohen, Stephen P. "South Asia: The Origins of War and the Conditions for Peace." *South Asian Survey* 4, no. 1 (1997): 25–46.

Connelly, Matthew. "Taking off the Cold War Lens: Visions of North-South Conflict during the Algerian War for Independence." *The American Historical Review* 105, no. 3 (2000): 739–769.

Dasgupta, P. "India's Commitment to Non-Alignment." *Indian and Foreign Review* 14, no. 14 (1977): 13–14.

Davis, Alexander E., and Vineet Thakur. "Walking the Thin Line: India's Anti-Racist Diplomatic Practice in South Africa, Canada, and Australia, 1946–55." *The International History Review* 38, no. 5 (2016): 880–899.

Davis, Richard. "Perspectives on the End of the British Empire: The Historiographical Debate." *Cercles* 28 (2013): 1–23.

Devetak, Richard. "'The Battle Is All There Is': Philosophy and History in International Relations Theory." *International Relations* 31, no. 3 (2017): 261–281.

Devji, Faisal. "Morality in the Shadow of Politics." *Modern Intellectual History* 7, no. 2 (2010): 373–390.

Devji, Faisal. "A Minority of One." *Global Intellectual History,* (2021): 1–7.

Dirlik, Arif. "The Bandung Legacy and the People's Republic of China in the Perspective of Global Modernity." *Inter-Asia Cultural Studies* 16, no. 4 (2015): 615–630.

Du Bois, W.E.B. "India." *Horizon* 1, no. 1 (1907).

Du Bois, W.E.B. "Tagore." *The Crisis* 13, no. 2 (1916): 61–62.

Du Bois, W.E.B. "Egypt and India." *The Crisis* 18, no. 2 (1919): 62.

Du Bois, W.E.B. "Gandhi and India." *The Crisis* 23, no. 5 (1922): 203–207.

Du Bois, W.E.B. "The Freeing of India." *The Crisis* 54, (1947): 301–317.

Dutt, V.P. "Detente and Non-Alignment." *India International Centre Quarterly* 3, no. 3 (1976): 59–64.

Edogun, Clifford. "The Emerging Ideological Trend in the Non-Aligned Movement: Some Reflections on the Havana Conference." *Africa Development / Afrique et Développement* 6, no. 2 (1981): 65–85.

Edwardes, M. 1965, "Illusion and Reality in India's Foreign Policy," *International Affairs*, 41(1), 48–58.

Engerman, David C. "The Second World's Third World." *Kritika: Explorations in Russian and Eurasian History* 12, no. 1 (2011): 183–211.

Fakhruddin, A. "Solidarity and Effectiveness of Non-Aligned Countries to be Preserved: Address to the Joint Session of the Parliament." *Indian and Foreign Review* 13, no. 7 (1976): 5–6.

Floyd, Rita. "Towards a Consequentialist Evaluation of Security: Bringing Together the Copenhagen and the Welsh Schools of Security Studies." *Review of International Studies* 33, no. 2 (2007): 327–350.

Gandhi, Indira. "Non-Alignment to Give a Lead in New Concept of Human Emancipation." *Indian and Foreign Review* 13, no. 22 (1976): 13–15.

Gandhi, Rajmohan. "Prime Minister's Address at NAM Bureau Meeting." *Indian and Foreign Review* 22, no. 14 (1985): 8–9.

Gerits, Frank. "'When the Bull Elephants Fight': Kwame Nkrumah, Non-Alignment, and Pan-Africanism as an Interventionist Ideology in the Global Cold War (1957–66)." *The International History Review* 37, no. 5 (2015): 951–969.

Getachew, Adom, and Karuna Mantena. "Anticolonialism and the Decolonization of Political Theory." *Critical Times* 4, no. 3 (2021): 359–388.

Ginat, Rami. "India and the Palestine Question: The Emergence of the Asio-Arab Bloc and India's Quest for Hegemony in the Post-colonial Third World." *Middle Eastern Studies* 40, no. 6 (2004): 189–218. https://doi.org/10.1080/0026320042000282946.

Goodwin, Geoffrey. "The Expanding United Nations: I-Voting Patterns." *International Affairs (Royal Institute of International Affairs 1944-)* 36, no. 2 (1960): 174–187.

Gopal, Sarvepalli. "What is Non-Alignment?" *India International Centre Quarterly: Role of Non-Alignment in a Changing World* 3, no. 3 (1976): 3–7.

Gopal, Sarvepalli. "Role of Nonalignment in a Changing World." *Indian and Foreign Review* 13, no. 15 (1976): 11–12.

Goswami, Manu. "Imaginary Futures and Colonial Internationalisms." *The American Historical Review* 117, no. 5 (2012): 1461–1485.

Graham, Sarah Ellen, and Alexander E. Davis. "A "Hindu Mystic" or a "Harrovian Realist"? US, Australian, and Canadian representations of Jawaharlal Nehru, 1947–1964." *Pacific Historical Review* 89, no. 2 (2020): 198–231.

Guilhot, Nicolas. "Imperial Realism: Postwar IR Theory and Decolonization." *International History Review* 36, no. 4 (2014): 698–720.

Gupta, Akhil. "The Song of the Nonaligned World: Transnational Identities and the Reinscription of Space in Late Capitalism." *Cultural Anthropology* 7, no. 1 (1992): 63–79.

Gupta, S.R. "Nonalignment: A Principled Stand in World Affairs." *Indian and Foreign Review* 13(21), 11–12.

Halliday, Fred. "Review of "The Soviet Union and the Strategy of Non-Alignment in the Third World", by Roy Allison." *The Slavonic and East European Review* 68, no. 3 (1990): 591–592.

Halliday, Fred. "Three Concepts of Internationalism." *International Affairs (Royal Institute of International Affairs 1944-)* 64, no. 2 (1988): 187–198.

Holloway, Steven. "Forty Years of United Nations General Assembly Voting." *Canadian Journal of Political Science/Revue canadienne de science politique* 23, no. 2 (1990): 279–296.

Hameed, Abdul Cader Shahul. "20 Years of the Non-Aligned Movement." *Indian and Foreign Review* 18, no. 9 (1981): 8–9.

Hansen, Lene. "A Case for Seduction? Evaluating the Poststructuralist Conceptualization of Security." *Cooperation and Conflict* 32, no. 4 (1997): 369–397.

Harshe, Rajen. "India's Non-Alignment: An Attempt at Conceptual Reconstruction." *Economic and Political Weekly* 25, no. 7/8 (1990): 399–405.

Herz, John H. "Idealist Internationalism and the Security Dilemma." *World Politics* 2, no. 2 (1950): 157–180.

Howard, Harry N. "Review of "The New States of Asia: A Political Analysis", by Michael Brecher." *Middle East Journal* 18, no. 2 (1964): 261.

Howard, Neil. "Freedom and Development in Historical Context: A Comparison of Gandhi and Fanon's Approaches to Liberation." *Journal of Pan African Studies* 4, no. 7 (2011): 94–108.

Houston, John A. "Latin America in the United Nations." *United Nations Studies*, No. 8 (1956): 298–299.

Huysmans, Jef. "Revisiting Copenhagen: Or, On the Creative Development of a Security Studies Agenda in Europe." *European Journal of International Relations* 4, no. 4 (1998): 479–505.

Huysmans, Jef. "Defining Social Constructivism in Security Studies: The Normative Dilemma of Writing Security." *Alternatives* 27, no. 1 (2002): 41–62.

Huysmans, Jef. "Minding Exceptions: The Politics of Insecurity and Liberal Democracy." *Contemporary Political Theory* 3, no. 3 (2004): 321–341.

Huysmans, Jef. "What's in an act? On Security Speech Acts and Little Security Nothings." *Security Dialogue* 42, no. 4–5 (2011): 371–383.

Ikenberry, G. John. "The End of Liberal International Order?" *International Affairs* 94, no. 1 (2018): 7–23.

Imlay, Talbot C. "International Socialism and Decolonization During the 1950s: Competing Rights and the Postcolonial Order." *The American Historical Review* 118, no. 4 (2013): 1105–1132.

Imam, Zafar. "Soviet View of Non-Alignment." *International Studies* 20, no. 1–2 (1981): 445–469.

Jacobsen, Kurt. "Some Aspects of UN Voting Patterns." *Proceedings of the International Peace Research Association,* (1967): 315–346.

Jayaprakash, N.D. "India and the Bandung Conference of 1955–II." *People's Democracy (Weekly Organ of the Communist Party of India (Marxist)), XXIX* 23 (2005). Accessed 26 October 2014. http://archives.peoplesdemocracy.in/2005/0605/06052005_bandung%20conf.htm.

Jones, Matthew. "A "Segregated" Asia?: Race, the Bandung Conference, and Pan-Asianist Fears in American Thought and Policy, 1954–1955." *Diplomatic History* 29, no. 5 (2005): 841–868.

Kaczmarska, Katarzyna, and Stefanie Ortmann. "IR Theory and Area Studies: A Plea for Displaced Knowledge about International Politics." *Journal of International Relations and Development* 24, no. 4 (2021): 820–847.

Kalter, Christoph. "From Global to Local and Back: The 'Third World' Concept and the New Radical Left in France." *Journal of Global History* 12, no. 1 (2017): 115–136.

Kamola, Isaac. "IR, the Critic, and the World: From Reifying the Discipline to Decolonising the University." *Millennium* 48, no. 3 (2020): 245–270.

Kaviraj, Sudipta. "An Outline of a Revisionist Theory of Modernity." *European Journal of Sociology* 46, no. 3 (2005): 497–526.

Kaviraj, Sudipta. "On the Enchantment of the State: Indian Thought on the Role of the State in the Narrative of Modernity." *European Journal of Sociology* 46, no. 2 (2005): 263–296.

Keenleyside, Terence A. "Prelude to Power: The Meaning of Non-Alignment Before Indian Independence." *Pacific Affairs* 53, no. 3 (1980): 461–483.

Keenleyside, Terence A. "Diplomatic Apprenticeship: Pre-independence Origins of Indian Diplomacy and its Relevance for the Post-independence Foreign Policy." *India Quarterly* 43, no. 2 (1987): 97–120.

Khan, R. "NAM and Global Powers." *World Focus* 6, no. 7 (1985): 13–16.

Khilnani, Sunil. "Nehru's Faith." *Outlook*, 9 December 2002.

Kidwai, MS. "Nonalignment in the Changed Context." *Indian and Foreign Review* 20, no. 6 (1983): 11–13.

Kona, Swapna Nayudu. "Swadeshi Ink on Swadeshi Paper: Jawaharlal Nehru's Rajneeti Se Door." *Global Intellectual History* 2, no. 3 (2017): 389–407.

Kripalani, Acharya J.B. "For Principled Neutrality-A New Appraisal of Indian Foreign Policy." *Foreign Affairs* 38, no. 1 (1959): 48–60.

Lal, Deepak. "Indian Foreign Policy, 1947-64." *Economic and Political Weekly* 2, no. 19 (1961): 879–887.

Lawler, Peter. "The Good State: In Praise of 'Classical' Internationalism." *Review of International Studies* 31, no. 3 (2005): 427–449.

Levi, Werner. "Indian Neutralism Reconsidered." *Pacific Affairs* 37, no. 2 (1964): 137–147.

Lee, Christopher J. "At the Rendezvous of Decolonisation: The Final Communiqué of the Asian-African Conference, Bandung, Indonesia, 18–24 April." *Interventions* 11, no. 1 (2009): 81–93.

Lijphart, Arend. "The Analysis of Bloc Voting in the General Assembly: A Critique and a Proposal." *American Political Science Review* 57, no. 4 (1963): 902–917. https://doi.org/10.2307/1952608.

Logan, Rayford W. "Is There An Afro-Asian Bloc?" *Current History* 40, no. 234 (1961): 65–110.

Logan, Rayford W. "The Operation of the Mandate System in Africa." *The Journal of Negro History* 13, no. 4 (1928): 423–477. https://doi.org/10.2307/2713843.

Lüthi, Lorenz M. "Non-Alignment, 1946–1965: Its Establishment and Struggle against Afro-Asianism." *Humanity: An International Journal of Human Rights, Humanitarianism, and Development* 7, no. 2 (2016): 201–223.

Lüthi, Lorenz M. "The Non-Aligned Movement and the Cold War, 1961–1973." *Journal of Cold War Studies* 18, no. 4 (2016): 98–147.

Maitra, Sankar N. "A New Look at Foreign Policy." *Economic and Political Weekly* 2, no. 17 (1967): 793–796.

Malhotra, Inder. "India and the Nonaligned Movement." *World Focus* 6, no. 9 (1985): 29–31.

Malkki, Liisa. "Things to Come: Internationalism and Global Solidarities in the Late 1990s." *Public Culture* 10, no. 2 (1998): 431–442.

Malkki, Liisa. "Citizens of Humanity: Internationalism and the Imagined Community of Nations." *Diaspora: A Journal of Transnational Studies* 3, no. 1 (1994): 41–68.

Manley, Michael. "Third World under Challenge: The Politics of Affirmation." *Third World Quarterly* 2, no. 1 (1980): 28–43.

Manno, Catherine Senf. "Majority Decisions and Minority Responses in the UN General Assembly." *Journal of Conflict Resolution* 10, no. 1 (1966): 1–20.

Mantena, Karuna. "Another Realism: The Politics of Gandhian Nonviolence." *American Political Science Review* 106, no. 2 (2012): 455–470.

Mantena, Karuna. "On Gandhi's Critique of the State: Sources, Contexts, Conjunctures." *Modern Intellectual History* 9, no. 3 (2012): 535–563.

Mantena, Karuna. "Gandhi and the Means-ends Question in Politics." *Occasional Papers of the School of Social Sciences* 46 (2012): 1–25.

Maslow, Will. "The Afro-Asian Bloc in the United Nations." *Middle Eastern Affairs* 8, no. 11 (1957): 372–377.

Mastny, Vojtech. "The Soviet Union's Partnership with India." *Journal of Cold War Studies* 12, no. 3 (2010): 50–90.

Maxwell, Neville. "Jawaharlal Nehru: Of Pride and Principle." *Foreign Affairs* 52, no. 3 (1974): 633–643.

Mazower, Mark. "An International Civilization? Empire, Internationalism and the Crisis of the Mid-Twentieth Century." *International Affairs* 82, no. 3 (2006): 553–566.

McCallum, JA. "The Asian Relations Conference." *The Australian Quarterly* 19, no. 2 (1947): 13–17.

McCann, Gerard. "Where Was the Afro in Afro-Asian Solidarity? Africa's 'Bandung Moment' in 1950s Asia." *Journal of World History* 30, no. 1 (2019): 89–123.

McConnell, Fiona. "Rethinking the Geographies of Diplomacy." *Diplomatica* 1, no. 1 (2019): 46–55.

McDonald, Matt. "Securitization and the Construction of Security." *European Journal of International Relations* 14, no. 4 (2008): 563–587.

McSweeney, Bill. "Identity and Security: Buzan and the Copenhagen school." *Review of International Studies* 22, no. 1 (1996): 81–93.

Mearsheimer, John. "The False Promise of International Institutions." *International Security* 19, no. 3 (1994): 5–49.

Mehta, Pratap B. "Cosmopolitanism and the Circle of Reason." *Political Theory* 28, no. 5 (2000): 619–39.

Mehta, Pratap B. "A New Foreign Policy?" *Economic and Political Weekly* 38, no. 30 (2003): 3173–3175.

Mehta, Pratap B. "World Religions and Democracy: Hinduism and Self-Rule." *Journal of Democracy* 15, no. 3 (2004): 108–121.

Mehta, Pratap B. "Still Under Nehru's Shadow? The Absence of Foreign Policy Frameworks in India." *India Review* 8, no. 3 (2009): 209–233.

Mehta, U.S. "Gandhi on Democracy, Politics and the Ethics of Everyday Life," *Modern Intellectual History*, vol. 7, issue 2 (2010): 355–371.

Mehta, Uday Singh. "Gandhi and the Common Logic of War and Peace," *Raritan* 30, no. 1 (2010): 134–155.

Menon, Dilip M. "Bandung Is Back: Afro-Asian Affinities." *Radical History Review* 119, (2014): 241–245.

Mišković, Nataša. "The Pre-History of the Non-Aligned Movement: India's First Contacts with the Communist Yugoslavia, 1948–50." *India Quarterly* 65, no. 2 (2009): 185–200. https://doi.org/10.1177/097492840906500206.

Misra, Kashi Prasad. "Towards Understanding Non-Alignment." *International Studies* 20, no. 23 (1981): 23–37.

Mphaisha, Chiscpo J.J. "Non-Alignment and the New Economic Order." *Indian and Foreign Review* 18, no. 11 (1981): 8–9, 21.

Mukherjee, Mithi. "'A World of Illusion': The Legacy of Empire in India's Foreign Relations, 1947–62." *The International History Review* 32, no. 2 (2010): 253–271.

Nawaz, Mohammad. "Afro-Asians and the United Nations." *Pakistan Horizon* 15, no. 1 (1962): 42–48.

Neal, Andrew W. "Foucault in Guantánamo: Towards an Archaeology of the Exception." *Security Dialogue* 37, no. 1 (2006): 31–46.

Nehru, Jawaharlal. "Changing India." *Foreign Affairs* 41, no. 3 (1963): 453–465.

Nehru, Jawaharlal. "The Unity of India." *Foreign Affairs* 16, no. 2 (1938): 231–243.

Neuhold, Hanspeter. "Permanent Neutrality and Non-Alignment: Similarities and Differences." *India Quarterly* 35, no. 3 (1979): 285–308.

Newcombe, Hanna, Michael Ross, and Alan G. Newcombe. "United Nations Voting Patterns." *International Organization* 24, no. 1 (1970): 100–121.

Newman, Edward. "Critical Human Security Studies." *Review of International Studies* 36, no. 1 (2010): 77–94.

Nolan, Mary. "The Rise and Fall of Internationalism." *Public Books*, 10 July 2013.

Official, Indian. "India as a World Power." *Foreign Affairs* 27, no. 4 (1949): 540–550.

Ogley, Roderick C. "Voting and Politics in the General Assembly." *International Relations* 2, no. 3 (1961): 156–167.

Ollapally, Deepa, and Rajesh Rajagopalan. "The Pragmatic Challenge to Indian Foreign Policy." *The Washington Quarterly* 34, no. 2 (2011): 145–162.

O'Malley, Alanna. "Ghana, India, and the Transnational Dynamics of the Congo Crisis at the United Nations, 1960–1." *The International History Review* 37, no. 5 (2015): 970–990. https://doi.org/10.1080/07075332.2015.1051082.

Oommen, Tharailath Koshy. "The Non-Aligned News Pool: Correcting the Imbalance in News Flow." *Indian and Foreign Review* 18, no. 2 (1980): 13–15.

Ørvik, Nils. "Defence against Help-A Strategy for Small States?" *Survival: Global Politics and Strategy* 15, no. 5 (1973): 228–231.

Pandit, Vijayalakshmi. "India's Foreign Policy." *Foreign Affairs* 34, no. 3 (1956): 432–440.

Parekh, Bhikhu. "Nehru and the National Philosophy of India." *Economic and Political Weekly* 26, no. 1/2 (1991): 35–39, 41–48.

Parker, Jason. "Cold War II: The Eisenhower Administration, the Bandung Conference, and the Reperiodization of the Postwar Era." *Diplomatic History* 30, no. 5 (2006): 867–892.

Parmar, Inderjeet. "The US-Led Liberal Order: Imperialism by Another Name?" *International Affairs* 94, no. 1 (2018): 151–172. https://doi.org/10.1093/ia/iix240.

Pauker, Guy J. "The Rise and Fall of Afro-Asian Solidarity." *Asian Survey* 5, no. 9 (1965): 425–432. https://doi.org/10.2307/2642492

Pitts, Jennifer. "Political Theory of Empire and Imperialism." *Annual Review of Political Science* 13 (2010): 211–235.

Power, Paul F. "Indian Foreign Policy: The Age of Nehru." *The Review of Politics* 26, no. 2 (1964): 257–286.

Prakash, Gyan. "Writing Post-Orientalist Histories of the Third World: Perspectives from Indian Historiography." *Comparative Studies in Society and History* 32, no. 2 (1990): 383–408.

Qureshi, Yasmin. "Pakistan's Foreign Policy – A Quarterly Survey." *Pakistan Horizon* 37, no. 1 (1984): 3–10.

Rai, KB. "India and Bloc Voting in the General Assembly." *The Indian Journal of Political Science* 25, no. 3/4 (1964): 117–23.

Rajan, Mannaraswamighala S. "India and World Politics in the Post-Nehru Era." *International Journal* 24, no. 1 (1968): 138–158.

Rajan, Mannaraswamighala S. "Jawaharlal Nehru and Non-Alignment." *Indian and Foreign Review* 18, no. 8 (1981): 10–12, 19.

Rajan, Mannaraswamighala S. "The Non-Aligned Movement: The New Delhi Conference and After." *Southeast Asian Affairs*, (1982): 60–72.

Rana, Swadesh. "The Changing Indian Diplomacy at the United Nations." *International Organization* 24, no. 1 (1970): 48–73.

Rao, P.V. Narasimha. "Non-Alignment in Today's World." *Indian and Foreign Review* 17, no. 16 (1980): 9–12.

Rao, P.V. Narasimha. "Non-Alignment in a Multi-Polar World." *Indian and Foreign Review* 18, no. 5 (1980): 9–10.

Rao, P.V. Narasimha. "Non-Alignment in Today's World." *Indian and Foreign Review* 19, no. 7 (1982): 9–11, 15.

Rao, P.V. Narasimha. "Non-Alignment in Today's World- II." *Indian and Foreign Review* 19, no. 8 (1982): 9–12.

Reddy, S. "New Government Will Follow a Dynamic Foreign Policy: Non-Alignment and Friendship with Neighbours." *Indian and Foreign Review* 17, no. 8 (1980): 7–8.

Rieselbach, Leroy N. "Quantitative Techniques for Studying Voting Behavior in the UN General Assembly." *International Organization* 14, no. 2 (1960): 291–306.

Roxborough, Ian. "Review: The Global Cold War: Third World Interventions and the Making of Our Times by Odd Arne Westad." *The American Historical Review* 112, no. 3 (2007): 806–808.

Ruggie, John Gerard. "Territoriality and Beyond: Problematizing Modernity in International Relations." *International Organization* 47, no. 1 (1993): 139–174.

Sagar, Rahul. "State of Mind: What Kind of Power Will India Become?" *International Affairs* 85, no. 4 (2009): 801–816.

Saksena, K.P. "Afghanistan Conflict and the United Nations." *International Studies* 19, no. 4 (1980): 661–79. https://doi.org/10.1177/002088178001900407.

Saksena, K.P. "Non-Alignment and the United Nations." *International Studies* 20, no. 1–2 (1981): 81–102. https://doi.org/10.1177/002088178102000107.

Sarkar, Sumit. "Subalternity, History and the Global." *An Interview by Déborah Cohen, Urs Lindner, in Actuel Marx* 50, no. 2 (2011): 207–217.

Scalapino, Robert A. ""Neutralism" in Asia." *American Political Science Review* 48, no. 1 (1954): 49–62.

Schmidt, Brian. "Political Science and the American Empire: A Disciplinary History of the 'Politics' Section and the Discourse of Imperialism and Colonialism." *International Politics* 45, no. 6 (2008): 675–687.

Schneer, Jonathan. "Hopes Deferred or Shattered: The British Labour Left and the Third Force Movement, 1945–49." *The Journal of Modern History* 56, no. 2 (1984): 198–226.

Schou Tjalve, Vibeke. "Designing (de) Security: European Exceptionalism, Atlantic Republicanism and the 'Public Sphere'." *Security Dialogue* 42, no. 4–5 (2011): 441–452.

Sen, Tansen. "The Intricacies of Premodern Asian Connections." *The Journal of Asian Studies* 69, no. 4 (2010): 991–999.

Shamim, M. "The Colombo Non-Alignment Summit – An Appraisal." *Indian and Foreign Review* 13, no. 22 (1976): 16–18.

Shimazu, Naoko. "Diplomacy as Theatre: Staging the Bandung Conference of 1955." *Modern Asian Studies* 48, no. 1 (2014): 225–252.

Shukla, Vidya Charan. "Information Media in the Non-Aligned World – The New Delhi Charter." *Indian and Foreign Review* 13, no. 20 (1976): 16–20.

Singh, Dinesh. "Non-Alignment and the New International Economic Order." *Indian and Foreign Review* 18, no. 24 (1981): 7–11.

Singh, Dinesh. "The Non-Aligned Movement: Aftermath of the Delhi Conference." *Indian and Foreign Review* 18, no. 12 (1981): 10–11.

Srivastava, Neelam. "Towards a Critique of Colonial Violence: Fanon, Gandhi and the Restoration of Agency." *Journal of Postcolonial Writing* 46, no. 3/4 (2010): 303–309.

Singh, Hira. "Confronting Colonialism and Racism: Fanon and Gandhi." *Human Architecture: Journal of the Sociology of Self-Knowledge* 5, no. 3 (2007): 341–352.

Singh, Sinderpal. "From Delhi to Bandung: Nehru, 'Indian-ness' and 'Pan-Asian-ness.'" *South Asia: Journal of South Asian Studies* 34, no. 1 (2011): 51–64.

Soward, Frederick H. "The Changing Balance of Power in the United Nations." *Political Quarterly* 28, no. 4 (1957): 317–327.

Stolte, Carolien, and Harald Fischer-Tiné. "Imagining Asia in India: Nationalism and Internationalism (ca. 1905–1940)." *Comparative Studies in Society and History* 54, no. 1 (2012): 65–92.

Stritzel, Holger. "Towards a Theory of Securitization: Copenhagen and Beyond." *European Journal of International Relations* 13, no. 3 (2007): 357–383.

Subrahmanyam, Krishnaswamy. "Alternative Security Doctrines." *Bulletin of Peace Proposals* 21, no. 1 (1990): 77–85.

Gandhi, Mohandas K. "On Revolutions." *Young India*, 1 March 1928.

Getachew, Adom. "A Fuller Freedom: The Lost Promise of Pan-Africanism." *The Nation*, 29 October 2019.

"Nehru Condemns Pacts." *The Hindu*, 13 November 1956.

Khanna, R.G. "Non-Alignment: Looking Back." *The Times of India*, 4 March 1983.

Khilnani, Sunil. "Dialogues with Liberalism." *The Times of India*, 19 November 2011. http://articles.timesofindia.indiatimes.com/2011-11-19/edit-page/30415438_1_liberal-party-term-liberal-liberal-ideas.

Lawrence, W.H. "Truman Relieves McArthur of All His Posts; Finds Him Unable to Back US-UN Policies; Ridgway Named to Far Eastern Commands." *New York Times*, 11 April 1951. http://www.nytimes.com/learning/general/onthisday/big/0411.html#article.

Malhotra, Inder. "Belgrade to New Delhi: New Vistas for the Non-Aligned." *Times of India*, 24 February 1983.

Mehta, Pratap B. "People of the Past." *Indian Express*, 15 August 2013. http://archive.indianexpress.com/news/people-of-the-past/1155521/.

Nanporia, N.J. "India and Non-Alignment." *Swarajya*, 18 January 1979.

"Early Indian Government Receives Much Criticism from Soviet Russia." *New Times*, 10 August 1948.

"Excerpts From U.N. Security Council Debate on the Indian Invasion of Enclaves." *The New York Times*, 19 December 1961. https://www.nytimes.com/1961/12/19/archives/excerpts-from-un-security-council-debate-on-the-indian-invasion-of.html.

Noorani, Abdul Ghafoor. "Nehru and the Cold Wars." *Frontline*, 14 February 2004.

Raghavan, Srinath. "Beyond Victimology." *Outlook India*, 2012. http://www.outlookindia.com/article/Beyond-Victimology/282578.

Russo, Peter. "38th Parallel & After? Mediation by Asian Neutrals May Be Solution." *The Argus*, 22 August 1950. http://trove.nla.gov.au/ndp/del/article/22899041.

"UN Admits Bomb Fell on Korea." *Red Eagle*, 23 January 1952. http://news.google.com/newspapers?id=OJItAAAAIBAJ&sjid=fp0FAAAAIBAJ&pg=6719%2C1040730.

Subrahmanyam, Krishnaswamy. "Global Reach of the Non-Aligned." *Times of India*, 17 March 1983.

"Move to Exclude India?" *The Sydney Morning Herald*, 24 August 1953. http://trove.nla.gov.au/ndp/del/article/18387570.

Time Magazine. "The Congo: Exit Raj." 2 June 1961. http://content.time.com/time/magazine/article/0,9171,826993,00.html.

Time Magazine. "UNCURK in Seoul." 4 December 2014. http://content.time.com/time/magazine/article/0,9171,813950,00.html.

Wright, Quincy. "Afro-Asian Bloc Cool to India." *The Christian Science Monitor*, 26 November 1962.

Wright, Quincy. "India Loses Support among Third World Nations." *Tribune*, 17 December 1971.

Articles

Békés, Csaba. "The 1956 Hungarian Revolution and World Politics." Working Paper No. 16, Cold War International History Project, Woodrow Wilson International Center for Scholars, Washington D.C., 1996.

Chen, Jian. "The Sino-Soviet Alliance and China's Entry into the Korean War." Working Paper No. 1, Cold War International History Project, Woodrow Wilson International Center for Scholars, 1992.

Floyd, Rita. "When Foucault Met Security Studies: A Critique of the 'Paris School' of Security Studies." *BISA Annual Conference at the University of Cork*, Ireland, 18–20 December 2006.

Goswami, Manu. "Revising the Geography of Modern World Histories." *New Research in Modern Trans-Regional History Lecture Series*, University of York, 9–19 February 2018.

Kamola, I. "IR, the Critic, and the World: From Reifying the Discipline to Decolonising the University." *Millennium: Journal of International Studies*, vol. 48, no. 3, 245–270, 2020.

Kaul, Triloki Nath. "The Idealist and the Revolutionary." Nehru Memorial Lecture, London, 1983. https://www.cambridgetrust.org/assets/documents/Lecture_10.pdf.

Khilnani, Sunil. "Looking for Indira Gandhi." *India-Seminar*, August 2004.

Khilnani, Sunil. "Making Asia: India, China and the Struggle for an Idea." Jawaharlal Nehru Memorial Lecture, 3 November 2012. http://www.cambridgetrust.org/assets/documents/Lecture_33.pdf.

Menon, Dilip M. "Bandung Is Back: Afro-Asian Affinities." *Radical History Review*, vol. 2014, no. 119, 241, https://doi.org/10.1215/01636545-2402153

Mishra, Pankaj. "Ahmet Hamdi Tanpinar and the Waiting Room of History." *The Guardian*, 28 February 2015.

"Nehru Charges US Flouts Asia." *The Spokesman Review*, 18 September 1953. http://news.google.com/newspapers?nid=1314&dat=19530918&id=by9WAAAAIBAJ&sjid=JeYDAAAAIBAJ&pg=7186,3307603.

Ramesh, Jairam. "How India and Canada Manage Diversities." *The Hindu*, 26 April 2007. http://www.thehindu.com/todays-paper/tp-opinion/how-india-canada-manage-diversities/article1833713.ece.

Sen, Tansen. *The End of Pan-Asianism? India, China, and the Asian Relations Conference in 1947*. Talk at King's College London, 10 March 2014.

Acknowledgements

Sunil Khilnani's *The Idea of India* inspired me to study modern India, so being under his tutelage for the doctorate was a privilege. Claudia Aradau took me on when my project had only the faint stirrings of something passable, but her brilliance and her kindness brought to life the thesis on which this book is based. Also, at King's, at the Department of War Studies, I had wonderful conversations with Mats Berdal, who encouraged me to continue working on peacekeeping, and Vivienne Jabri, who asked me to "let the archive speak". Mervyn Frost, the Head of Department when I began the PhD, was also always very supportive. I must also thank the department as a whole – the emphasis on war as worthy of study has meant a lot to how this project is positioned and how a lot of my other writings from this time came together. I was fortunate to have conversations with those at, and those passing in and out of, the India Institute – Jahnavi Phalkey, Ian Jack, Christopher Bayly and Tansen Sen freely gave of their time. At the viva, Odd Arne Westad and Andrew Hurrell pieced together thoughts on what the book would look like. I do hope I have not disappointed them.

Arne has unstintingly supported me and encouraged me, and I can only hope to pay it forward. After London, I did go through a period of having my ambitions dwarfed by a series of incredible events. In those tough times, I was saved by the mentorship of Tarak Barkawi, who is rightly lauded for his immense intellect and celebrated for his incredible generosity. Tarak has been a teacher to me and a mentor in the truest sense of the word. Faisal Devji does not possess a single unkind streak in his person. I am always deeply moved by his munificence – he is what my father used to call, in a now outmoded way, "a good man". I am filled with gratitude towards Arne, Tarak and Faisal, who have had such a formative influence on my work, but who are, first and foremost, such decent and lovely people that I feel fortunate to have been around.

In London, Cambridge, and now in Singapore, I've had some enormously rewarding interactions to do with ways of thinking about this book, from writing it to publishing it: Quentin Skinner helped me articulate my thoughts over lunches at the British Library; I don't think he knows how pivotal those interventions were to this project. David Armitage, who wears his brilliance so lightly, has always cheered me – and this book – on, for which I am so thankful. Sudipta Kaviraj is the most articulate thinker I have read and the gentlest interlocutor I have had. I will never forget that he cut short a holiday and drove back into the city in the middle of the summer to meet with a student. Conversations with Shruti Kapila began at a conference on Foucault, and I should've known then that I would return to her time and again for her wise counsel. Naoko Shimazu has helped me navigate a world I knew very little of; I am indebted to her. Carolien Stolte and Su Lin Lewis brought me into another world altogether and through them, I have met some incredible historians producing fascinating writing. Kama Maclean has indulged my ideas time and again, including a long speech on Nehru's 100 volumes, which I never thought would see light of the day. When I came to the study of the Cold War, the first people I learnt from were Svetozar Rajak, Jovan Čavoški and my dear departed friend Andreas Hilger, whose sense of humour I miss terribly. I am also thankful to Christian Ostermann for being as excited as I was about obscure stories on India in the Cold War. Manu Bhagavan, who put together a fantastic project on this theme, has always made time to answer my questions. I am grateful for these friendships.

At Yale-NUS, I am thankful to Joanne Roberts, David Jacks, Edward John Driffill and Chris Howell for supporting my professional goals while the book project was culminating. Chin Hao-Huang, Steve Monroe, Steven Oliver and Bittiandra Chand Somaiah have been the loveliest colleagues. In Singapore, more widely, I would also like to thank Tan Tai Yong, Sinderpal Singh and Kanti Bajpai, who helped me settle in when I first arrived, and Jonathan Rigg and Tim Bunnell, both from the Asia Research Institute.

But it all began in Delhi. Pratap Bhanu Mehta, my first teacher, asked me to get in touch with a scholar who had just returned from England – King's as it turned out – to begin work at the Centre for Policy Research. At our first meeting, Srinath Raghavan handed me ten books and asked me to return when I had read them. Since then, Pratap and Srinath have always been what feels like an intellectual home. Also in Delhi, I had the great privilege of listening to the reminiscences and insights offered by India's erstwhile diplomats – Eric Gonsalves, Arundhati Ghose, Lalit Mansingh, Salman Haidar, Shyam Saran, Shivshankar Menon and Maharaja Krishna Rasgotra – who were all enormously enthusiastic about and helpful with this project. I am indebted to them and will forever treasure the joy with which they spoke of Nehru's India. I cannot not remember with fondness P.R. Chari and Gurmeet Kanwal, who are no longer with us, but who got me started in Delhi on all sorts of projects that eventually culminated in my body of work.

My tryst with archivists began with a lecture by the late Mushirul Hasan in his office at the National Archives of India. So much of this book would not have been possible unless, against all odds, the staff, especially at Teen Murti, had made it possible for me to work. I must also thank, amongst others, the archivists at the United Nations Archives and Records Management Section in New York, the Butler Library Special Collections at Columbia University, and the National Archives at Kew, London.

Saneet Chakradeo, Kanishkh Kanodia, Chiki Sarkar, Rhea Gupta, Nishtha Kapil, Vandana Menon, Bhavi Mehta, Ajith Kumar, Attaul Munim Zahid worked on aspects of the book. I owe a debt of gratitude to them and to Parth Phiroze Mehrotra, whose enthusiastic reception of this project has galvanized me.

And then there are those who scolded, cajoled and encouraged me into finishing this book – Menaka Guruswamy, Devika Rege, Rohan Mukherjee, Sana Aiyar, Rahul Rao, Sarnath Banerjee, Constantino Xavier: thank you! Arunabh Ghosh, Benjamin Siegel, Rahul Sagar and Avinash Paliwal have been very generous with professional advice. Gayatri Uppal, Arkaja Singh and Mathew John, along with Madhavi Katuri, Shreya Katuri, Srishti Katuri and Srinagesh Katuri, opened their homes to me when I would visit from London, in the dead of winter, to go hibernate in the archives and emerge triumphantly with the tattered remains of forsaken files. The girls – Ritika Prasad, Zareen Bharucha, Rachana Nakra – are family. Pragya Vats, Puja and Shivraj Anand, Raghu Karnad, Meraj Shah, Zoha Waseem, Pinal Patel, Shweta Rangnekar, Snober Sataravala and Liyaan Sataravala, Yamini and Ajit Patel, Chitra and Virender Sethi, Tripti Bhadauriya and Manish Pratap, Shailey Hingorani and Malini Kannan, have all been sources of support and encouragement throughout the decade it took to write the book. I am forever grateful.

I am also thankful to my new family, Renuka and Amit Sharma, Megha and Aditya Sharma, and Sarla Inamdar, for being excited about the book. I am grateful for the unfailing backing I have received from Shakuntala Issar, my daughter's great-grandmother – and a confidante like none other.

The interiority of politics is only allowed to some. I was born into a family where people described themselves as political animals. They also described themselves as Gandhian. This has made writing this book terrifying. I never thought that my father's many anecdotes were anything, but I now realize that I carry his life as a civil servant in my mind and I think it stops me from resorting to the shrill cynicism that could easily be justified in today's political climate. My mother taught me that scholarly pursuits were a privilege and a duty. My father's first lesson was to bite the hand that feeds me – he was the most anti-establishment figure I knew, a true polemicist. Unbeknownst to him, I started to write this book so he may read it. I can scarcely believe he's gone. I owe you everything, Amma and Nana.

First came Adhiraj, then came Surasti. I am grateful to both for celebrating every little inch I moved forward with the book. Every good word spoken about *The Nehru Years* belongs to them as much as it does to me.

Fortune presents gifts not according to the book. My path has ebbed and flowed much more than I could have ever imagined. But I am here now.

Index